The Giriama and
Colonial Resistance in Kenya,
1800-1920

And the Giriama said, "Who will give away his son to go and
be killed? Try taking the chicks."
Chembe [Champion] took a chick and the hen flapped
and attacked Chembe.
And the Giriama said, "Do you see what the hen has done? If you take our sons,
we will do the same."
And that is how the war started in Vitengeni.

GIRIAMA HISTORICAL TEXTS:
Hawe Karisa Nyevu Makarye and
Ishmael Toya (Jilore),
15 December 1970

The Giriama and Colonial Resistance in Kenya, 1800-1920

CYNTHIA BRANTLEY

UNIVERSITY OF CALIFORNIA PRESS
Berkeley • Los Angeles • London

University of California Press
Berkeley and Los Angeles, California
University of California Press, Ltd.
London, England
© 1981 by
The Regents of the University of California
Printed in the United States of America

1 2 3 4 5 6 7 8 9

Library of Congress Cataloging in Publication Data

Brantley, Cynthia.
  The Giriama and colonial resistance in Kenya, 1800-
1920.

  Bibliography: p.
  Includes index.
  1. Giryama (African people)—History.   2. Kenya—
History—To 1963.   I. Title.
DT433.545.G55B7   967.6′203   81-524
ISBN 0-520-04216-6   AACR1

To my family

Contents

Maps

Preface

This study was begun, literally, on a footnote. In their discussion of African resistance to British colonialism in Kenya prior to the Mau Mau rebellion of the early 1950's, Carl Rosberg and John Nottingham mentioned the rebellion by the Giriama of Kenya's coastal hinterland.[1] In 1970, filled with enthusiasm and innocence, I set out to investigate, for my dissertation, this little-known rebellion.[2] I gradually discovered the extent of the task. Few published materials existed on the Giriama, and no anthropological study of them was available.[3] Studies of the coastal Afro-Arab communities, which were closely interwoven with the history of the Giriama, left an incomplete picture even though C.S. Nicholls, A.I. Salim, and F.J. Berg had recently written theses that extended beyond Reginald Coupland's focus on British efforts to end the slave trade,[4] aiming, rather, to explain the participation of Swahili-speaking peoples in coastal affairs.[5] The history of Kenya's hinterland remained a void.

Once I was in the field, the gap in African history that I was trying to fill began to seem a chasm. In contrast to the rich Portuguese and Swahili records of the Zambezi valley, which went back as far as the sixteenth century, written documentation offered only intermittent glimpses of the peoples of the Kenyan hinterland. Although the British established their first consul in Zanzibar in 1841 and the first missionaries came to Rabai in 1844, it was not until the Imperial British East Africa Company came to the coast in 1888, shortly before the establishment of the British East Africa Protectorate in 1895, that written accounts began to be kept. I was forced to fall back on what is in fact the major source of evidence for Giriama history—the rich Giriama oral tradition.[6]

My original study, focused on the Giriama political system, attempted to explain how a noncentralized society could provide the organizational basis for resistance. By the time of the rebellion in 1914, however, that political system was undergoing serious transition; I discovered that it had not been the basis for organization. Nor had any underlying religious system served

ix

this purpose. I concluded that cultural and psychological explanations must have accounted for the violent Giriama response.

I was wrong. Certainly, cultural differences between the Giriama and the British underlay the inability of the two peoples to come to terms, but these differences are in themselves an insufficient explanation for the intense resistance. An examination of the Giriama economy in relation to the East African coastal economy and a more precise investigation of the circumstances surrounding initial colonial economic demands enabled me to set the Giriama rebellion in a completely new context. I came to see the Giriama as a significant part of a changing coastal economic network and to understand the economic factors that informed the colonial government's goals and the Giriama response to efforts at implementation.

This book looks at change within Giriama society over a span of many years. By bridging the gap between the precolonial and the colonial periods in Kenya it tries to make clear that political control in the colonial period was primarily a means of expanding Britain's plan for economic capitalism; by exploring the Giriama rebellion in terms of the complex and varied economic constraints on Giriama society in 1913, and thus highlighting economic rather than formal political grievances, it may contribute to resistance historiography; and by examining the responses of people drawn into the network of international capitalism, it attempts to demonstrate the implications of that involvement not just for those Giriama individuals who were active in trade but for the Giriama society as a whole. Finally, it is my hope that this study will inspire future historians to delve more deeply into other cases of African resistance.

Acknowledgments

Although the author is fully responsible for the end product, a work such as this incurs debts which are impossible to repay. Contributors to the formulation of the ideas and those who facilitated access to materials are too numerous to mention. My deepest appreciation goes to the Giriama, who were always willing to share their hospitality and their history. Their experiences have given them every reason to distrust outsiders and to refuse to answer a constant barrage of questions from a stranger, but instead they welcomed me and they took our joint effort seriously; I shall remain forever grateful. Victor Gona Kazungu and Wilson Nguma shared in many phases of the field research; I value their contributions highly.

I am grateful to the Republic of Kenya, President's Office, for permission to conduct this research project; to the University of Nairobi, which made its library and archive facilities available to me and with which I was affiliated as a Visiting Research Fellow; to the Fulbright-Hays Fellowship Program for Doctoral Dissertation Research; to the United Presbyterian Church, for a Presbyterian Graduate Fellowship; to the United States Government, for National Defense Educational Act loans which made my graduate training possible; and to the University of California, Davis, for supporting extended research in Kenya in 1974 and in London in 1977 and 1978.

Many archivists and librarians gave me invaluable assistance in locating materials. Special thanks must go to Nathan Fedha and Robert Kubuko of the Kenya National Archives, Nairobi; Rosemary Keen of the CMS Archives, London; and the staffs of the Public Record Office, London; the British Museum; the Royal Commonwealth Society; the University of London, the Institute of Commonwealth Studies, London; the Maxwell School of Citizenship and Public Affairs in Syracuse, New York; and Rhodes House, Oxford.

I am most thankful for the guidance, encouragement, and patient criticisms of T.O. Ranger and E.A. Alpers, who nurtured this study. I give special, deep appreciation to Mary Bolton, for her scholarship, support, patience, and caring. I thank Jocelyn Murray, who shared my first investigative project on the Giriama and whose bibliographic and editorial skills have improved this work considerably; Penny Kanner, for her rigor and special inspiration; and Ron Hart, for the part he shared.

Special thanks go to Tom Spear for his contributions on Giriama hinterland trade, for sharing several stages of work with me, and for providing useful assistance throughout. I appreciate Marcia Wright's tough criticism, and Ruth Rosen's skilled assistance and support. I am grateful to Fred Cooper, who sent me a draft of a chapter in a forthcoming book in answer to a request for more information; to Inez Jarrick, who assisted me in obtaining access to materials; to Don Rothchild, who freely shared his work in progress on Kenya with me; David Parkin, for sharing his special knowledge about the Giriama; Peg Strobel, Chris Ehret, Bill Bowsky, Arnold Bauer, Miriam Wells, Dick Curley, and Ed Steinhart, who read drafts at various stages; Arnold Temu, for his loan of cyclostyled archival excerpts; Fred Morton, who allowed me to copy some of his notes; Mr. and Mrs. J. Milton-Thompson of Kaloleni, who lent me the CMS Log Book and other materials in their possession; John Lonsdale, who gave me access to comparative Nyanza material; Allen Isaacman, who sent me work in progress; Robert Maxon and Ann Frontera-Riol, for mailing me copies of their theses; Suad Joseph, for many fruitful hours of discussion; Karl and Elizabeth Thür for special, warm hospitality; and to B.E. Kipkorir, G. Muriuki, B.A. Ogot, Jean Hay, Alice Gold, A.T. Matson, Sally Stockley, Lewis Greenstein, Leo and Hilda Kuper, Ginny and Harry Smith, Barbara Zoloth, Doris Herrscher, and Richard Fields for their support.

I conducted research for this book simultaneously with a number of young scholars who were addressing similar general questions (about African initiative, African resistance, oral tradition, traditional African religion, ecological changes, and underdevelopment) and who pored over many of the same archival materials in Kenya and England. Each of us would have benefited enormously from the extractions and interpretations of the others; yet, under the pressure of scholarly timetables, each of us has produced our work in comparative isolation. Still, the availability of their dissertations, private correspondence with several of them, and, in many cases, warm conversations have contributed greatly to this work. I am appreciative of both their direct and indirect assistance.* The increasing body of literature on African resis-

*T.T. Spear, "The Kaya Complex: A History of the Mijikenda Peoples of the Kenya Coast to 1900" (Ph.D. dissertation, University of Wisconsin, 1974); Marguerite Helen Ylvisaker, "The Political and Economic Relationship of the Lamu Archipelago to the Adjacent Kenya Coast in the Nineteenth Century" (Ph.D. dissertation, Boston University, 1975); Hollis Merritt, "A History of the Taita of Kenya to 1900" (Ph.D. dissertation, Indiana University, 1975); William Francis McKay, "A Precolonial History of the Southern Kenya Coast" (Ph.D. dissertation, Boston University, 1975); Margaret Strobel, "Muslim Women in Mombasa, Kenya, 1890-1973" (Ph.D. dissertation, University of California, Los Angeles, 1975); Frederick Cooper, *Plantation Slavery on the East Coast of Africa* (New Haven, Connecticut, 1977); R.F. Morton, "Slaves, Fugitives, and Freedmen on the Kenya Coast, 1873-1907" (Ph.D. dissertation, Syracuse University, 1976);

tance in East, Central and Southern Africa* and the recent analyses by Richard Wolff, Anthony Clayton and Donald Savage, Colin Leys, and E. A. Brett include pertinent views on the colonial economy that have been of assistance to me in this study.†

I am especially grateful to the Rotary clubs of Southeast Texas and to Rotary International, for the fellowship they granted me in 1966, under which I first experienced Africa and its rich heritage; to my students at Alameda High School, Lakewood, Colorado, who indulged me in 1966 when I was a beginning teacher whose enthusiasm for Africa was much greater than my knowledge; to my fellow graduate students at the University of California, Los Angeles, for criticisms and support, and to many of my colleagues at the University of California, Davis, who supported this effort; to Charlyn Fishman for her suggestions for improvements to the original manuscript; and to Cheryl Riggins, Bobbie Figy, Jeanne Etzler, Evelyn Echevarria, and Anik Gentry for their careful typing. The support given me by all of my family was faithful and loving.

Peter Koffsky, "A History of Takaungu, East Africa, 1830-1896" (Ph.D. dissertation, University of Wisconsin, 1977); Ann M. Frontera, *Persistence and Change: A History of Taveta* (Waltham, Massachusetts, 1978); Robert Strayer, *The Making of Mission Communities in East Africa* (London, 1978).

*T. O. Ranger, *Revolt in Southern Rhodesia, 1896-7* (London, 1967); Julian Cobbing, "The Absent Priesthood: Another Look at the Rhodesian Rising of 1896-1897," *Journal of African History* 18:1 (1977): 61-84; John Iliffe, "The Organization of the Maji Maji Rebellion," *Journal of African History* 8:3 (1967): 495-512; Gilbert C. K. Gwassa, "The German Intervention and African Resistance in Tanzania," pp. 86-122 in *A History of Tanzania*, ed. I. N. Kimambo and A. J. Temu (Nairobi, 1969); Shula Marks, *Reluctant Rebellion: The 1906-1908 Disturbances in Natal* (Oxford, 1970). Allen Isaacman's recent works that concentrate on "the secondary states" and on "social bandits" have been more successful in exploring organization than economic conditions: Allen Isaacman, *The Tradition of Resistance in Mozambique: Anti-Colonial Activity in the Zambesi Valley, 1850-1921* (Berkeley, 1976); idem, "Social Banditry in Zimbabwe (Rhodesia) and Mozambique, 1894-1907: An Expression of Early Peasant Protest," *Journal of Southern African Studies* 4:1 (October 1977): 1-30. See Lorne Larson, "A History of the Mahenge (Ulanga) District, c. 1860-1957" (Ph.D. dissertation, University of Dar-es-Salaam, 1976), for an example of the role of local economic conditions in the Maji Maji rebellion.

†Richard D. Wolff, *The Economics of Colonialism: Britain and Kenya, 1870-1930* (New Haven, Connecticut, 1974); Anthony Clayton and Donald C. Savage, *Government and Labour in Kenya, 1895-1963* (London, 1974); Colin Leys, *Underdevelopment in Kenya: The Political Economy of Neo-Colonialism* (Berkeley and Los Angeles, 1975); E. A. Brett, *Colonialism and Underdevelopment in East Africa: The Politics of Economic Change, 1919-1939* (London, 1973).

Giriama Terms

Fisi	Literally, *hyena*; the most sacred Giriama oath. Also, the medicine men who are qualified to administer the oath.
kambi	Council of elders, councillors.
kaya (pl. *makaya*)	Fortified clearing in which the Mijikenda built their homes; also refers to the political system developed during residence in the *kaya.*
Kirao	Ritual to elevate me to councillor status.
kore	Blood-money, to be paid to the family of a murdered person by the one who killed him.
liwali	The Afro-Arab officer in charge of a town.
mahaji	A Giriama who has converted to Islam.
Mganga (pl. *waganga*)	Medicine man.
Mijikenda	Nine closely related tribes, of which the Giriama are the largest.
mtoro (pl. *watoro*)	Runaway slave.
Mung'aro	Ritual for installing one rika and retiring another.
mwanandia	Ambassador from the kaya.
Mwanza M'Kulu	Ritual designating young boys as an age-set.
nyere	Giriama youth, usually serving as warriors.
rika	Group of thirteen age-sets that make up a ruling generation.
sub-rika	Each of the thirteen age-sets that comprise a rika.
Vaya	Secret society of Giriama elders who participate in the judicial process.

Abbreviations

A.D.C.	Acting District Commissioner
A.G.	Acting Governor (East Africa Protectorate)
AR	Annual Report
CMS	Church Missionary Society
CO	Colonial Office
CP	Coast Province
CRP	Colonial Records Project (Rhodes House, Oxford)
D.C.	District Commissioner
D.O.	District Officer
FO	Foreign Office
GHT	Giriama Historical Texts
IBEAC	Imperial British East Africa Company
IJAHS	International Journal of African Historical Studies
JAH	Journal of African History
JRAI	Journal of the Royal Anthropological Institute
JRAS	Journal of the Royal African Society
KAR	King's African Rifles
KFI	Kilifi District Records (KNA)
KNA	Kenya National Archives
LNC	Local Native Council
MAL	Malindi District Records (KNA)
MSA	Mombasa District Records (KNA)
P.C.	Provincial Commissioner
PRB	Political Record Book
PRO	Public Records Office (London)
PP	Parliamentary Papers (London)

1
Introduction

Until recently, colonial African scholarship has focused on colonial goals; as
a result, the conditions under which Africans were forced to respond to the
colonial economy have been left in obscurity. My first inclination was to try
to tell the African side of the story. In the end, I realized that to understand
the colonial encounter, the goals, challenges, and perspectives of the Africans
had to be integrated with those of the colonial power. I have tried to achieve
this goal by combining a history of the Giriama, who inhabit Kenya's coastal
hinterland, with a case study of their 1914 rebellion against the British colonial government. Through its examination of the interwoven cultural zones
of the coastal enclaves and the hinterland peoples, this study demonstrates
the problems that arose in 1912 when British colonial agents, after establishing a settler economy up-country, returned their attention to the coast, where
their imperial efforts had begun in the 1890s.

At least four groups inhabited Kenya's coast and hinterland. First, the
communities of Muslim Afro-Arabs had been the earliest allies of the British,
but their economy, which was dependent upon grain plantations maintained
solely through slave labor, declined as a result of the British campaign against
the slave trade. Since the British needed their Afro-Arab allies as administrative agents, however, they made the abolition of slavery a gradual process
and were careful to offer compensation for freed slaves.

Second, the hinterland had a long history of runaway slaves, who either
formed separate communities, rushed for protection to the Church Missionary Society missions at Freretown and Rabai, or were assimilated into Giriama
society. Those who obtained their freedom in the later years often continued
working on their ex-owners' land as squatters. From the British administrative perspective, ex-slaves were disruptive and required special attention.

Third, the small, scattered homesteads of the Giriama and their other

Mijikenda neighbors occupied the major portion of the coastal hinterland. In the early twentieth century, these Giriama were the most productive of the peoples in the coastal region. They were reluctant to convert either to Islam or to Christianity. This meant that the mediation between the colonial and the African culture, which in other societies was performed by missionaries, was here lacking, and most direct encounters took place in an atmosphere of mutual ignorance.

Fourth, directors of European companies came to the coast to revive the agricultural production of the area and found themselves caught between the proven productivity of the past and the present lack of labor. These Europeans were dependent upon British colonial assistance to gain initial legal access to the land, and then to obtain a sufficient number of laborers to make their efforts successful.

Under the scheme of early colonial economic development, these groups were not left to develop economic arrangements among themselves. Instead, the colonial administration was expected to intervene on behalf of British capitalists. What follows is the story of their unsuccessful attempt at that intervention.

Three major questions present themselves. The first is: What kinds of political and economic experience helped, or failed, to prepare the Giriama for British colonization? Did some African societies have a choice of numerous responses to colonial demands, while others were limited by their experience to one or two possibilities? If societies that we tend to regard as single entities are in fact complex combinations of peoples, organized, often temporarily, on the basis of age, clans, territory, or economic endeavor, then what factors determine their responses and who has the authority to articulate them? Might those very cleavages within the society have had a significant influence on the perceived options?

Chapter 2 examines the agrarian adaptations of the Giriama and the changes in their political system in an attempt to suggest some answers to the first question. The second question, which stems directly from the first, concerns the organizational basis for the 1914 Giriama rebellion against British colonialism. It has long been assumed that societies need hierarchies, bureaucracies, and stratifications in order to rebel, but when the Giriama rebelled they had none of these organizational forms. They did not draw on a traditional military system—their military organization was designed to offer defense when necessary, but was neither permanent, aggressive, nor particularly strong. Nor did they draw on a political bureaucracy to organize all Giriama—their traditional political organization, based on councils of elders, reflected regional and economic differentiation, and some local councils had been victims of the British practice of co-optation. Neither did innovative religious leaders draw upon traditional religious forms to design organized rebellion—Giriama religion lacked priests, territorial or spirit-possession cults, or even an innovative leader to translate old customs, such as the

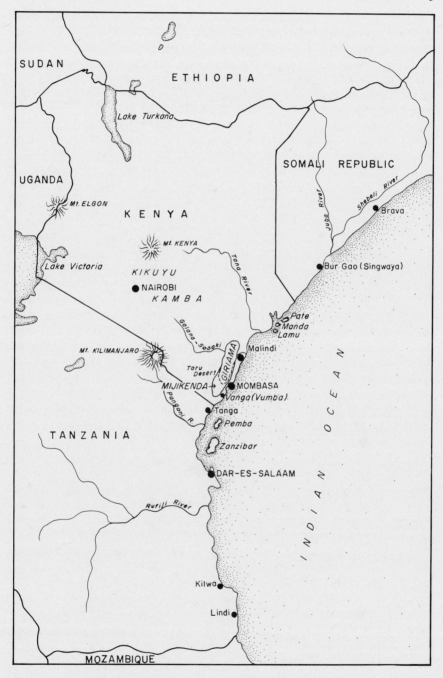

Map 1.   The East African coast.

eradication of witchcraft, into new forms in order to mobilize the Giriama into rebellion. Since they lacked a political, military, or religious basis for organizing rebellion, what can account for the fact that the Giriama responded as they did?

Certainly they felt their grievances deeply; they had been asked to pay taxes, to provide labor, and to evacuate portions of their land for the benefit of the Europeans, and they were being forced to settle in permanent locations, thereby losing the mobility which had contributed to their economic success. However, other Africans had faced these same demands from the British and by 1912 had complied. Certainly the presence of government troops following an initial skirmish was more provocative than it was frightening, but it would be irresponsible to conclude that the British had caused the Giriama rebellion by bringing in armed forces. Why, then, did the Giriama choose to fight?

The third question is that of the ramifications of rebellion for the Giriama. At one time, the generally accepted interpretation of all African resistance to colonialism was that it was due to lack of political sophistication; the conclusion to be drawn from this was that the rebels reaped no rewards.[1] Critics of this view pointed out that Africans who resisted may not have won the encounter, but they did receive special benefits and consideration from the colonial powers, who respected the Africans' willingness to fight and feared that they might fight again.[2] Did the Giriama rebellion fail simply because they were overpowered by British forces, or because the aim of Giriama fighting—to be able to continue as producers and traders in their existing economy (as opposed to the British aim of transforming them into wage-laborers)—was undermined by the conditions and consequences of warfare? Finally, did the Giriama ultimately derive any special benefits or respect from the British because they had demonstrated their willingness to fight?

In order to determine why the Giriama chose rebellion in 1914, and to assess the impact of that rebellion, this study explores the development of the Giriama, from 1800 to 1920, in the context of the environmental, economic, political, and social changes that occurred along the coast and in the newly formed British Protectorate. Giriama economy, politics, and society all underwent drastic changes around mid-century, as the Giriama dispersed from the fortified clearing (Kaya Giriama) in which they had all lived. The prosperity they enjoyed in the period of the 1850s through the 1870s suffered a setback in the 1880s. During the 1890s, they regained prosperity but also encountered increasing disruption, for the British declared a formal protectorate over the coast, hinterland, and far interior in 1895. Between 1900 and 1912 the coastal economy became isolated from the mainstream, and the economic independence of the Giriama made a striking contrast to the growing economic dependence of Africans in the interior.

Administrative intervention in Giriama affairs did not come until 1912; it immediately stimulated the first phase of rebellion, in 1913. This was followed by severe reprisals and an attempt at reconciliation, which failed. The Giriama undertook open warfare in August 1914, and the aftermath—the year of the fine in 1915, the struggles of Giriama deprived of their Trans-Sabaki lands, the subsequent changes in administrative policy—was even more traumatic than the war itself. The political behavior of the Giriama and of other noncentralized societies, when faced with a newly formed colonial economy, can best be understood when the direct conflict between African and colonial economic systems is itself clearly understood.

In order to have a context for the history of the Giriama, it is useful to see them in their modern environment. The Giriama are agriculturalists, cattle-keepers, and traders who dominate the woodland plateau in Kenya's immediate coastal hinterland, between the town of Mombasa and the Malindi/Mambrui complex.* Numbering approximately 150,000 in 1969 and occupying almost 2,500 square miles—mostly in scattered patrilineal, patrilocal homesteads—today they are the major population in Kilifi District, Coast Province.[3]

Giriama homesteads are linked primarily by footpaths. The road from Mombasa to Malindi has been paved for many years, but only in the last few years has the spur road into Kaloleni been topped; a network of dirt roads joins small administrative centers such as Ganze, Hadu, Kinarani, and Vitengeni. The only semiurban population is at Kaloleni in the southeast, where cash crops foster a concentrated residence pattern. Recently, a few government-sponsored resettlement schemes have moved some Giriama nearer to the coast, to Mombasa, Takaungu, Malindi, and Mambrui; a few have gone to Nairobi. Many of these relocated Giriama have become converts to Islam, and some have been incorporated into the Swahili population, abandoning their Giriama identity. The vast majority of the Giriama, however, remain in the coastal hinterland.

In this coastal hinterland, even during the dry season when no moisture falls from the sky and the maize in the fields suffers and threatens to die before maturing, the air that reaches just beyond the Kenya coast from Mombasa to Malindi is hot and humid. Most Giriama spend their days in the fields, walking the lengthy footpaths that join the rather small, isolated clusters of homesteads, or sitting under baobab trees discussing the day's events.

The Giriama participate only minimally in the wage-labor market. Their economy is based on their own grain production, and agricultural labor is primarily women's work. Most cultivation is still done with hand hoes, hatchets, and digging sticks. The chief crops are maize, millet, eleusine, beans,

*When the British first formed a protectorate in 1895, the Giriama area was a part of Seyyidie Province, sharing portions of Malindi and Nyika districts. By 1909, Mombasa and Malindi districts had been expanded to incorporate Nyika District. In 1924, Mombasa District was again reduced to the immediate area of Mombasa, and Kilifi District replaced Malindi District: S. H. Ominde, *Land and Population Movements in Kenya* (Evanston, Illinois, 1968), pp. 4-9 and map, p. 6; "Kenya: Report on the Regional Boundaries Commission" App. 6, Map 1 (PP: C. 1899).

sorghum, pulses, tobacco, and rice. A few areas grow cotton; at Kaloleni and in the government settlements coconut trees are cultivated for *tembo* (palm wine) or copra (for oil), and scattered orange and cashew trees offer cash income. Most families have a few goats and chickens, and some Giriama have herds of cattle which are tended by young boys.

The Giriama have been only casually attracted to mission education. As a result, their literacy rate is low and few Giriama have continued their education as far as University. The majority of the population still speak kiGiriama rather than kiSwahili, though the languages are extremely close linguistically.* Those who speak English live mostly in the areas of the old mission stations, in the south at Kaloleni and Mwabayanyundo and in the north around Jilore. Although some of the younger generation have adopted Western dress, most Giriama still wear imported cloth wrappers; the elders wear a waist cloth and carry a walking stick; and some Giriama women still wear the traditional short, layered skirts which resemble ballet tutus. (Once made of grass, these are now made of cotton cloth.)

Today the Giriama are represented in local government by appointed chiefs, but most daily government is still conducted by local councils of elders. More and more land is being held individually, but registration of land has not yet begun. In the reopened kaya, a general assembly for all Giriama theoretically meets to deal with general problems, but in fact a few representatives maintain this center, acting as spokesmen for the Giriama when called upon to do so.

The Giriama are the largest of the cluster of nine peoples who call themselves Mijikenda.† The others are the Digo, Duruma, Rabai, Ribe, Kauma, Kambe, Chonyi, and Jibana. They have shared a cultural and linguistic relationship in the Mombasa hinterland for several centuries, but they lacked any cooperative political organization until the late 1940s, when they assumed a collective political identification by choosing the name *Mijikenda* and forming the Mijikenda Union.**

The Giriama, with other Mijikenda, were one of the leading groups in

---

*KiGiriama is one of the Mijikenda languages within the Sabaki subgroup of the northeastern Bantu. Sabaki, a name suggested by C. Ehret and used subsequently by Thomas Hinnebusch, includes three languages, Mijikenda, Pokomo, and Swahili: Thomas Hinnebusch, "The Shungwaya Hypothesis: A Linguistic Reappraisal," in *East African Cultural History*, ed. J. Gallagher (Syracuse, New York, 1975), pp. 1-42. This finding has been independently confirmed by Derek Nurse and G. Philippson. KiGiriama was originally regarded as a dialect of the Nyika language of the northeastern Bantu: see Clement M. Doke, *Bantu: Modern Grammatical, Phonetical, and Lexicographical Studies since 1860* (London, 1945), pp. 1, 42, 43, 46, and Malcolm Guthrie, *The Classification of the Bantu Languages* (London, 1948), p. 43.

†The Giriama's own term, *Makayachenda*, the nine makaya, was changed by them to *Midzichenda*, but the Swahili term *Mijikenda* is best known and has now been accepted by the Mijikenda themselves. Most accounts referred to these people collectively as the Nyika, a term they now consider derogatory.

**The Mijikenda Union was formed for self-identification, in response to the nationalist movement in Kenya that was intended to counteract growing political and land demands made by the Afro-Arabs of the coast.

KADU (Kenya African Democratic Union), the opposition party to KANU (Kenya African National Union). Prior to Kenyan independence KADU supported regionalism rather than federalism for the new government. The promising Giriama politician and leader of KADU, Ronald Ngala, helped to incorporate his party into KANU at the time of independence, after which he served in several high ministries. His recent and untimely death has cost the Giriama their representation in current national politics.

In an attempt to halt African migration and make land available for settler use, the colonial officials early on established reserves for African occupation. Except for the Taru Desert to the west, which serves as a natural boundary, these colonially imposed boundaries for the Giriama define their borders today: the area of Kaya Giriama and Kaloleni to the south, the lush tropical coastal strip to the east, and the hinterland to Mambrui in the Trans-Sabaki to the north (though some Giriama have gone to the Tana River valley to live). The Giriama, like other Kenyan peoples, have developed a political economy suited to the conditions of their new life and environment, and they have adapted to the changes wrought by climate, by outsiders, and by their own sense of tradition and new options. Like other Kenyan peoples, they initially viewed the British as no more than a passing group of traders, or, at most, as religious, military, or political representatives. They had no way of knowing the degree to which these people from so far away were to change the dimensions of Giriama life.

2
Nineteenth-Century Adaptation,
1800-1890

In the nineteenth century, the scope and direction of the Giriama economy underwent a major transformation. Significant modifications were necessary in their political system, and these were connected, in varying degrees, with the political economy of Afro-Arab communities along the coast. This all took place during a period of British interference in Afro-Arab dominance of the Indian Ocean. By the time the British declared a protectorate over the area in 1895, the coastal economy had altered completely.

To understand the Giriama reaction to the imposition of colonial authority it is necessary to become familiar with the changes made by the Giriama in their political organization and economic system. In the first period (called the kaya period), which lasted until about mid-century, all the Giriama lived in or near their fortified clearing (*kaya*) in the Mombasa hinterland. Their traditional political system, called the kaya system, was one in which a permanent council of elders, representing all six clans, oversaw the operation of the Giriama as trading middlemen between the coastal enclave of Mombasa and the interior. This period, the culmination of several centuries of relationships with the coast and interior, supplied the Giriama with political and economic experiences that they later adapted to the conditions they encountered in the second half of the nineteenth century.

The period from mid-century until 1890 is called the Godoma period, because many Giriama moved from the kaya area to the Godoma region of the hinterland of Takaungu. As Giriama dispersed northward from their kaya, economic changes forced them to abandon their traditional role as trading middlemen and instead to become producers in a market economy. The elders in council lost both their power to regulate behavior and their privilege as main beneficiaries of Giriama economic prosperity. The last decade of the Godoma period was characterized by quarrels between Giriama

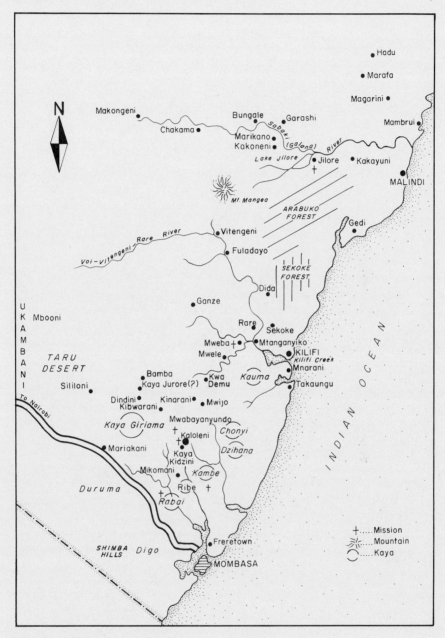

Map 2.   Giriama expansion.

and their trading allies, disruption of the political process, serious famines, and another phase of migration, again northward, into the valley of the Sabaki River—a move that brought them into the newly established British sphere.

THE KAYA PHASE

At the beginning of the nineteenth century, the world and experiences of most Giriama were restricted to the immediate environs of their fortified kaya in the Mombasa district, where they grew grain and kept cattle. They governed themselves through a ruling council of elders and successfully developed a middleman/trader role between Mombasa and the hinterland beyond their kaya. The elders determined the terms of this trade, redistributed the society's wealth, and served in regulatory and judiciary capacities.[1] At this time there were probably about 5,000 Giriama; their population was the largest of any of the Mijikenda peoples then, as it is today.*

The Giriama had as neighbors other Mijikenda, who lived close to the coast. Their makaya dotted the dense forests that covered a ridge rising 800 feet parallel to the coast and 12 miles inland. From the Shimba Hills south of Mombasa to Kilifi Creek to the north, the makaya were situated in the following order: Digo, Duruma (at Mnyenzeni), Rabai, Ribe, Kambe, Jibana, Chonyi, and Kauma. The Giriama, however, had chosen not to occupy this most fertile portion of the Mijikenda zone when they arrived in the area several centuries earlier; they had opted to clear less dense forest, twenty miles inland, in order to keep cattle as well as to grow grain and, perhaps, to draw upon the hunting abilities of their Waata allies and to foster trade. By choosing this environment they were exchanging the generous ridge rainfall of 35 to 45 inches for the 25 inches of annual rainfall of the drier forest, but the absence of the tsetse fly further inland made cattlekeeping possible.

The pastoral Oroma, traditional enemies of the Mijikenda for two centuries or more, grazed their cattle in the area surrounding the Giriama fortifications, and frequently stole Giriama cattle. The Giriama stayed within their fortifications as much as possible, but the constant threat of the predatory Oroma meant that Giriama kept cattle only at great risk.[2]

The Giriama, like all the Mijikenda, were primarily agriculturalists. In the nearby fields they cultivated the traditional staple crops of millet (*mawele*), sorghum (*mtama*), eleusine (*wimbe*), cassava, beans (*kunde*), sweet potatoes, pulses (*pojo*), and yams, and they also grew tobacco and castor beans. Since they practiced swidden agriculture to clear virgin woodland and to provide nutrients from the ashes, the Giriama could use land for no more than three years before leaving it fallow for approximately ten more, to allow nutrient recovery. This extensive use of land gradually pushed their farming further and further from the kaya, to the protection of which they returned each night. The Giriama were also hunters and trappers, using special pits and

*For a full discussion of Giriama demography, see Chapter 3, pp. 51-53.

snares as well as bows and arrows, but to acquire ivory they relied mostly on trade with Waata hunters. Most families kept goats, sheep, and chickens, and some acquired cattle. Each family made its own pottery and baskets, as well as bows, arrows, and arrow poison; blacksmiths produced hoes, knives, axes, and arrow tips. The major import, palm wine for rituals, came from the Digo, who initially had the only coconut trees.

The Giriama government had been formed by a combination of clan and age organization: the council of elders included the most senior men of the society, while representing all kin groups. The kaya had originally been settled according to membership in six patrilineal clans, but these clans were not all of equal size. Only through clan membership did each Giriama acquire kaya identity. Over the years, the clans had been divided into subclans and further divided into lineages; the number of clans had always remained at six, but as the Giriama population grew, they created new subclans, assimilated new members, and redivided. Reciprocal social relations, particularly births, marriages, and funerals, occurred at the subclan level. For most daily activities the lineage was the significant association; farming units and homesteads normally included three generations.*

In order to keep larger clans from dominating smaller ones, the Giriama divided the society by age as well as by clan descent. Through initiation into age-sets and eventual promotion of an age-set into a ruling generation (*rika*), Giriama men passed through clearly marked stages, from childhood (*umundo*), to warriorhood (*nyere*), to responsible adulthood as councillors (*kambi*). Respect, power, and control were maintained by the kambi, who as members of a ruling rika sat in public council to determine the regulations of the society and to adjudicate conflict.

The elders' position of power in Giriama society was renewed periodically, through their control over the complex rituals that advanced a man's status. Young boys were initiated into age-sets through the ritual of *Mwanza M'Kulu*, a new ruling rika was installed through the elaborate celebration of *Mung'aro*, and elders were advanced to kambi through the training of *Kirao*. Ruling elders controlled all these ceremonies and, with them, the transfer of power.[3]

In difficult situations, ruling elders were assisted by the members of a secret society, the *Vaya*, to which the most prestigious Giriama elders belonged. Vaya judicial procedures could be conducted in secret and the most powerful Giriama oath, *Fisi* (*hyena*), could be administered only by the twelve Fisi medicine men, who came from the Vaya ranks and represented all six clans.† Giriama elders, sitting in council and supported by the Vaya secret society, maintained order and exerted power over the entire Giriama population. The fact that the Giriama lived in such close proximity to one another facilitated the elders' control; to escape from the protection of the kaya was virtually impossible until the middle of the nineteenth century.

*Since the Giriama have not retained clan histories—their emphasis is on the present— genealogical subclan links can seldom be traced.

†Giriama men have three other secret societies, Habasi, Kinyenzi, and Gohu, but none of the others has a specific role in the governmental process.

The Mombasa Alliance

As the Giriama and other Mijikenda developed separate ethnic identities in the Mombasa hinterland, they maintained ritual, cultural, and economic links, but the most significant relationship for the Giriama was that with the coastal Afro-Arabs, which grew to be one of mutual support. Centuries before, the relationship between the Mijikenda and the Mombasa population had been hostile. The Mijikenda had frequently attacked the island, disrupting island life and threatening the existence of the vulnerable population. To prevent such raids, the Afro-Arabs had paid substantial tribute to the Mijikenda and eventually gained them as allies.*

It had been crucial, for three reasons, for the Mombasa population to develop amicable relationships with her hinterland peoples. The greatest threat to Mombasa's existence came from the sea, particularly from the Portuguese and from Arabs. The Afro-Arabs of Mombasa had needed Mijikenda assistance in protecting themselves from these potential conquerors. Their dependence on the Mijikenda extended beyond protection, however. Since only a limited amount of grain could be grown on the island, the Mombasa population negotiated a regular supply of grain from the hinterland peoples. Moreover, the economic basis of Afro-Arab communities on the East African coast was exportation of goods from Africa's interior. The inhabitants of Mombasa, unable to acquire these goods directly, had always depended upon the Mijikenda to provide them. In exchange for these three sorts of services, the Mombasa peoples had paid regular tribute to the Mijikenda, had offered the Mijikenda the right to participate in Mombasa politics, and had paid for the privilege of trading with Mijikenda representatives who came to Mombasa. In this way, the Mijikenda established a stable relationship, based on military, political, and economic alliances.

Mijikenda participation in Mombasa politics supported a stable climate for trade. The major gain for the Mijikenda in trading food to Mombasa was not the cloth, beads, and iron wire they received in return (some of which they kept and some of which they traded again to the Digo for palm wine) but protection against famine, which hit this area of East Africa periodically. During these times of drought and famine, the Arabs and Swahili, who had access to grain brought from the sea, were willing to provide famine relief for their political and trading allies. The Giriama were more susceptible to droughts than the

---

*Rezende's observation in 1634 was that "they [Mombasa Swahili] are like prisoners of the Mozungullos Caffres [Mijikenda], because they have to pay them in large tribute in cloth in order to be allowed to live in security": J. M. Gray, "Rezende's Description of East Africa in 1634," *Tanganyika Notes and Records* 23 (June 1947): 12. Portuguese records verify that by 1592 some Mijikenda had allied with Mombasa in a struggle against Malindi, and a few years later Mijikenda raids on the island were so serious that, after an unsuccessful attempt to fortify Makupa on the mainland, the Portuguese were forced to pay tribute to the Mijikenda; Justus Strandes, *The Portuguese Period in East Africa* (Nairobi, 1961), pp. 168-69: Gray, "Rezende's Description," pp. 9-24. Mijikenda assisted a Mombasa rebellion against the Portuguese in 1631-32: Strandes, *Portuguese Period*, p. 179. In 1720, Mijikenda assisted Mombasa in the expulsion of the Portuguese: Strandes, *Portuguese Period*, p. 253.

ridge-kaya Mijikenda, and had more to gain from such protection. Conversely, the Giriama were the most significant trading partners for Mombasa, for they provided the major items for export—ivory, gum copal, rhinoceros horns, cattle, and hides.[4]

Until the late eighteenth century, it was through their alliances with interior peoples that the Giriama obtained the goods with which they supplied Mombasa. They obtained ivory primarily from the Waata, who hunted the fringes of the forest and followed the herds of elephants. Waata exchanged tusks for food and resting-places in Giriama homes. Most of the cattle were obtained from Oroma who, through Waata mediation, met Giriama at a market place in Biryaa on the fringe of the Taru Desert and traded their cattle for beads and for chains that Giriama women fashioned from iron received at Mombasa. This trading relationship was uncertain, for the traditional enmity between the Giriama and the Oroma often flared up, but due to the mutual alliance with the Waata, this trade increasingly expanded. Over the years, the trade between Mombasa and the interior was regularized: the Giriama traded grain, sesame, and tobacco from their shambas, gum copal and timber collected from the forests, and ivory, rhino horn, hippo teeth, cattle, hides, honey, and beeswax obtained from the Waata and Oroma, in exchange for salt, cloth, beads, and iron from the coast.[5]

By controlling access to the interior and by delivering goods directly to the coast, the Giriama dominated Mombasa's trade. In the second half of the eighteenth century the Giriama began intermittently to send caravans to Chagga territory, around Mount Kilimanjaro, and to trade with Kamba in the highlands near Mount Kenya, offering arrow poison and coastal trade-goods in exchange for ivory and cattle. These hazardous journeys across the Taru Desert, which risked the hostility of the Kwavi and Oroma who commanded the territory, were the first stage in opening up the interior beyond the desert barrier. Traveling in small caravans, the Giriama dispersed to individual Kamba homesteads, where they drew upon long-term blood-brotherhood trading relations that afforded mutual protection. Although this trade involved great risk, the profitable exchange for ivory on the coast and the acquisition of cattle made the effort worthwhile.[6]

In the late eighteenth century Kamba traders from Kitui began to connect their internal markets with Mombasa, bringing caravans to the coast in order to trade directly with the Giriama. Eventually the network of exchange the Giriama had created in Ukambani was replaced by long-distance Kamba caravans that brought a large volume of trade goods, especially ivory, directly to the markets just outside Mombasa, and there the Giriama acted as middlemen between the Kamba and the coastal Swahili. The Giriama continued to go in small groups to Ukambani for cattle, and Biryaa, the major Giriama-Oroma market on the fringe of the Taru Desert, continued to receive Kamba ivory. Loss of the bulk of the highland ivory trade did not relegate the Giriama to a secondary trading role, however; using their Waata allies as intermediaries, they intensified their ivory trade with the Oroma, and there was still ample ivory in the northern coastal hinterland. The long-distance Kamba caravan trade supplemented rather than supplanted Giriama trade, and the two peoples continued their amicable relationship.[7]

The Maasai, the Oroma, and Migration

Through the early part of the nineteenth century the political system within the kaya was stable and strong. The Giriama elders controlled use of communally held lands, distribution of cattle for bridewealth, and—through their appointed agent, the *mwanandia*—trade with the coast. The proceeds from all trade went to the elders for redistribution; in this way they maintained control over the youthful warriors, who could never gain significant power by participating in defensive warfare. Young Giriama men were dependent upon their fathers for status (through membership in the kambi council and in secret societies), and for bridewealth (which would allow them to marry and to establish their own homes). Elders in council held power over the society as a whole; and each elder in his homestead held power over his sons. The elders accumulated cattle; they and their wives wore imported cloth and beads; and they dominated the rituals and the supply of palm wine—all of which served to enhance Giriama prestige and power in general, and the position of the elders in particular, well into the early part of the nineteenth century.[8]

By the early nineteenth century the Giriama were reaping benefits both from the firmly established political system inside their kaya and from regularized political trading relationships with Mombasa and with their inland neighbors, but beginning in the late 1830s and continuing through the middle of the century, both internal and external conditions changed so drastically that the Giriama were impelled to begin a slow, and eventually prosperous, migration northward. Externally, altered relationships between the Giriama and the neighboring Oroma, as well as the development of Arab-owned, slave-worked coastal plantations, modified trading patterns and set the stage for upheaval. Internally, the kaya system itself decreased in effectiveness.

Changing patterns of trade and agriculture, and conflict among the interior peoples—in particular the Oroma and Maasai groups called Kwavi—restricted Giriama movement but gave them new options. The Giriama had always recognized the advantages of living beyond the protective fortress of their kaya, for the surrounding area offered additional land for cultivating their grains and tobacco and sesame, while living outside the kaya made trading contacts easier. But peaceful conditions were a prerequisite to leaving the communal and physical protection of the kaya, and though in prior centuries the Giriama had experienced short periods of minimal threat from raiders, for the most part their caution was well-advised. Over the centuries many agricultural peoples, such as the Kikuyu, Kamba, Shambaa, Pare, Chagga, Taveta, Taita, and other Mijikenda, had found refuge from pastoral raiders in highland areas, on hilltops, and on ridges. The Giriama were one of the few peoples who hid in a lowland forest. Intermittent Maasai and Oroma raids had taught them to be wary, and most agricultural people kept cattle only at considerable risk.

The Giriama, the Kamba, and the Oroma were all influenced by repercussions from the nineteenth-century Maasai civil wars. From about 1815 to 1875, various groups of Maa-speaking (Maasai) peoples throughout Kenya became locked in civil war. Those Maasai called Kwavi had ravaged the Vanga hinterland south of Mombasa, but in the 1830s, the Kwavi were defeated so severely by other Maasai that the resulting peaceful conditions facilitated inland trade from the coast at Vanga. Far west of Mombasa, however, the Maasai were able to recover, and from the 1840s onward their raids along the coast from Mombasa as far north as the Sabaki River brought periods of harassment to the hinterland and, on a few occasions, to Mombasa itself.[9]

During the nineteenth century the Oroma, confronted by strong enemies such as the Maasai and Somali and, to some extent, the Kamba, lost their dominant position in the coastal hinterland. Maasai attacks concentrated on the Oroma cattle, because from them the Maasai could restock their herds. Between 1858 and 1867 Maasai raiders defeated the Oroma along the Sabaki River; in the 1860s the Oroma were suffering cattle raids by the Kamba in what had been neutral territory;[10] and in the north, between the Juba and Tana rivers, Oroma trading and territorial dominance was being effectively challenged by Somali.[11] The Oroma started to retreat northward and found themselves in isolated pockets, sometimes entirely stripped of their cattle and dependent on their long-standing alliance with the Waata. Many Oroma became agriculturalists in order to survive, and they were increasingly receptive to trade with their former enemies, the Giriama.[12]

For the Giriama, the main result of these changes was to open land for cultivation. For the first time Mijikenda, particularly the Giriama, had the option of clearing permanent homesteads outside their makaya. The Giriama transformed their former hostile relationship with the Oroma into one of alliance, in the hope that the Oroma would not regain their strength.

The Oroma decline did become permanent; by the 1860s they had lost any chance of recovery. Sometime after 1865, as one story goes, the Oroma were victims of a Somali trap designed to gain dominance over them. The Somali invited the Oroma in the northern part of the coast to a deceptive "love feast" in the Tana River valley, at which they assassinated 2,000 Oroma leaders, captured 8,000 women and children, and raided 30,000 cattle.* The final blow came in the 1890s, when the scattered and disorganized Oroma lost almost all their cattle to rinderpest. Most of the surviving Oroma became clients of the Somali.

---

*There is controversy regarding this "love feast" incident. See C. W. Hobley, *Kenya: From Chartered Company to Crown Colony* (London, 1970), pp. 176-77; I. M. Lewis, "Somali Conquest of the Horn of Africa," *Journal of African History* 1:2 (1960): 226; and Kenneth Mac-Dougall, "Notes on the Decline and Extermination of the Gallas," 31 March 1914 (KNA: DC/MAL/2/3).

Had the decline of the Giriama's major enemy, the Oroma, been the only change, the Giriama would probably have limited their expansion to the immediate area of their kaya, as the Chonyi and Rabai had done under similar circumstances. But other conditions were changing as well, and the combined effect was to encourage the Giriama to move well beyond the immediate environs of their kaya to small, scattered homesteads, separating this once cohesive people.*

Modifications in relationships among Africans in the coastal interior were matched by changes in the economy and politics of the coast. In the nineteenth century, as Arabs, Indians, Europeans, and Americans came in greater numbers to the East African coast to participate in trade, they in turn influenced the volume of export and became embroiled in political issues of trade control. As a result, the Giriama trading and political network, drawn ever more closely into this far-reaching capitalist expansion, was radically modified.

The Coastal Trade

At the beginning of the century, coastal trade focused not only on the Mombasa exchange, in which the Giriama played an indispensable role, but also on other towns and islands off the coast. Kilwa, to the east of Lake Nyasa on the southern East African coast, had long been a primary source of slaves exported to Arabia. Zanzibar, a large island southeast of Mombasa with an excellent harbor and a permanent group of Arab traders, had become a coordinating center for much of Kilwa's trade. Zanzibar and the nearby island of Pemba offered agricultural potential as well. The islands of the Lamu Archipelago (Lamu, Manda, and Pate), sources of ivory and sesame, were often in competition with each other and with Zanzibar, Mombasa, and Kilwa for trading dominance. In the nineteenth century these centers, which for centuries had generally traded as independent entities, expanded into a single network as the East African coast supported a rich and complex

---

*The beginning date of the Giriama dispersal remains uncertain. Descendants of those Mazrui Arabs who first arrived in Takaungu reported the Giriama to be still in their kaya in 1834: Kenneth MacDougall, "Notes on the History of the Wanyika," Kilifi District Book, compiled 31 March 1914 (KNA: CP 75/46). In 1845 Krapf, who never mentioned a kaya, visited several Giriama hamlets near Mombasa, among them "Kerima Hamlet" (Giriama) of Babai Korura (8-10 cottages) and Mikomani (20 cottages), which he was told was the largest Giriama community outside "Embirria" (Biryaa), where he mistakenly understood the majority of the Giriama to reside (Krapf, CMS: 5/016/166). In his journey along the trade route to Ukambani in 1849 Krapf met many Giriama, but he mentions no Giriama communities there (Krapf, CMS: CA 5/016/174). Thus it appears that by mid-century the Giriama had at most begun to spread into a few homesteads in the direction of Mombasa. The Giriama apparently followed the same pattern as their Digo and Duruma neighbors, who had moved westward from their makaya to take advantage of cattlekeeping and trade in the late eighteenth century. The Rabai built additional makaya, but did not stray, because they had planted valuable coconut trees and were tapping them for palm wine to sell to the Mijikenda: T. T. Spear, "The Kaya Complex: A History of the Mijikenda Peoples of the Kenya Coast to 1900" (Ph.D. dissertation, University of Wisconsin, 1974), chap. 4.

commercial empire, dominated by Omani Arabs, financed by Indians, and provisioned from Africa's interior.[13]

The Arabs were primarily traders, but in an attempt to diversify their sources of income, to make full use of the dhows which could carry all types of goods from the East African coast, and to enjoy profits in their new homeland, they began to turn to agriculture, using slaves exclusively not only to do the clearing and cultivating but for much of the supervision as well. Although very few slaves had ever been captured for sale from the Mombasa hinterland, slaves—most of them from Kilwa, which was further south—had been a major East African export in the late 1700s. With the closing of the French markets, the volume of exported slaves declined; thereafter, most exported slaves went to Arabia and Brazil. In an attempt to find a substitute for slaves as a major trade item, in the 1830s the sultan developed clove plantations on Zanzibar and Pemba islands. Climate and conditions there were perfect for delicate clove trees, but planting, cultivating, and harvesting were all labor-intensive.* The resultant demand for slaves as laborers in the 1840s again increased the volume of slave trade; now, however, the largest volume of slaves was traded directly to Zanzibar rather than being exported to Arabia.

The clove plantations were well established by the 1840s, when the sultan made this island the capital of his empire. Zanzibar was a perfect staging place because the sultan drew on previous successful trade in ivory and slaves from Kilwa on the southern mainland, on the loyalty of Zanzibar's Arab inhabitants, and on the island's own agricultural potential.

The success of agriculture on Zanzibar encouraged the Arabs to cultivate on the mainland. Zanzibar's cloves, and mainland products such as maize, coconuts, sesame, and millet, ushered in a new economic phase for the coast. In subsequent decades, plantations worked exclusively by slaves became permanently established, and slaves became even more crucial to the East African economy as agricultural laborers than they had been as an item of trade.[14]

This commercial empire was formed under the astute leadership of an Omani Arab, Seyyid Sa'id bin Sultan Al-Busaidi. The Busaidi had been the ruling dynasty in Oman since the 1740s. Seyyid Sa'id inherited the throne in 1807, at the age of eleven, and within a few years had brought his grasp of commerce and his penchant for organization to bear on the exploitation of the Indian Ocean network. The link between Oman in Arabia and the East African coast was based on the predictable and constant monsoon winds which every year carried sailing vessels from Oman to and from ports on the East African coast. Successful maritime trade from Muscat, Oman's capital and port on the Persian Gulf, was due to its central position in Arabian, Persian, and European trade. With the decline of Portuguese influence in the

---

*Picking the clove bud from the end of the branch without breaking the branch itself is a delicate job. There are two harvest seasons, and each tree has to be picked several times each season; then the buds have to be separated from the stems and dried for approximately six days before being collected for sale.

Indian Ocean in the eighteenth century and an increasing demand for slaves, ivory, and other African items such as hides, grains, sesame, and copal, the Omani Arabs were drawn to East Africa.[15]

In the early part of the nineteenth century Seyyid Sa'id forcefully incorporated the numerous independent islands and towns of the East African coast into a single East African commercial empire. His navy forced into submission the Arabs of such islands as Lamu, Pate, and Pemba and the mainland centers of the Somali, Bajuni, and Kilwa coasts. The last major Busaidi struggle to win coastal control was the fight with the Mazrui, who commanded Mombasa.[16] The Mazrui had been powerful enough, with Mijikenda support, to stave off numerous attacks from various outsiders over the years, but in 1837, despite help from their hinterland Mijikenda allies, the Mazrui were forced to turn over control to the sultan.[17]

Following the Busaidi take-over of Mombasa, Giriama and other Mijikenda lost their privileged role in Mombasa trade and their special political connections. Furthermore, they suffered from Busaidi animosity for having assisted the ousted Mazrui. Mijikenda support of the Mombasa Mazrui had been a significant factor in the previous unsuccessful efforts of the Busaidi to control Mombasa. The Busaidi launched slave-raids against the Giriama, who had recently been weakened by famine. Worst of all, the Busaidi broke a long-standing pawning agreement. As was the custom, the Mijikenda had pawned some of their wives and daughters to families in Mombasa as collateral for the following year's crops. Under normal conditions the Mazrui would, upon payment, have returned these people; instead, the Busaidi sent some of these pawned Mijikenda to Arabia as slaves.[18]

The Busaidi also broke the pattern of Mombasa dependency on the Mijikenda for food. The Mijikenda had for several centuries supplied the inhabitants of Mombasa with food, and although some Swahili and their slaves cultivated small plots on the mainland early in the century, British observers in 1824 remarked on Mombasa's limited agricultural production.[19] Now, using large forces of slaves residing in small communities on the mainland, the Mombasa population began to cultivate extensive maize and rice fields, and encroached on the Mijikenda lowland farms.[20] When an 1845 British ban on exporting slaves to Arabia increased the number of slaves available locally, Mombasa inhabitants enlarged their farms. By the late 1840s Mombasa was able to export grain, most of which was grown by slave labor, though some was obtained through traders from Mijikenda.[21] Although economic relations were eventually restored between the Busaidi and the Mijikenda, Mombasa ceased to be dependent on the Mijikenda either for protection or for food. Kamba were bringing goods directly from the highlands to Mombasa; Mombasa traders began to send some of their own caravans up-country; and the inhabitants of Mombasa were able to feed themselves. The position of the Giriama as trading middlemen to Mombasa had been seriously undermined.

THE GODOMA PHASE

The end of Giriama dominance in Mombasa coincided with a change in their relationship with neighboring Oroma which provided them with new interior trading partners and with land on which to establish permanent farms outside the kaya. As a result, although some Giriama remained participants in kaya-Mombasa trade, a new economic phase began that was centered not in the kaya but in an area to the north, called Godoma, which formed the hinterland of Takaungu town.

Some Mazrui Afro-Arabs had left Mombasa after their defeat in 1837 and settled at Takaungu, a town thirty-five miles to the north on the coast, just south of Kilifi Creek.[22] This move offered the Giriama an opportunity to maintain old trading alliances in a new place. In order to respond to this attractive opportunity, however, the Giriama political system, which had been dominated by elders, had to give way to a younger group of enterprising men. The cohesive society that had once occupied the small area inside the kaya was to become dispersed over a large area.

The Mazrui moved to Takaungu intending to combine trade and agricultural production; naturally, they wanted to retain their Giriama trading alliance. They encouraged the Giriama to bring ivory and other goods to Takaungu, offering a new port for Giriama goods and expanding the volume of trade. Mazrui development of plantations fed into a grain-trading network and tempted Giriama to grow maize for export. The Giriama, no longer mere middlemen in the trade from the coast to the interior, became producers of grain as well as collectors of new trade items such as rubber and gum copal, which were available in the forests of Biryaa and Arabuko-Sekoke north of Takaungu. From the 1850s and 1860s, when the Giriama began moving into the Takaungu hinterland, until the final abolition of the slave trade in 1876, Giriama prosperity steadily increased.

Many Giriama began moving northward from their kaya, building small homesteads on land vacated by Oroma, in hidden woodland locations with nearby clearings for cultivation. Eventually they expanded into three regions. The area immediately to the north and east of the kaya was called Weruni, and already contained many Giriama farms. A region to the northwest called Biryaa developed around the trading center of Biryaa and became a particularly good region for grazing cattle. By far the greatest number of Giriama, however, moved into Godoma, a northern region crossed from west to east by the river system of the Ndzovuni, Rare, and Vitengeni rivers, which flowed together at Mtanganyiko into the salty waters of Kilifi Creek.[23]

These moves were not easy. Water was scarce: the rivers usually ran dry months before the rainy season began again, and the threat of drought was ever-present. The Giriama developed a number of ways of coping with this problem: they tended to settle in areas where the vegetation was an indicator of sufficient rainfall for crops; they dug waterholes called *mitsara* (which, however, often became brackish); and, since they now occupied varied eco-

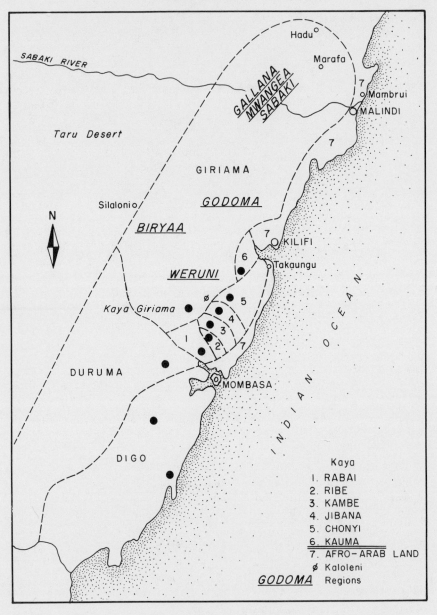

Map 3.   Nineteenth-century Giriama expansion in relation to other Mijikenda.

logical regions, rather than the restricted area of the kaya, at least a part of the population now had food to share with those who were most affected by drought.[24] As they separated, they developed networks of communication so that they would be able to assist one another. Moreover, extended trading operations made possible the purchase of grain during famine.

The new options opened to the Giriama allowed them to deal more successfully with Maasai cattle-raids, which from the 1850s until the late 1880s intermittently plagued the Giriama, Kamba, and Oroma. The hilltop makaya, as well as Mombasa, attracted attacks from Maasai. Some herdsmen chose to move away from the area of the raiding, and others gave up their cattle to the raiders so they could remain to cultivate their crops, but many Giriama found that they could simply hide from the raiders, since Maasai raiding parties never stayed in one area for any length of time.[25] They even became better able to deal directly with their enemies. For years Giriama had felt themselves no match for the Oroma, but now some succeeded in fighting Maasai raiders. In fact, Fungo wa Gona, the kaya spokesman in the early 1870s, became the best-known Giriama hero by leading Giriama in defense against a Maasai attack.[26]

The Maasai threat encouraged many Giriama to keep on the move. Rapid migration was possible because they did not always have to clear land for cultivation; sometimes they found a protected clearing with fertile land nearby. Time was saved by using maize as the staple crop.* Unlike millet, which had been the staple until the early part of the nineteenth century, maize could produce crops twice a year.[27] This shorter planting period facilitated Giriama mobility and promoted their chances of survival.

As the demand for trade goods increased along the coast, the Giriama expanded their trading operations, seeking new sources and meeting the demands for new products. For ivory the Giriama continued to rely on Waata, who remained the major source throughout the nineteenth century. As they moved northward they encountered more and more Waata and thus acquired more ivory.[28] By 1845 the Giriama controlled the market at Biryaa, where they coordinated Oroma, Swahili, and Kamba trade. The Giriama continued their exchange of cloth and tobacco for Oroma livestock and ivory, and they also became brokers for Swahili, mainly from Mombasa, who annually traveled to Biryaa. The Giriama received a portion of the profits as the Swahili exchanged cloth for cattle and ivory. They remained brokers for the Kamba ivory brought to Biryaa, and some Giriama still led caravans to the Kitui Kamba region and to Chagga to collect ivòry and cattle for sale at the coast.[29]

In addition to amassing ivory and livestock for trade, the Giriama began

*Maize did not spread throughout Kenya until the end of the nineteenth century. The history of its introduction to the coastal hinterland and its eventual replacement of millet as the staple food crop remains obscure. The Portuguese brought maize to East Africa, and it probably came to the Mijikenda hinterland from the island of Pemba: A.C.W. Wright, "Maize Names as Indicators of Economic Contacts," *Uganda Journal* 31:1 (March 1949): 66-67.

to acquire other items for exchange at the coast. Hippo teeth and rhino horn came from hunting, and Giriama collected wild rubber and gum copal. Gum copal, which was used in making varnish, was particularly prized by Americans, and although the Mijikenda had collected it for trade at Mombasa since the 1770s, by the 1840s the bulk of this trade had been transferred to Takaungu and to Mtanganyiko, an inland port on Kilifi Creek.*

Takaungu

Takaungu had begun to develop as a trading center when a group of Mazrui moved to Takaungu to escape close Busaidi control. The mainland around Takaungu offered good agricultural potential; the creek provided access for dhows from Arabia; and the town was protected from seaborne enemies.

In the Takaungu system the Afro-Arabs established grain plantations—mostly millet and sesame—along the coast. Landowners acquired vast numbers of slaves (from Kilwa, through Zanzibar) who served as domestic servants, artisans, sailors, and fishermen, as well as cultivators for their new plantations.[30] Because the Busaidi take-over of Mombasa threatened the Giriama trading relationship there, the extension of the trading partnership between the Giriama and their long-term allies the Mazrui at Takaungu was welcome to the Giriama. By contracting an alliance with the Giriama, for their part the Mazrui assured themselves access to indigenous commodities.[31] Moreover, the relationship of interdependence between the Giriama and the Takaungu Mazrui allowed Takaungu considerable independence from the sultan. Local Kauma and Chonyi, who occupied the ridge just behind Takaungu and had little interest in trade, also welcomed the Giriama, who increased food production.

The earliest written accounts of Takaungu come from J. Ludwig Krapf, who represented the Church Missionary Society and who in 1844, at Rabai, started the first mission station in East Africa. His 1845 reports depict Takaungu as a town of 40 to 50 heads of families and 3,000 to 4,000 slaves, most of whom worked grain plantations.[32] He documented Takaungu as an increasingly prosperous town of Arabs, Swahili, and Indians.

But Takaungu had been born out of animosity toward Sultan Seyyid Sa'id at Zanzibar, and despite its prosperity there were several conditions that made its position tenuous. Since the early 1850s Takaungu had been in competition with Malindi. The sultan, who wanted mainland plantations, had reestablished Malindi after it had been abandoned for two centuries following Oroma raids in the late 1660s. The Washella Swahili from Lamu Island and the Bajuni Swahili from the Lamu Archipelago, as well as Omani and Hadrami Arabs, used thousands of slaves imported from Kilwa via

*Takaungu trade included goods brought to two subsidiary entrepôts, Mtanganyiko and Konjora, located where the Rare River enters Kilifi Creek. Takaungu plantations produced sorghum and sesame; maize, gum copal, sorghum, sesame, and ivory came from the Mijikenda: Spear, "Kaya Complex," p. 155.

Zanzibar to cultivate grain around Malindi and to plant extensive areas in coconut, mango, and orange trees.[33] In 1861, 150 Baluchi soldiers, sent by the sultan to protect the Malindi inhabitants from the Oroma, watched over 50 freedmen and more than 1,000 slaves.[34] Since Malindi had no agricultural peoples in her immediate hinterland, more land was available than there was labor to clear. The absence of interior peoples, however, prevented Malindi settlers from gaining access to interior trade goods and encouraged an economy entirely dependent on the production of grain.

Takaungu responded to Malindi competition by encouraging Giriama grain cultivation and setting up outposts for the collection and exportation of maize. Giriama fitted well into their new role as producers; a few extraordinary men, such as Yaa wa Medza and Ngonyo wa Mwavuo had several hundred slaves working on their grain plantations.[35] Yaa wa Medza had converted to Islam, which probably improved his access to slave markets; however, when he later became involved in an inland Christian community he lost his wealth. Ngonyo wa Mwavuo, who was born a Digo but became a Giriama by joining the Akiza Giriama clan, enjoyed ever-increasing prosperity through trading and grain production. His father had begun operations in Rare, northwest of Mtanganyiko, and Ngonyo expanded to Dida, just to the north.

Before 1873, few direct reports of the Giriama in the hinterland exist, but some conclusions can be drawn from the evidence at the coast. We know that Giriama grain added substantially to Takaungu's exports; we also know that many Giriama acquired slaves, because runaways from Giriama account for the majority of the slaves who came to Rabai for refuge.[36] Therefore we can conclude that some portion of Giriama expanded their economic opportunities by using slave labor.* Indeed, many Giriama slaves were incorporated into Giriama society, either through marriage or through becoming attached to a Giriama clan.[37]

Prosperity and Conflict

Since the advantages of living outside the kaya must have been obvious even before they were tested, why did the Giriama remain so long within the confines of that forest clearing? And how is it that the kaya period produced the energy to reformulate Giriama society in conditions of dispersal? Surely the need for new land to cultivate and the attractiveness of the Biryaa-Takaungu trade route had been evident before mid-century. The Giriama relationship with the Oroma had changed by that time: despite some intermittent fighting, both the Oroma and the Giriama had profited from their trading exchange.

The Giriama had originally settled in their fortified kaya for protection and in order to form a new society. Ethnicity was determined by membership

---

*Agricultural labor had long been "women's work"; as slaves were increasingly used for this work, it became even more degrading to a Giriama male to work in the fields.

in the kaya. Since they no longer needed organized protection from the marauding Oroma and since new economic opportunities extended beyond the kaya, an exodus from the kaya seemed reasonable, but this threatened the political structure. Elders, who had the most to gain from keeping the system intact, would lose much of their control if they allowed people to move away. Younger men were frustrated because they were rarely called upon to fill their rôle as warriors.

The kaya was geographically isolated from the trade routes, which had moved further north. It was the young Giriama men who had most to gain from migration: as traders they would have many new opportunities. They could keep some of the trading profits for themselves; they could pay bride-wealth without their fathers' help; and they could, therefore, marry earlier and start their own homes even though their fathers were still heads of the main households. It was politically disadvantageous for younger Giriama to continue to permit the older men to control their lives, and it was economically unsound for them to turn over the trade goods they collected without sharing in the profits. It was this generational conflict—between the elders restraining migration from the kaya and the younger Giriama struggling to remove the restrictions on their lives—that delayed the Giriama migration.

In the process of changing trade patterns, the Giriama elders lost their basis for control over Giriama trade with the coast. Since the kaya was no longer located between the trade source and the port, the elders lost their special political position in Mombasa politics. By moving out of the kaya to reside in the Takaungu hinterland, young Giriama traders removed themselves from the control of the elders, improved their trading opportunities, and also placed themselves in a position to collect additional products, such as the gum copal that was abundant in the Arabuko-Sekoke forest just north of Kilifi Creek, as well as in the Biryaa and Godoma forests. Some traders became sufficiently prosperous to purchase slaves.

The conflict between the elders, who had the prestige and power, and the younger men, whose trading efforts and connections with the hinterland peoples were mainly responsible for the prosperity of the kaya, was most easily solved by migration, which avoided confrontation while it fostered continued Giriama prosperity and retained the elders' prestige. Once the elders recognized the economic benefits of expansion and saw that restricting people to the kaya would result only in political constraint, Giriama began to move outside the kaya quickly and in large numbers.[38]

But the Godoma trading network and agricultural production that made the Giriama increasingly prosperous had its core well outside Giriama control. The Giriama were dependent upon the security and prosperity of Takaungu, where difficulties were multiplying. Internal struggles developed: the Mazrui split into factions and founded independent settlements up and down the coast.[39] These internal squabbles were further stimulated by the interest of some of the factions in joining another Mazrui leader from Gazi, south of Mombasa, who aimed to keep the sultan's coastal dominions in upheaval.

This leader, Mbaruk bin Rashid, persisted in attempting to lead all Mazrui in a fight against the sultan.[40]

The slave supply was also threatened. The sultan, under British pressure to abolish the slave trade, increased restrictions on slave-trading, restrictions that the Takaungu population joined others on the coast in opposing. Moreover, slaves were prone to escape from Takaungu and other plantation areas and to move into the hinterland, where they established separate farming communities. Takaungu planters were compelled either to accept these losses or to mount expensive expeditions to try to recover them. The runaways became potential supporters for Mbaruk or other rival factions and sometimes raided their former masters' crops.

In 1865, following a succession dispute in Takaungu over the position of the *liwali* (governor), the new liwali made peace with the sultan and allowed Zanzibari soldiers to be quartered in Takaungu.[41] By linking Takaungu's commercial network more directly with that of the sultan, Takaungu opened up more trade. As a result, Takaungu inhabitants increased their contacts with the Giriama and other Mijikenda in their hinterland, and Swahili caravans began to go in larger numbers directly from Takaungu into the interior to get goods from the highlands.

This prosperity was accompanied by new difficulties. The firmer the link of Takaungu with the sultan, the greater became Mbaruk's attempts at intervention and disruption around Takaungu.[42] In addition, the sultan himself had become less and less powerful in the Indian Ocean as Europeans, especially the British, gathered strength there. As demands by the French and Germans forced the sultan to depend on Britain, and as Britain insisted more strongly on total abolition of the slave trade, the Omani commercial empire, the plantation agricultural system, and, ultimately, the Giriama Godoma economic prosperity were all to weaken.

BRITISH INVOLVEMENT

The sultan's coordinated commercial empire along the coast, which he controlled from Zanzibar, masked an increasingly intense British involvement in East African affairs. Britain's interest had emerged slowly from the new economic phase of industrial capitalism that had been launched in Europe around 1780, when the economies of western Europe, led by Great Britain, began to undergo a basic transformation from rural agrarianism to urban industrialism. Britain's Industrial Revolution had stimulated cumulative economic growth that went beyond Europe's internal resources to create new demands on overseas economies. The search for raw materials, markets for manufactured products, and food for workers led Europe far outside her own boundaries. New technological advances—particularly steam power and railways—assisted rapid production and made the transportation of raw and finished goods cheaper, easier, and faster.

Britain had a specific purpose in East Africa: to acquire raw materials and luxury items in exchange for mass-produced, machine-made goods, particularly cloth, that could be sold in bulk. Trade linked the wealthy industrial nations to the poor agrarian societies of East Africa. Although East Africa was responsible for only a minuscule portion of Britain's annual economic growth rate of 5.03 percent between 1820 and 1880, British concern for political dominance and humanitarian causes as well as economic profits made East Africa an arena for British involvement.[43]

From 1800 to 1870 in East Africa, a long-term international exchange continued among the forces of the Arabian Peninsula, southwestern Asia, northeastern Africa, and northwestern India. The principal intermediaries in this Indian Ocean/Red Sea/Persian Gulf/Eastern Mediterranean trade were Arab and Indian, rather than Western European; nevertheless, East Africa became an attractive area for future Western investment. As the Western European international economy brought new vitality to Egypt, Syria, and India, East Africans felt secondary reverberations. The increasing volume of Afro-Asian trade attracted European and American traders directly to East African ports, initiating direct interchange between this region and Europe. The rapid expansion of trade along the islands and coastal towns of the East African coast is indicated by the fivefold increase in customs revenues between 1804 and 1859. After 1841, when the sultan channeled all trade through Zanzibar, the external trade is more easily measured: by 1862, it had reached 200,000 Maria Theresa dollars annually, excluding slaves.[44]

Increase in trade volume, widespread use of money, and availability of firearms helped to change the character of trade in the African interior. American, French, German, and British agents came to the Indian Ocean to tap this wealth, and it was the British, through political involvement, who were to have the greatest impact on the sultan's domains. The Busaidi rulers of Oman had early in the century formed an alliance with the British for protection of the Persian Gulf, easing a British political alliance with Zanzibar. The British wanted to maintain their dominance in world trade and to obtain the best trading advantages for investors and private companies, but they also opposed the slave trade, and it was to bring about the abolition of this trade that Britain's intense involvement with East Africa began. British humanitarians argued that abolition was Britain's responsibility and that it could be accomplished by replacing the slave trade with legitimate trade. Thus the British, coming to East Africa with both political and economic goals, met head-on a society thriving on plantation agriculture supported by slaves.

Abolition of the Slave Trade

In 1807 Britain had declared the slave trade illegal and prohibited British subjects from trading or transporting slaves from Africa. Although most of the initial attention was given to West Africa, which supplied the bulk of exported slaves, the Indian Ocean trade also drew considerable attention because of the large number of slaves that had been sold to Ile de France (Mauritius) and Bourbon Island (Réunion) since the end of the eighteenth century. When France ceded Mauritius to Britain at the close of the Napoleonic wars, the British put the 1807 act into effect there.[45] The first move was to send letters to Seyyid Sa'id in Oman, urging him to ban the slave trade in his dominions. This action was taken by at least three British agents: the governor of Bombay in 1815, England's African Institution (which became the Anti-Slavery Society) in 1820, and the governor of Mauritius in 1821. Such interventions were without result, primarily because British moral arguments were not applicable to Islamic society, which permitted slavery, and because the sultan derived considerable revenue from taxing the slave trade.[46]

Ironically, the British began protesting the slave trade at the same time that cloves were being planted at Zanzibar and Pemba with the intention of diverting the economy away from slave-trading (although those plantations actually increased internal demand for slaves). The sultan had to accede to the British urgings, because British sea-power dominated the area and because he was accepting British protection. In 1822 Seyyid Sa'id signed a treaty prohibiting sale of slaves to any Christian nation. In exchange for this sacrifice of part of his revenue and the measure of unpopularity it earned him among his subjects, the sultan gained British support in Oman and kept peace in East Africa. Seyyid Sa'id moved his capital to Zanzibar in 1840; the British sent a consul the following year. This move enabled Britain to exert even greater pressure to end the slave trade. At the time, the number of slaves retained in Zanzibar and Pemba for use on clove plantations was on the upswing. A treaty of 1845 between the sultan of Zanzibar and the British to end shipment of slaves to Arabia turned out to be unenforceable, and the volume of the slave trade rose. Local demand for slaves increased annually, as agricultural development in cash-crop plantations expanded beyond cloves to mainland cultivation of coconuts, grains, and sesame, with total dependence on slave labor.*

Following an economic boom in the 1850s and 1860s in Europe, the British began to face far-reaching changes at home, several of which converged to bring pronounced economic instability to Western Europe. Indus-

---

*The Moresby Treaty of 1832 prohibited sale of slaves to Christians. Many of Moresby's original intentions were apparently modified in the Arabic translation of his treaty, including the provisions for the punishment of offenders. The treaty had been intended to end shipment of slaves from East Africa to Mauritius; however, although it ended open sale of slaves to most Europeans, non-Christian British subjects were not affected: Christine Stephanie Nicholls, *The Swahili Coast: Politics, Diplomacy and Trade on the East African Littoral, 1798-1856* (London, 1971), p. 223; J.M. Gray, *The British in Mombasa, 1824-1826* (London, 1957), p. 30.

The 1845 treaty, which was to come into effect in 1847, called for Seyyid Sa'id to prevent slaves being exported from his dominions in Africa. In addition, he was to prohibit the importation of slaves from anywhere in Africa to his Asian and Arabian possessions, and to encourage his Arabian neighbors to do the same. Although this treaty gave the British authority to search cruisers, its major impact was to ban public sale of slaves without curtailing private sales: Nicholls, *Swahili Coast*, pp. 239-41.

trialization had spread well beyond Britain. The increase in production brought subsequent declines in prices and interest rates; intense competition was generated as the nations of Europe struggled to improve or at least maintain their relative positions. It was in this setting that the powers of continental Europe retreated from liberal free-trade policies and attempted to use cartels in the domestic market to restrict competition. The British, whose trade was greater by far than that of any other power at the time, responded defensively—initially, to maintain a dominant position and, eventually, for survival. Efforts to respond to the trade barriers in Europe led Britain to ensure the security of British trade with such peripheries of the international economy as sub-Saharan Africa, where in 1880 Britain's trade was still three times the value of the combined trade of France, Germany, Holland, Portugal, the U.S.A., and India.[47]

When Sultan Seyyid Sa'id died in 1856, the dual empire encompassing Oman and East Africa was, with British assistance, divided between his two sons: one son, Thwaini, became sultan of Oman and the other, Majid, became sultan of Zanzibar.[48] From then on the fortunes and the security of the sultan of Zanzibar, isolated from his homeland, would become more dependent on the British, who continued to press for a final end to the slave trade. In 1870 Sultan Majid died and was succeeded by his son, Burghash. Although Burghash had made concessions to the British in order to become sultan, he was determined not to assist with abolition in any way. His subjects, whose livelihood was dependent on slave-run plantations, protested abolition strenuously.[49] Circumstances worked against him, however. The devastating hurricane of April 1872, which destroyed two-thirds of the clove plantations and wrecked the sultan's entire shipping fleet, undercut Burghash's independence. John Kirk, the new British consul to Zanzibar, took advantage of the situation to force Burghash to sign the 1873 treaty that prohibited shipment of slaves from the mainland and closed all the slave markets in the sultan's territories. In addition, Burghash bound himself to arrange for prohibition and abolition of the export of slaves from all his dominions.[50]

The immediate result of the 1873 abolition of the sea trade in slaves was that a land trade sprang up almost overnight. In order to supply the mainland slave centers of Mombasa, Takaungu, Malindi, the Lamu Archipelago, and the island of Pemba (whose clove plantations escaped the ravages of the 1872 hurricane), slave caravans moved up the coast from Kilwa. Since slaves could not be taken further north to Arabia by sea, they became more plentiful on the East African coast than they had ever been, and prices fell. With the influx of additional cheap labor, plantation owners along the coast and Giriama in the hinterland were able to expand their cultivation; Takaungu alone got 5,000 slaves from the overland route in 1873/74.[51]

The expanded slave-trade that brought cheaper labor to the coast was short-lived. In 1876 the British forced the sultan to make two proclamations that prohibited all land traffic in slaves. These pronouncements, supported by the formation of the sultan's first army, under the direction of British

Lieutenant William Lloyd Mathews, immediately made it difficult for slave caravans to come to the coast from the interior. Stringent military support subsequently made the decrees impossible to ignore,[52] and the slave trade dwindled to nothing.

Hinterland Upheaval

The decline of plantation agriculture and the end of the slave trade led to upheaval in the Giriama economic system. Most of the disruption was centered around the runaway slave communities in the hinterland and the growing frustrations of the Mazrui Arabs of Takaungu, who saw their prosperity collapsing around them. The Giriama were caught in the middle.

The end of the trade in slaves meant that any new labor force had to come either from the direct interior or the immediate hinterland. Owners improved their treatment of slaves in order to prevent them from running away, but soon the Mazrui desperately needed more laborers. A few clandestine caravans were sent deep into the interior seeking slaves, but a logical source was the communities of runaways who had ensconced themselves inland. The Giriama had never liked these runaways in their midst—particularly because their own slaves were apt to join them—and the existence of such communities began to attract greater numbers of coastal slaves, a situation that aroused the ire of Takaungu owners.[53]

The largest community of runaways in Godoma began as a Christian settlement. In 1879 David Koi founded Fuladoyo, just south of Mount Mangea at a place on the Vitengeni River that, unlike most of the hinterland, had a permanent source of sweet water. His first followers were Giriama, but when he accepted runaways late that year, both the Giriama and the Mazrui were angry that their runaway slaves were allowed to live there, and relations became strained.[54]

In the Malindi interior at Lake Jilore, Merikano, and far inland at Makongeni—all along the Sabaki River—runaways found in the river's fertile valley hiding places where they could farm. Their Malindi and Takaungu owners tried to raid these runaway communities, but the runaways simply scattered: many made their way to Rabai, and others regrouped after the attackers had gone.[55] Since it had been British pressure that had brought about action to end the slave trade, runaways expected British support. They were wrong. After the 1873 decree abolishing the sea trade in slaves, the Church Missionary Society, which had had only limited success in converting Mijikenda from the time of their first mission effort in 1844, made a commitment to provide refuges for freed slaves.[56] The Society's main center was at Freretown, just outside Mombasa, but freed slaves and some of the early runaways as well were accepted at Rabai. Working with freed slaves and accepting runaways were two different matters. So long as slavery itself was still legal, the CMS was jeopardizing the position of the British government by harboring runaways, and thereby offending slaveowners. The missionaries were therefore under strict orders from the British government to refuse to accept runaways, in order not to provoke hostility from the sultan's subjects. The first runaways from Malindi tried to contact the CMS, but the combination of the attitude of the Oroma, who discouraged Europeans from entering Oroma territory on the Sabaki, and the British prohibition of CMS harboring of runaways prevented any missionary assistance in the Malindi hinterland.[57]

The communities at Makongeni and Fuladoyo served as the main centers for runaways from Malindi and Takaungu, respectively. Fuladoyo, which by 1883 had grown to 600-700 inhabitants, was the most convenient settlement for the Mazrui to raid for laborers. In 1883 Takaungu Mazrui forces stormed Fuladoyo, but captured few runaways; they scattered the runaway population throughout the hinterland, where they threatened Mtanganyiko and Konjoro trading centers. The Fuladoyo founder, David Koi, was recognized by some Giriama who, to assure the Mazrui that Giriama were not assisting the runaways, captured Koi and delivered him to the Mazrui, who promptly tortured and killed him.[58]

The abortive attack on Fuladoyo was followed by total war by the Mazrui upon Fuladoyo runaways; raids and plundering intensified. In January 1884, Mbaruk of Gazi tried to persuade the Fuladoyo runaways to join his forces, but without success. By March, 800 runaways who had again settled at Fuladoyo asked for British protection. Salim, the liwali of Takaungu, offered special concessions to runaways who would return to the coast to work, but they refused his terms.[59]

Mazrui frustration mounted as their efforts to control labor resources failed. Although the alliance with the Giriama kept a precarious balance throughout the Fuladoyo conflict, the relation between the Mazrui and Giriama gradually became more unstable. Two factors adversely influenced the alliance. While at first the Giriama and the Mazrui seemed to be suffering from the same problem—loss of many of their slaves to these communities, with little chance of replenishing their supply—it was the Mazrui who resorted to recapture as the best method for arresting the decline of their labor-hungry plantations. They were also increasingly tempted by the prospect of kidnapping Giriama into slavery.[60]

The Mazrui suffered much more from the loss of their slaves than did the Giriama, whose family-centered agriculture and trade could continue without slave labor. The Takaungu Mazrui became increasingly dependent on Giriama exports to maintain their economy, but the Giriama had less need to funnel their goods through Takaungu, particularly since other Mazrui settlements north of Takaungu were nearer to the Giriama, who continued to move northward in Godoma.

Out of desperation, the Takaungu Mazrui tried to force the Giriama to continue the grain monopoly once held by Takaungu. They sent a double-aimed expedition to capture runaways at Fuladoyo and to force the Giriama to submit to them in order to secure the grain trade. For the first time, Giriama and runaways joined forces. Together they drew the Takaungu forces into the waterless country, and then remained elusive while making guerrilla-type attacks on the Mazrui. The Mazrui forces lost over 250 men, not in open confrontation but in the traps of the desertlike hinterland. The peace terms that resulted from this encounter marked a turning point: the Fuladoyo runaways received many captured arms and the concession that they would be recognized by the Mazrui as free people. The Giriama thereafter dictated most of the terms of their trade and sold increasing amounts of grain to Indian traders who came from Mombasa to Mtanganyiko. They moved northward in larger numbers into the Rare Valley and traded with other Mazrui towns south of Malindi. The Giriama had demonstrated the resiliency of their economic and political system under pressure from much better-armed enemies.[61]

This Giriama victory was short-lived, however, for it was followed by one of the most serious famines ever to hit East Africa. The Giriama called it *Mwakasenge*, and it apparently lasted from 1884 through 1885.[62] It was a time of tremendous hardship for all peoples, for with the drought and the lack of food, many Giriama were led to pawn or sell potential laborers—their slaves, their children, their wives, themselves—in order to get food. The Giriama were not able to escape this disastrous famine, but they were in a better position than their coastal neighbors to survive it with the least possible amount of permanent damage. The runaways were less fortunate, and there was a substantial revival of the slave trade in 1884. The imperatives of famine and war increased the demand for slaves, as well as the supply, but the Giriama suffered least of all.*

SUMMARY

The Giriama had begun the nineteenth century with a cohesive and stable political economy, but it was soon disrupted by changing external conditions. As increasingly more Giriama left the population concentration around their kaya, they had to make agrarian adaptations and political modifications, few of which were determined by the ruling elders, who therefore stood to lose their control over the population and the economy.

In this new (Godoma) phase of their economy, many Giriama became prosperous by diversifying and intensifying their trade and production to such an extent that Takaungu's plantation economy depended on supplements from the Giriama. When the abolition of the slave trade imposed hardships in Takaungu, the Giriama felt the repercussions. Rather than sub-

---

*Ironically, mainland production reached its peak during this last surge of labor supply even though slave supplies in general diminished. Between 1884 and 1887, Malindi's exports increased 38 percent: Frederick Cooper, *Plantation Slavery on the East Coast of Africa* (New Haven, Connecticut, 1977), p. 97. By the end of 1885, when the famine ended, Mbaruk's scattered men, regrouping at Fuladoyo, found that only 600 had survived: R.F. Morton, "Slaves, Fugitives and Freedmen on the Kenya Coast 1873-1907" (Ph.D. dissertation, Syracuse University, 1976), p. 192.

mit to Takaungu demands, they shifted to an alliance with runaways and fought successfully against their old Mazrui allies. Although they continued their cultivation through periods of warfare, not even the Giriama could escape suffering during the Mwakasenge famine. Nor could they avoid the constant raiding and fighting which followed. But compared to the others—runaways, Mazrui and Malindi planters, and other Mijikenda—the Giriama had excellent resources for recovery. By the late 1880s, the relationship with the Mazrui of Takaungu had been mended. Ngonyo wa Mwavuo accepted two of the Takaungu liwali's sons, Aziz and Mbaruk, as blood brothers. The Takaungu liwali, at great expense to himself, was accepted into a Giriama secret society, and Giriama *mahaji* (converts to Islam) were allowed to settle around Mazrui towns.[63]

By enduring the hardships of war and famine, the Giriama had reinforced their solidarity, which had been threatened by the magnitude of their migration. Many moved into the Sabaki River valley, where they could farm more successfully than on the Godoma plateau. The Malindi inhabitants, like those of Takaungu in earlier years, welcomed these producers and traders into their hinterland. While the Giriama as a people tended to avoid Malindi town, they were willing to send their produce there and to continue coordination of trade goods from this spacious hinterland, where their economy was to recover and flourish.

3

Sabaki River Prosperity, 1890-1900

With the 1890s a new phase of the Giriama economy began, one in which the Giriama recovered their prosperity and dealt successfully with the political consequences of continuous migration over a distance that finally stretched to more than a hundred miles. The Giriama, settling on both banks of the Sabaki River, came to dominate the Malindi and Mambrui hinterlands. The Giriama conflict with the Takaungu Mazrui and the impact of the Mwaka-senge famine in the mid-1880s had encouraged Giriama to move toward the Sabaki River, where they could cultivate its fertile valley. This river, which the Oroma had called the Gallana, was a much more dependable source of water than was the Rare River complex of Godoma. While the abandoned fields and untended trees of Malindi and Takaungu were only a reminder of former abundance, Giriama trade with the interior flourished and their new fields were ripe with grain.

This is not to say that they enjoyed unmixed blessings. The decade proved to be one of trouble. There was a series of natural disasters; the Imperial British East Africa Company representatives demanded laborers and imposed trade restrictions; the British government declared a protectorate in 1895; and an Anglo-Mazrui war disrupted the entire coast and hinterland in 1895 and 1896. By the end of the century, permanent British presence was assured, but since initial Giriama encounters with British agents had been mediated by mutual Afro-Arab allies and were regarded as trading exchanges, the British presence appeared deceptively innocuous to the Giriama; the full meaning of the Protectorate lay far in the future.

ECONOMIC RECOVERY

The first Giriama migrants to the Sabaki Valley did not find it empty. After a war in 1889/90, the Kauma had gained from the local British official permission to cross the river.* They settled in a fortification near the plantations of Magarini. *Wataro* (runaway slaves) communities still existed at Jilore, Makongeni, and Magongoni. Some Giriama joined these communities, and others established separate homesteads; they quickly came to dominate the area both numerically and economically.

Migration of Giriama into the Malindi hinterland helped to prevent the decline of that town's economic base. Malindi's economy had been totally dependent on grain production, and after the 1860s the town had become the granary of the East African coast. With her hinterland virtually unpopulated—except by Oroma, who claimed the land but were only sparsely occupying it, and by Waata who hunted there—Malindi's plantation developers were able to expand their holdings up and down the coast and into the river valley unrestricted. In the 1850s and 1860s, when slaves were plentiful, the size of a plantation had been dependent upon the number of laborers available to clear and cultivate the land. Unlike Mombasa, where land was restricted and an urban community had supported itself by trading for several centuries, and unlike Takaungu, which combined substantial inland trade and plantation agriculture, Malindi's economy was almost exclusively one of cultivation.[1]

By the time the Giriama moved to the Malindi hinterland, around 1890, the town and the plantations had both declined. Malindi had grown from a deserted area in 1860 to the site of thriving plantations of 6,000 slaves by 1873. This rapid growth owed much to the relative solidity of the grain market as slaves continued to be supplied—approximately 1,000 a year until 1880—but the abolition of the slave trade had initiated a decline there as elsewhere on the coast.[2] In the late 1870s and early 1880s, Malindi plantation owners had tried to exploit the hinterland peoples as labor; the fact that some Giriama were captured and sold explains their reluctance, even years later, to go into Malindi town.[3] The years between 1884 and 1888 marked the zenith of Malindi's prosperity. In 1884 Malindi's exports of agricultural produce were worth 275,000 Maria Theresa dollars; in 1887 they were worth 381,800 dollars. At its height, Malindi's population combined with that of Mambrui probably totaled 5,000 slaves in addition to a free population of 1,000, of which 202 landowners shared 30,887 acres.[4] An 1890 estimate indicates approximately 400 free inhabitants and a much-reduced slave population.† Most of the plantations had fallen into disuse, but there were patches of coconut, mango, orange, and other trees whose fruit was consumed locally.[5]

The Giriama were particularly fortunate to be occupying the fertile Sabaki Valley, not only because the town of Malindi offered continued access to

---

*The Kauma had apparently requested to be allowed to move after conflict with the Giriama during the Makufu famine in 1889/90, when the Giriama had sold captive Kauma women and children as slaves in exchange for food: Arthur Champion, "History of the Wagiryama," Rabai, n.d. (KNA: KFI/13).

†Morton has calculated that 41,412 slaves remained on the coast by 1890: Morton, "Slaves," p. 402.

imports and a chance to sell their produce, but because the decade of the 1890s was a disastrous one throughout East Africa, and the river valley offered greater chances of surviving the serious famines which opened and closed the decade. Periodic droughts during the intervening years threatened even greater loss of productive capacity. Rinderpest, a disease deadly to cattle, moved from the coast to the plains, devastating almost 80 percent of the cattle herds. Pastoral peoples such as the Oroma and Maasai, losing the cattle that were their only livelihood, starved and died. Many agricultural groups whose economies were disrupted had barely recovered before they were hit by another disaster—an epidemic of smallpox. Again, the Maasai and the Oroma were struck particularly hard.[6]

This decade also saw the great immigration of Europeans into the East African interior. British agents forged their way into the Kenya interior to Buganda, depending on African allies to provide guides, porters, food, and security, and launching punitive expeditions against Kamba, Kikuyu, Nandi, Bugusu, and a few other tribes who failed to cooperate. When the Imperial British East Africa Company followed the Swahili trade routes inland, and when in 1895 the British declared the British East African Protectorate, it meant that the British were in Kenya to stay and that African options had become severely restricted.

The Giriama weathered both the natural disasters and the British incursions better than many of their up-country neighbors. The British inland route bypassed Giriama, and smallpox missed the main Giriama population, but the rinderpest epidemic killed virtually all Giriama cattle.[7] This loss of cattle was particularly hard on those Giriama who had made their homes in Biryaa, although no Giriama cattlekeepers were totally dependent on their herds. Moreover, two elements of their economy, agriculture and trade, actually expanded during the decade of the 1890s.

Once a substantial number of Giriama had reached the valley of the Sabaki River, it became a granary so successfully cultivated that the Giriama there were able to exchange food and grain with other Mijikenda, with Oroma, with Waata, and with Taita during the two famines of Makufu (1889/90) and Magunia (1899/1900). Though individual families were hard-hit and some became dependent on creditors or other Giriama, the fact that the Giriama and those ex-slaves who became squatters on their former masters' coastal lands had the greatest opportunity for producing grain meant that some benefited economically from famine conditions. Trade demand for rubber and gum copal—two products the Giriama had successfully collected since the 1860s—also increased.* The Giriama thus had access to incoming capital, which some of them used to begin restoration of their cattle herds. No longer in competition with Oroma for land, the Giriama had access to virtually the entire Sabaki Valley. Even the first encounters with Europeans were not to cause the drastic changes for them that they caused for many others in East Africa.

*Both Takaungu and Malindi exports of these products increased.

THE IMPERIAL BRITISH EAST AFRICA COMPANY

Until 1888 the Giriama had glimpsed white men only rarely, as occasional missionary travelers through Giriamaland or as passing strangers in the streets of Mombasa or Malindi, and most Giriama had no contact at all with white men. But the Europeans—and after 1886 this meant the British—were interested in the coast and the interior for a number of reasons, and although the nature and extent of their involvement changed year by year, Britain became directly involved in East Africa after 1888. Britain's initial involvement on the East African coast was due to the need to protect the vital trading operation with India; British representatives were led inland in an indirect way. When the Suez Canal was built in 1869, Britain wanted sufficient influence over Egypt to ensure that the canal remained open and safe. When the security of the headwaters of the Nile was threatened with intervention from the French and possibly from Menelik of Ethiopia, and when direct access from Egypt seemed impossible because of the Mahdi's control of the Sudan, the British Foreign Office decided that a secondary attempt to get to Buganda should be made through East Africa from Zanzibar. The longstanding relationship of the British with the sultan at Zanzibar eased the transition to a new period in which the coast came to be viewed as a launching depot to the interior.[8]

The arrival of representatives of the Imperial British East Africa Company and the establishment of a European-run mission station at Lake Jilore affected some of the Giriama directly, although in a limited way. The British East Africa Company, under William MacKinnon, was granted a concession from the sultan of Zanzibar in 1887 (Britain did not grant the company a royal charter until 1888). The concession gave the company full charge of the investments along the ten-mile strip of coast that the sultan claimed, under the condition that they take the responsibility of administration and guarantee to the sultan customs revenues equivalent to those he had been receiving in the past.[9]

The main goal of the Imperial British East Africa Company was to make a profit for itself while maintaining administration in the name of Britain. Its tasks were immense. In 1888, the year that Seyyid Khalifa succeeded Burghash as sultan, the company purchased from the liwali of Takaungu a tract of land at Kilifi for a station to supplement those at Mombasa and Malindi. The company's representatives particularly feared a coastal rebellion like that the Afro-Arabs, led by Bushiri, had made that same year against the Germans on the coast of German East Africa.[10] Aware of the long-term animosity between the Mazrui and the sultan, the company's agents made little attempt to enforce the sultan's wishes in Mazrui territory. When the company director learned that, contrary to policy, the African missionary in charge of Rabai had given shelter to large numbers of runaway slaves, thereby outraging their Afro-Arab owners, he agreed to pay compensation in order to free 1,421 of the slaves.[11] In 1890, to prevent rebellion and to conciliate the Afro-Arabs, the company allowed some of its troops to assist the Mazrui in raids on runaway communities in the Sabaki Valley.[12] These cooperative raids were only moderately successful, but they made it clear that the company's commitment to end the slave trade did not necessarily imply ending slavery.

Although the company drew upon all coastal resources, their major interest lay in Buganda, with its populous areas and promise of large profit. The company placed its main effort on securing an 800-mile route from the coast to Buganda, an endeavor that was to prove costly rather than profitable. In their search for a route that would avoid the inhospitable Taru Desert, George MacKenzie, the director of IBEAC in Mombasa, hired Frederick Lugard to survey a possible northern route along the Sabaki River. As the need to improve communications with Buganda became urgent, it was realized that a railway line would eventually be required, so Lugard was empowered to explore the feasibility of building a railway there as well. In 1890, the year the British government declared a protectorate at Zanzibar, Lugard traveled inland along the river and established several stockades, the largest of which was at the watoro community at Makongeni (about forty miles directly inland from Malindi). He ultimately reached Kikuyu territory by this shorter, less dangerous route.

If the railway had followed Lugard's route, the subsequent history of the Giriama might have been very different, for Malindi, not Mombasa, would probably have been the chief port for Kenya, with the Giriama taking a central role in its provisioning. But J. R. L. MacDonald, chosen as the chief engineer to survey the preliminary railroad route, concluded that the vagaries of the river and the density of the brush made it difficult to build a railroad there. Instead he selected the southern, Swahili caravan path inland through the Taru Desert.[13] Close as the Giriama were to Mombasa, this route to the interior bypassed their lands.

It was clear that whether company officials wished it or not, they would, at least initially, be dependent upon the Africans along their route to Buganda. Here the experience of the Giriama was very different from that of the up-country Africans. The relationship between the Giriama and the company revolved around the company's efforts to take over the local ivory trade and to revive the agricultural economy of the coast, rather than to promote the servicing of British caravans. The headquarters staff at Mombasa and officers stationed at Takaungu and Malindi collected customs duties, and their main hope of recovering the company's large investment rested upon the revitalization of coastal agricultural estates. By 1890 the labor shortage had brought plantation production to a standstill, with a consequent loss of revenue at the ports.[14]

In 1891 a company employee, W. W. A. FitzGerald, arrived to explore the coastal lands and to suggest ways in which they might be profitably developed. FitzGerald first made his headquarters west of Mambrui at Magarini, where he was charged with reestablishing production of the Magarini Plantations of Suleman bin Abdulla, whose land had been confiscated after his participation in a rebellion in Witu. FitzGerald initially hired Abdulla's slaves, but he tried to encourage Giriama to come and work at the plantation.

He was particularly impressed with the Giriama living around Lake Jilore, where the Church Missionary Society had opened its first European-staffed mission among Giriama in 1890: "The Wa-Giryama around Jelori alone number over three thousand; they are intelligent, industrious, and keen agriculturalists; their blacksmith's work too is particularly good. They make their own hoes, and I was shown some necklaces of iron of remarkably good manufacture."[15] FitzGerald attempted to settle slaves from Makongeni at Jilore. Had he succeeded, the situation at Jilore would have come to resemble that at Freretown and Rabai, where the needs of the ex-slaves took precedence over those of the local people, but nothing came of it. Instead, Jilore was to become a major center of Giriama production.

FitzGerald meant to make such a success of Magarini that it would provide a stimulus for European planters to come to recover the granary of the coast, and IBEAC agents looked to the Giriama as the major potential source of labor. Although FitzGerald asked the Giriama to become laborers, there was little need for them except at Magarini. They were more impressed with his offers of seed and a program to begin an experimental plantation at Jilore from which they could harvest the produce,[16] but for reasons not made clear, FitzGerald's plan was never implemented. In any case, the Giriama had other indications that his requests for labor were not very serious. Watoro coming to the communities along the Sabaki during the Makufu famine in the early part of the decade had offered, in response to a request from Lugard, to work for the company to buy their freedom, but the company failed to provide work.[17] A few were briefly employed on the Taru road, and some worked on the railroad; most, under the stress of the famine, migrated to the Sabaki Valley but found no work there. At one point late in 1891, Lugard returned to Fuladoyo to find it abandoned; when the rains came, however, the people did return to try once again to cultivate.[18]

The company was unable to coordinate its efforts to develop the coast while they were primarily concerned with reaping the profits from Buganda. There were incidents, too, that reminded company officials that they were in a precarious position vis-à-vis the local people. A few Giriama shared Jilore with the missionaries and ex-slaves and saw the company as their protectors, but the majority of the Giriama in the Sabaki Valley viewed the Europeans as intruders. On 30 October 1891 officials at Jilore and Malindi received warnings that Oroma, assisted by Giriama, were preparing to attack. The missionaries were hurriedly evacuated from Jilore, and when British officers demanded support, the potential defense force grew. By 10 November, a full camp of armed Giriama were joined at Sekoke Hill by 300 Kambe. Some Kauma and Chonyi declared themselves ready to take up arms for the company, and Baluchi soldiers were requested from Mombasa. One officer threw sticks of dynamite into the river, killing the fish, in order to convince the Africans of the superiority of British weapons. All these preparations proved to be unnecessary, for the threat turned out to be a hoax conceived by some Giriama who hoped to scare the Europeans away. The perpetrator of the false alarm was caught, arrested, and sent to Mombasa for trial.[19]

For the moment, conflict between British and Giriama at Jilore had been averted, but this did not mean that the Giriama welcomed British intervention. The hoax showed that within a year of their first extended exposure to Europeans—in the persons of the CMS missionaries and company officials—some Giriama were making it very clear that they wanted nothing to do with them. Even those Giriama who supported the company were not primarily acting to protect the mission; few were converts. Rather, they thought the main enemy was the Oroma, whom they feared. They wanted to protect their agricultural area around Jilore, and they had ample evidence that the company had superior forces. The Giriama at Jilore were not supporting the company so much as they were protecting their own interests. Four years later, when the British found themselves involved in conflict with a faction of Mazrui at Takaungu, the Giriama living in the immediate neighborhood of Jilore mission quickly lent their support to the British, but the majority of Giriama initially opted to support their old Afro-Arab allies.[20]

TRANSFORMATIONS IN GIRIAMA POLITICS

In order to understand what was likely to happen in a Giriama-British conflict, it is necessary to examine the ways in which the Giriama political system had become modified since the kaya phase. Having spread over a wide area extending from the kaya to Weruni, Biryaa, Godoma, and now to the Sabaki Valley, the Giriama, living in small homesteads, had developed new mechanisms for dealing with threats to their society. During the period of migration, confrontations with the Maasai and the Mazrui, and even the Jilore conflict, were localized, and there was little need for an all-Giriama response. A new political form, developed since the dispersal began, allowed them to respond to the new economic situation and changed demographic conditions by modifying the kaya system, but it had limited capacity to respond effectively to the British.

The most notable change outside the kaya was in local adaptations of the council system. The elders' rôle as arbiters became modified in the homestead and the community. The homestead's founder became the primary decision-maker. Krapf has written that "every man of wealth and of a large family and relations considered himself a headman."[21] When several homesteads were clustered together, the first founder theoretically had no direct authority beyond his own family. In communities, men who had been initiated as elders still sat in council to rule. Just as a kaya spokesman had represented the Giriama as a group to outsiders, so did one man frequently become the primary representative of the community. To formalize community councils, clearings were designated in which the elders would gather to settle arguments. When disputes arose between communities, the elders in the two communities sat in council to settle the conflict. It was important to have as many as possible of the six clans represented, and the clansmen of those involved in the dispute excused themselves from the proceedings. If this council could not solve the problem, representatives were usually sent to the kaya, where some of the remaining kambi, Vaya, and Fisi took up the matter.[22]

Although the Giriama tried to maintain close communication among homesteads, they were more isolated from each other than they had ever before been. The Giriama in these dispersed homesteads eventually grouped into four regional areas: Weruni, around the kaya, became a pastoral area—cattle were grazed there until they fell victim to Maasai raids, and subsequently sheep and goats found nourishment in this unreplenished agricultural area; Biryaa, bordering on the Taru Desert, also became a grazing area and remained the main trading center for cattle when most of the population had settled further north; Godoma became the agricultural hinterland that served Takaungu; and the Mangea-Gallana region incorporated the fertile Sabaki River valley of Malindi's hinterland. Since the regions had different economic bases, people within one area had little reason to communicate with those from other areas.

The kaya center helped to overcome this tendency toward isolation, but it soon became more symbolic than practical.[23] After the councils of elders had been formed within the homesteads, regional councils met to arbitrate conflicts within each region. The elders who remained in the kaya were called upon only when conflicts could not be resolved within a region. Thus, the kaya was shunted to the periphery of Giriama agricultural development and trade. A kaya spokesman remained in residence, supported by his entourage—the elders of the six clans—but these elders, who had traditionally played an active role to ensure that each clan was represented on any important council, became merely symbolic reminders of the need for equal representation.[24]

The status of the kaya itself was also changing. When everyone lived within the kaya boundaries, consensus and unity had produced a successful Giriama political organization, but a society ruled by a single council of elders was dependent upon all elders being available at any given time. Once the Giriama had migrated from the kaya, the functioning of a single council became impossible. The council could still be convened at the kaya as the highest court of appeal, but much judicial power was transferred to the homesteads.

The kaya changed from the core of Giriama population and government into the Giriama ritual center and a symbol of Giriama unity. As the storehouse of all medicines and the burial ground of the ancestors, the kaya became sacred. Giriama elders who kept traditional knowledge convened there when called upon, and the council that met there served as the ultimate authority in judicial matters when cases were brought on appeal, but the kaya had lost its central function.[25]

After the 1880s few Giriama of any age lived in the kaya, though many remained in the surrounding area. A Digo or Waata or Watoro could become assimilated into a Giriama clan without ever having visited Kaya Giriama. People had not originally left the kaya as clan groups, and the clans, as a result of their being so diffused throughout the society, ceased to be an active part of social organization. Elders no longer held control over distribution of land among the clans, and land abandoned by one clan member could be claimed by another. In these dispersed settlements, many reciprocal relationships were conducted on the subclan level, so subclans served the population beyond the family. Family residences were often held for only two generations, since the younger men, attracted by the availability of new land, tended to move away and start their own homes.[26]

The main internal conflict in Giriama society had always been intergenerational. During kaya days, the initiated councillors held considerable power over the young men, and fathers exercised control over their sons. Once the Giriama had scattered over an area covering almost 1,500 square miles, a council's power over any member of a region was much reduced, since migration and further arbitration were possible alternatives. Although age was still the basis for power in local areas and the elders received generous gifts for their services in council, they no longer controlled the community's wealth. Lower-ranking men could acquire greater wealth than their elders; with an independent income, sons were not dependent upon their fathers for bridewealth, so they could marry earlier and become heads of households. Young men could use their wealth to acquire supporters—through patronage, debt, investment, and sometimes slavery—and remove themselves from the restrictions of local councils. Under these circumstances, a young man could form his own council and become the elder spokesman.

These conflicts between men of different ages and the shifts in traditional relationships between wealth and power were exacerbated by the fact that membership on councils became ambiguous. In order for these councils to function with initiated kambi, it was necessary for rituals to be continued so that men could be elevated to councillor status.[27] This proved to be difficult, for several reasons. Locally, men who founded homesteads, even though they were not councillors, had authority over the homestead members; if disputes arose within the community, such a man would represent his people. For this reason some of the younger men came to put little stock in councillor initiation. On the other hand, one way to ensure a position of authority was to be an initiated councillor, so the Giriama became ambivalent concerning this ritual.

For the Giriama as a whole, conducting the Kirao ritual approximately every three years to install a new age-set as councillors was extremely difficult. The trip to the kaya was long and perilous for many, and the ceremonies involved considerable expense; moreover, time was precious, and the ceremonies took months. Kirao was a strongly communal ritual, and part of its purpose was to provide community recognition of new councillors so that everyone knew the ranking of the elders. When all Giriama lived inside the kaya, men and women participated in Kirao and the existing councillors shared their knowledge in a lengthy educational process. After the dispersal, the few old men who still lived in the kaya could not be expected to be the keepers of all the information; much of the tradition regarding council procedure was passed down to the local level.

Because the Kirao ritual remained necessary to install legitimate councillors, however, Kirao ceremonies continued, with two fundamental adaptations. First, representatives of the eligible elders went to the kaya for a much-shortened ceremony and then returned to hold secondary ceremonies in their local areas to initiate the qualified men who had remained at home. Second, under normal circumstances during kaya days, the Kirao ceremony had been held approximately every three years; the distance between Giriama homesteads and the kaya in the post-migration period forced the combination of two sets of initiates for each ritual, which was held only every six years.

Dispersal also made it harder to designate the age-sets that provided the basis for eventual elderhood. In kaya days everyone knew who had been born within a time period; under dispersed conditions it became a matter of guesswork. The kaya representative sent out the Mwanza M'Kulu drum approximately every three years to separate young men into age-sets, but since it took several months to reach all communities and since, for some unknown reason, age-sets were not named at this ceremony, members only understood their group in terms of the initiates who had come before and after them. This created confusion. Whereas, traditionally, members of age-sets had herded together, been warriors together, and were initiated as councillors together, following the dispersal period people acted in their community according to need rather than status.

The Giriama confronted another problem when it came time to initiate a ruling generation. A ruling generation had been installed around the 1830s. It was subsequently called Mkwavi, after the Kwavi who raided during the period of its service. After approximately forty years, all the age-sets within the Mkwavi ruling generation had become councillors and it was necessary to install the next ruling generation in order to continue to have legitimate councillors. Now, by Giriama tradition, no man could be initiated as a councillor unless he had danced the Mung'aro ritual that installed his ruling generation. In the 1870s it was time for the Mkwavi ruling generation to retire and for a new ruling generation to dance Mung'aro and establish their rule; only after that happened could elders be initiated as councillors. Therefore, despite the dispersal, the Giriama held a modified Mung'aro to install the new ruling generation. Although the Giriama conducted Mung'aro at Kaya Giriama, only a small percentage of the eligible men attended this Mung'aro ritual.* They then returned to their respective residences to initiate the others who were qualified.

Thereafter, elevation of the members of the thirteen age-sets within the new ruling generation to the position of councillors occurred every six years,

*Sometime during the early dispersal of the Giriama from the kaya, members of the Akiza clan started a new kaya near Mwabayanyundo. Some rituals of the late nineteenth century were held at both makaya simultaneously and spokesmen and their assistants were chosen for each kaya.

when two age-sets danced Kirao, under modified circumstances. The retirement of the generation of men who had ruled when the Giriama had fought
against the Kwavi raiders was, by tradition, combined with the installation
of the upcoming group of younger men who would represent the Giriama
through decades of migration. But because the next Mung'aro was not due
until after the turn of the century, and because the Giriama continued during
the intervening period to become even more dispersed, the special traditions
and knowledge of the ruling council were lost, and the Mung'aro of the 1870s
proved to be the last. The first need for legitimate spokesmen to represent all
the Giriama to the British arose in 1895; by that time it had proven almost
impossible to continue the old method of replacing councillors. The kaya was
virtually defunct. It had, however, served a valuable purpose as a source of
legitimation during a period of transition. This polity and sense of a charter
worked well in a time of considerable adaptation not only to varied ecological situations but to mounting commercial activity and potential for
marketing surplus grain.

The form of Giriama politics developed in the 1890s retained the use of
councils and adhered to the principle of age, but allowed for new members
who could not possibly have participated in the age-set system. People chose
those who had legitimate local authority to sit on a council or even to be its
head, and problems were dealt with locally. But even though the young men
of kaya days had chosen to leave the kaya and pursue their economic endeavors without the restraints of the elders, those same men, who had become
the elders in the 1890s during a period of resettlement, were unsympathetic to
the youth, who now perceived their position as one restricted by new constraints, mostly brought about by their fathers' control over trade. British-
sponsored economic changes had prevented young men from accumulating
wealth through slave-worked farms and had made the sale of ivory illegal.
Once again, the Giriama political system was dominated by generational
conflict, this time exacerbated by increasing British restrictions.[28]

THE ANGLO-MAZRUI WAR

The strains on the Giriama political system were felt most directly at the time of
the Anglo-Mazrui war, fought in 1895 to determine political control of the
coast. Trouble began when the huge difficulties of the IBEAC began to
surface and the British government considered whether or not to take complete charge of the East African territory. It had become clear that the limited
range of exportable produce, lack of navigable waterways to ship goods to
the coast from the interior, preoccupation with British rivalry with Germany,
and undercapitalization meant that the few resources that did exist were
exhausted in dealing with the matters at hand; nothing was available for
expanding trade. Moreover, company agents were notably inexperienced,
and many of them were highly ineffective.

Finally, the IBEAC, overwhelmed by the responsibilities of coastal development and the costs of the route to Buganda, and perhaps doomed from its inception as "poorly conceived, badly managed, and grossly undercapitalized," decided to withdraw from East Africa.[29] Although the British government wanted neither the costs nor the responsibility for the peoples and the territory between Mombasa and Uganda, they had no choice; they would have been shut out of Uganda had they not controlled that route.

When on 30 June 1895 the company's commission expired, Arthur Hardinge, who became the consul-general in Zanzibar and commissioner for the Protectorate, proclaimed the East African Protectorate under the auspices of the British Foreign Office. Britain took over the company's lease of the sultan's coastal strip by paying £11,000 rent and 3 percent interest on the £200,000 paid for the surrender of the original treaty.[30]

The Seeds of Rebellion

The new Protectorate officers inherited a rebellion instigated by some of the coastal Mazrui Afro-Arabs against the sultan and the British. This 1895 conflict focused on Takaungu and Gazi, but it involved communities all along the coast, from the Shimba Hills to Malindi. The Giriama were inescapably drawn into the eleven months of fighting. Ultimately, the leader of the 1895 rebellion was Mbaruk bin Rashid of Gazi, who had been trying to stimulate a Mazrui rebellion against the Busaidi Sultan since the early 1860s. In earlier years he had caused general unrest, relying on runaway slaves and other dissidents to swell his forces and create problems for the sultan by disrupting caravan trade and raiding plantations and towns along the coast. He had built a stronghold in the Shimba Hills at Mwele, where the sultan's forces, led by Lloyd Matthews, had on a number of occasions captured him and extorted from him promises of good behavior.[31]

Angry at the liwali of Takaungu's submission to the sultan in 1865, Mbaruk had tried unsuccessfully to get Takaungu dissidents to acknowledge him as the new leader of the Mazrui. As a leader Mbaruk was, however, respected and feared by the runaway slaves, who knew they were always welcome to join his group (they were not always given the choice), and by the hinterland Mijikenda, who were aware of his brutality against people who failed to support him. Therefore, when conflict arose over the new appointment of the liwali of Takaungu and another claimant was chosen over Mbaruk's nephew, Mbaruk was able to pursue his rebellion. Many coastal Afro-Arabs were from the outset angry about the establishment of a British protectorate; the conditions for conflict had been brewing for some time. For the British, coastal security was mandatory if the critical link with Uganda was to be maintained. Moreover, an open conflict gave Sir Arthur Hardinge, the British commissioner, a chance to replace most of the dissident Afro-Arabs with men more friendly to British goals.

When after 1895 the British government assumed authority for the sultan, one of their officers, Kenneth MacDougall, was given the responsibility of deciding upon the successor to the governorship of Takaungu. He chose

Rashid bin Salim, son of the deceased governor, over Mbaruk bin Rashid bin Khamis, the newphew of Mbaruk of Gazi. Young Mbaruk's father had been the liwali until his death in 1878, but the young Mbaruk, still a small boy at that time, was passed over in favor of his uncle, Salim bin Khamis. Mac-Dougall had worked well with Salim bin Khamis and knew that his son, Rashid, would be more favorable to British positions than Mbaruk the younger.

When the younger Mbaruk decided to protest, the Mazrui quickly divided into factions, motivated by complex combinations of individual pragmatism, new and old alliances, and political debts. The pervasive new condition that had to be considered was the rapidly growing European presence. Mbaruk was able to draw on his inheritance of slaves, arms, and the plantation at Konjora, as well as his ability to set up alliances with runaway slaves in the area. When the British troops arrived to fight against him, both parties burned crops and homes. The people who suffered the most from this were those living in the immediate hinterland between Takaungu and the Mijikenda territory. When these rebels finally sought protection in Gazi from the younger Mbaruk's uncle, the famed Mbaruk bin Rashid, the fighting expanded into a full-scale rebellion. Mbaruk bin Rashid led the British officers to believe that he would hand his nephew over to them, but instead he proclaimed a rebellion, established headquarters at a fortified village called Mwele about ten miles into the forest, and for the next year stirred up rebellious activity along the coast and hinterland from Vanga to Malindi, drawing supporters from among other Arabs, coastal Swahili, ex-slaves, and slaves.

The rebellion caused much disruption in the hinterland. In July 1895, Fuladoyo and Makongeni runaways dropped their allegiance with Mbaruk bin Rashid and moved into the hinterland of Malindi to escape the fighting.[32] The rebels were ruthless in their attacks on the slave and *mahaji* (Muslim Giriama) villages in the immediate hinterland of Takaungu. In January and February 1896, they attacked the Makonde settlement and the Tezo, Roka, and Uyombo areas. These areas were raided for all their resources and the slaves and mahaji were usually forced to flee or to join the rebels, or were taken into the Giriama country and sold there as slaves.[33]

The Giriama Rôle

The Giriama had been long-term allies of the Mazrui, and despite some years of animosity between the two over trade rights and several unsuccessful attempts by the Mazrui to get Giriama to work for them, in the late 1880s the Giriama had renewed this alliance, particularly with the Mazrui of Takaungu. Under the circumstances, then, it was logical that Mazrui would call upon their old Giriama allies to assist their rebellion, to feed and shelter them, to hide their arms, to become informants, and, of course, to refuse to assist British efforts against them. The Giriama contribution to the rebel effort consisted of supplying grain and storing what the rebels had confiscated, and allowing the rebels to hide in their villages. They bought cloth at the coast which they then sold to the rebels, receiving money and even donkeys in exchange.[34] Giriama who had become Muslims kept the rebels informed of British whereabouts and some Giriama allowed the rebels' slaves, disguised as Giriama, to cultivate small plots of land alongside their own farms.[35] By facilitating the sale of slaves that the rebels had captured, the Giriama were able to provide the rebels with income to buy food and arms, and at the same time the Giriama could enlarge their own supply of slaves. This Giriama assistance to the Mazrui made it impossible for the British to restrict rebel movements in the hinterland and to prevent embarrassing attacks on Malindi and Takaungu.

The Giriama were the first African peoples encountered by Protectorate forces, and the first whom they needed to bring over to their side. This is ironic, since the Giriama were also to be the last of the agricultural peoples of the Protectorate that the British forces fought. From the Giriama perspective, this conflict was just another defense of Mazrui domination of the coast against an outsider—this time British—and they were cooperating as they had many times before. For many centuries the Giriama had respected Arab domination of the coast and had been accustomed to the squabbling of various factions for control. They provided assistance to the Mazrui, but they did not actually take up arms for them.[36] Nothing in the Giriama experience led them to perceive that the overriding issue was the permanence of British administration.

For the British, however, there was no question as to what was at stake. Because the fighting focused on Takaungu, the initial British dealings were with nearby Giriama, but as time passed it became clear that, with the exception of people in the Jilore settlement, Giriama support for the rebels was widespread. For the British, gaining Giriama support became crucial to the resolution of the rebellion.

The British decided to back strong persuasion by force. Hardinge forbade the sale of cloth or food to the Giriama without special permission. In his efforts to understand the people with whom he was dealing, he was strongly influenced by a recently published vocabulary of the Giriama compiled by W. E. Taylor, who had served for two years in the late 1880s as an itinerant missionary for the CMS among the Giriama. Taylor had interpreted what he learned about the Giriama political system as if it were synonymous with the organization of Freemasonry, and he erroneously described three clan elders as owners of the land and leaders of the Giriama.[37] Hardinge made a visit to the kaya in search of these elders, but finding it inhabited by only a few old men, he concluded that the kaya must be insignificant. At the same time he decided that another of Taylor's revelations, the oath of the hyena, administered by special elders and regarded as the most powerful oath of the Giriama, was worthy of his attention and might be useful in bringing the Giriama into the British camp.[38]

Meanwhile, Kenneth MacDougall, working from Malindi, sent bribes and threats to all the surrounding Giriama homesteads, demanding that the Giriama renounce support for the rebels. For a month, MacDougall's forces demonstrated British Maxim guns and war rockets against the enemy, mainly in villages of slaves and Swahili who were actually fighting for the rebels. Using as headquarters a temporary government station constructed at Tandia, near the Rare River, MacDougall ordered the Giriama to send their "chiefs" to a meeting.[39]

Ngonyo wa Mwavuo: A Giriama/British Alliance

A dozen or so elders from the surrounding area appeared, but the most influential individual in the area, Ngonyo wa Mwavuo of Rare, refused to come. Ngonyo's rise to prominence had been unusual among the Giriama. Following the groundwork laid down by his father, Mwavuo, he had become independently wealthy through trade. He had accumulated wealth as an ivory trader, as a producer of grain for export, and as an intermittent participant in the slave trade. Over 1,200 people lived in his village, which was the largest Giriama settlement, and many of the inhabitants were slaves used as agricultural laborers. He had forty wives, several of whom were Oroma slaves.[40] Few Giriama villages even approached this size, and all the larger ones had several elders who shared the responsibilities in council. Ngonyo dominated his council and maintained the respect of Giriama in the surrounding area. Existing evidence indicates that no other Giriama had command of such a substantial number of people who were personally indebted to him. And once he had demonstrated his authority, he attracted rootless people who were willing to come to his support.[41]

Ngonyo frequently hid rebel leaders in his village, and he purchased some of the slaves the rebels had captured from Malindi plantations. Unable to ignore Ngonyo's disobedience to his orders, MacDougall ordered his arrest and detention in Takaungu. Ngonyo submitted willingly—in order to learn British intentions. MacDougall ordered his arrest for six months, but after a short period in Takaungu, Ngonyo reversed his position and agreed to support the British effort. Ngonyo was a realist who correctly interpreted British power and determination. He was an effective collaborator, but for himself, rather than for the Giriama as a whole. He did not want to lose his prominent economic position by sacrificing his holdings. He gambled and won his reward. With the assistance of Ngonyo's ability at persuasion, the British asked elders from the villages around Malindi to prevent continued Giriama harboring of rebels.[42]

Ngonyo told the fifty to sixty gathered elders that

he had been down to the coast and seen the power of government, its ships and maxim guns and that it would be madness on their part to mistake its [government's] forebearance for weakness and provoke a conflict with it. . . . [Some] recalled the vengeance [Mbaruk bin Rashid] had inflicted before on those who assisted his enemies.[43]

Ngonyo was telling his fellow Giriama that the British were stronger than Mbaruk and that they should fear the British, not the Arabs.

British officers failed to understand that Ngonyo and the Jilore mission
were exceptional: in both cases, individuals were able to influence the Giriama within their sphere, but this was atypical of the Giriama. When British
officers came to recognize Ngonyo as an example of chiefly influence who
could be useful to them, they took an exaggerated view of his power, believing that Ngonyo's support for the rebels explained all Giriama aid to Mbaruk.
Concluding that Ngonyo's power surpassed that of the weak elders in the
kaya, Hardinge felt his co-optation of Ngonyo to the British side had in itself
changed the Giriama relationship with the British. To confirm this he insisted
that the Giriama elders pledge their support to the British effort by swearing
the hyena oath. MacDougall's description indicates that the British officers
were pleased with the meeting:

In the end, the whole assembly [of northern elders] were induced to take a solemn
oath that they would throw in their lot with the government and not with the rebels
and that within 15 days they would clear them from their district and induce chiefs
[sic] of other divisions of Giriama to come to the same decision.[44]

However, Hardinge not only overestimated Ngonyo's power, he misunderstood the purpose of the hyena oath.[45] The British were using the oath in a
nontraditional manner, and they were asking the wrong people to administer
it. The hyena oath was a proscriptive oath, administered by one of six Fisi
medicine men who were members of the Vaya and who were traditionally the
representatives of the six Giriama clans. Most of these men had retained their
close affiliation with the kaya, but did not live there.[46] Since Hardinge had
chosen to ignore this group, none of these men attended the oath-swearing
ceremony (even though Mbaruk wa Nduria, one of the two official kaya
representatives, lived nearby); the evidence indicates that the Giriama participated in the entire ceremony simply as a performance for the British, who
felt the oath had made a significant difference.[47]

In fact the Giriama were agreeing to expel the rebels from their territory
for pragmatic reasons. Despite the fact that the war had been lucrative for
them at the expense of slaves and watoro in Takaungu's immediate hinterland, they understood the rebels to be losing their support in the face of
British forces, and the Giriama did not want to be punished by the British.
Moreover, they were frightened. Some young Giriama warriors had caused
trouble by openly attacking the British in nearby Tandia and were forced to
submit only by British military retaliation. By agreeing to British requests,
the elders were able to assure the British that they did not wish to fight; they
did not admit their lack of control over the younger men. To indicate their
good faith, the elders told one of the rebel leaders, Aziz, who had settled
down at Bamba, that he must leave, and they directed MacDougall's forces
toward Gabina to the west in Oroma country, where they understood other
rebel leaders had gone from Kirwitu.

The Giriama had declared their willingness to change sides none too soon.
MacDougall pushed his troops to the edge of the Taru Desert. Reinforced
British troops followed Aziz to Gabina, where the rebels withstood an attack

of over four hundred men. Aziz moved to Bamba, where he again scavenged among the Giriama for food. Meanwhile, reinforcements allowed Hardinge to launch a two-pronged attack from Mombasa and Vanga in the south.[48] In one last desperate attempt, Aziz moved again against the Takaungu hinterland, but found the area too unsafe. He finally moved southward, and he and Mbaruk escaped with twelve hundred followers into German East Africa, where they asked for and received asylum from Major von Wissman. Handing over their arms, they ended their rebellion. With no hope for reinforcements from Mbaruk, the mop-up of remaining rebels in the British territory then became easy.[49]

Effects of the War

As a result of the British encounter with the Giriama in this war with the Mazrui, British officers reached several mistaken conclusions about the Giriama people. Hardinge thought he had been right to ignore the kaya elders in favor of Ngonyo, and that the hyena oath had turned the tide, giving the British future Giriama support, whereas in fact the turning point came with the Giriama realization that the British were more powerful than Mbaruk. The Giriama changed sides judiciously, in order not to suffer as rebels to the British or traitors to Mbaruk. They did not interpret their support in this instance to mean that they would henceforth serve the British administration. Moreover, the oath, used improperly and offered by the wrong people (possibly with some duplicity on the part of the Giriama), influenced the Giriama very little, if at all. Hardinge was correct to interpret it as a powerful oath, however, for when in 1913 it was sworn by the Giriama to oppose the British, with the backing of kaya elders and the ancestors, it was highly effective.*

British officers also concluded that local elders wielded much greater power as individuals in their settlement areas than was actually the case, and they thought that Ngonyo had authority over all the Giriama elders. Ngonyo had been useful because of his persuasive powers, but he had no authority over Giriama outside his immediate neighborhood. In fact, Ngonyo was by birth a Digo, whose father had become a Giriama by joining a Giriama clan and then founding his own sublcan. Ngonyo had become independent in many ways, but because he was not a member of a Giriama age-set he had never been initiated as an elder. His power derived from his wealth and the Giriama accepted him as an elder, but he could not draw upon traditional authority. He became a British supporter in this rebellion after seeing the demonstration of British military power, and he was rewarded for his collaboration: he was allowed to clear new land north of the Sabaki River at Marafa, where he moved shortly after the rebellion. This area in the Trans-Sabaki, which the British hoped would be the center of European estates, was very slow to develop, so Ngonyo profited greatly from the move. He was able, from this isolated place, to collect ivory despite its illegality and to sell it surreptitiously through German East Africa. As a pioneer in the Trans-Sabaki, he cultivated

*See below, Chapter 5.

grain to be sold at Malindi and Mambrui. Although he became an officially gazetted headman in later years, he removed himself physically from British influence and demands for a number of years to come.[50]

The Anglo-Mazrui war had far-reaching repercussions for the entire Giriama coastal population. The economy of Takaungu had been dealt a hard blow. Land was confiscated from those on the losing side; the Mazrui slaves, whose condition had been improved in the late 1880s to discourage their running away, now became the victims of plundering and capture by rebels. The destruction of most of the agricultural areas on which the slaves were dependent was followed in 1896 by a famine called Bom Bom. This abrupt and violent reversal of their social and economic position brought much hardship. Many had fled or been resold into slavery, so the old ties with their masters were broken and they were isolated. Indian shops had also been victims of considerable raiding and plundering, as was evidenced by later requests for compensation from the government. Nineteen Indians from Mtanganyiko and Konjoro claimed damages on houses and goods. They not only benefited from the peace that followed, but they became prominent as collectors of goods within Giriama territory.[51]

Giriama profited from the misfortunes of Takaungu and the slaves. Giriama mahaji moved into the coastal lands to work their own farms; Giriama had sustained their grain production in the hinterland throughout the disruption, and they were able to expand their crops in the Trans-Sabaki; Indian traders became more prevalent in the interior. The rebellion had ended once and for all the upheavals caused by Mbaruk bin Rashid of Gazi; thus, there was less pressure on runaways and their relationship with the Giriama became one of cooperation rather than conflict.

Many of the runaways were given permission by the government to move to new settlements nearer the coast.* One group was supposed to move nearer the Arabuko-Sekoke forest, but instead they crossed the river. And in 1896 the commissioner at Malindi supervised a move of watoro from Makongeni to Ali Tete so that they would be nearer a market.[52] During and after the war, watoro abandoned their farms in large numbers. This was especially true at Kibokoni, Koeni, Konjora, and other areas close to Sekoke. Many slaves settled near mission stations.[53] The number who arrived at Rabai made the mission the largest recruiting station on the coast for porters, since to become a porter freed a man from the stigma of former slavery.[54]

Slaveowners asked the British government to assist in the recovery of these runaways, and they received verbal support from local officers and from Hardinge. Many of the officers then serving were ambivalent on the question of slavery. They had distinctly wanted the slave trade to end, but many were sympathetic to the slaveowners and did not wish to undermine the wealthy and influential Muslims of the coast. This intensified conflict between the

*The British government offered resettlement to many of the runaways to prevent them from joining Mbaruk: Kenneth MacDougall, "Notes on the History of the Wanyika," Kilifi District Book, compiled 31 March 1914 (KNA: CP 75/46).

mission stations and the administration.[55] Though the officers were willing to assist the slaveowners, in late 1897 Salisbury, the colonial secretary, ordered them to abandon any plans to recover runaways.[56]

IMPACT OF THE DECADE

Neither the natural disasters nor the British Protectorate per se had as great an impact as the Anglo-Mazrui war had on the Giriama. For them, the rebellion, welcomed by Hardinge as a convenient opportunity to depose the restive Afro-Arabs and to consolidate British power, launched a period of peace and security. Despite the fact that the British aim was to foster development of European plantations along the coast, to the Giriama land appeared to be opening up.

In 1897 in Malindi district there were only 2,836 Afro-Arabs, who owned 5,422 slaves; Giriama production accounted for most of Malindi's dwindling grain exports.[57] At the same time, exportation of wild rubber increased markedly as Giriama and freed slaves continued to collect it in large quantities.[58] The Giriama survived even the serious famine of 1898/99 more successfully than did most other peoples of the coast and hinterland. In most areas there were no harvests for over twenty months. Missionary records and the report of the Seyyidieh (Coastal) Provincial Famine Committee estimate that the famine affected over two million people and killed about forty thousand children.[59] All the slaves left Takaungu town, and by 1900 all but five hundred had left Takaungu subdistrict. Few of these slaves returned.[60]

The British imported sacks of grain for famine relief; for this reason the famine was known as Magunia, or the "sacks." Unlike most of the other peoples of the coast and hinterland, the Giriama benefited from the combination of the Mazrui war and the Magunia famine, in the sense that they were able to move into land that was opened up when the slaves and runaways abandoned communities such as Kibokoni, Konjora, and Koeni, in the immediate hinterland of Takaungu.[61] In addition, Giriama who had been able to store grain or who could purchase grain through Malindi were able both to sustain themselves and to assist less fortunate Giriama.

The last decade of the nineteenth century was a culmination of Giriama prosperity, which had been increasing throughout the century. The Giriama overcame setbacks by moving onto new land and locating themselves in advantageous trading positions. The recorded increase in Giriama population provides additional evidence of these nineteenth-century changes. To use these records, it is necessary to work backward from the present. Four records of Giriama population exist for the twentieth century. The most recent figure (1969) of 197,668 is somewhat inflated, because it includes a few thousand non-Giriama who lived in the Trans-Sabaki area.[62] The 1950 census gives the Giriama population as 111,844.[63] The Coast Province annual report for 1924 records 104,433,[64] and the political report of 1912 lists 60,000, but is not based on a thorough census.[65] In 1896 MacDougall estimated the Giriama

population to be 60,000 to 70,000, with no fewer than 2,000 elders. In all
these reports the Giriama are distinguished from the other Mijikenda, so we
can reasonably assume that these figures represent Giriama exclusively (except, as noted, for 1969).

We know that the Giriama have always been the largest of the Mijikenda
peoples, but we have no description or population estimate for the period
when they all lived inside Kaya Giriama. After visiting the makaya of other
Mijikenda in 1847, J. Rebman estimated their populations as Kauma, 1,000;
Chonyi, 1,500; Jibana, 1,000; Kambe, 1,500; and Ribe, 900.[66] If we accept
these population figures, it seems unlikely that in the middle of the nineteenth
century the Giriama numbered more than 5,000. My own observation of the
kaya and the designation made by Giriama on that occasion as to the widest
clearing ever encompassed within the kaya fortifications indicate a maximum
population of 5,000 to be a fair estimate.[67]

Figures from the 1969 census clearly indicate that the Ribe, Jibana, Kambe, and Kauma, who elected to stay within close range of their makaya and
who have populations ranging from 2,000 to 8,000, have restricted their
population by staying in their kaya areas, as compared to the Giriama, Digo,
and Duruma, who have migrated widely and have expanded their populations
to 197,668, 136,000, and 105,000, respectively.[68]

Several other factors account for the steady population increase among
the Giriama. Famine struck all the Mijikenda periodically, but only the
Giriama had the advantage of variable ecological zones so that they often had
food to share. As traders, moreover, Giriama had access to coastal sources
for food imports so that they could bargain against future profits, and their
political relationship with the Arabs made it possible for them to pawn wives
and daughters during times of famine, securing their return upon repayment
the following year.* Additional increases in population occurred through
continuous assimilation of peoples during the nineteenth century. Ex-slaves,
Waata, Oroma, and other Mijikenda joined Giriama clans. Some entered
Giriama families as dependents and others attached themselves to clans independently, but all were able to take advantage of Giriama trade, cattlekeeping, agricultural growth, and mobility.[69]

Like most of Kenya's peoples, the Giriama experienced population loss
during the famines and epidemics of 1884/85, 1889/90, and 1899/1901, but
their agricultural success made them less vulnerable than their neighbors. By

---

*The concept of pawning was misunderstood by many observers, who thought the Giriama
were selling their wives and daughters into slavery. During famines as early as Singwaya days, a
practice developed among the Kashur (Giriama ancestors) to pledge daughters or sisters or wives
to get food. If the debt was paid in the allotted time, the relatives were returned; if the debt
remained unpaid, the women became slaves: *Kitab al Zanuj*, I:253-56, as cited in T. T. Spear,
"The Kaya Complex: A History of the Mijikenda Peoples of the Kenya Coast to 1900" (Ph.D.
dissertation, University of Wisconsin, 1974), p. 171. The Giriama continued to offer relatives as
pawns to ensure future payment. Another alternative was to obtain brideprice for their daughters
early, by offering them in marriage to Swahili, but this had the disadvantage of losing the
daughter to Swahili society and to Islam.

the turn of the century, their proximity to the coast and the presence of British representatives there meant that food became available and most deaths were from disease.* The Giriama experienced some population losses in the Giriama rising of 1914 and losses of Giriama serving in the Carrier Corps in World War I, but assimilation continued, and years of drought were relieved by imported food so that they rarely resulted in loss of life. Often followed by extremely productive years that allowed debts to be repaid and the population to be fed, droughts ceased to be the prelude to famine and loss of life. The Giriama in the late nineteenth century had access to good land and they welcomed people who became Giriama; this increased their agricultural production and their dominance of the hinterland. Only in the mid-twentieth century have the Giriama experienced population pressure on their land.[70]

In the course of demographic, economic, and political modifications, the meaning of Giriama identity changed. At the beginning of the century Giriama defined themselves as the descendants of the people who had lived within the confines of the kaya clearing in the Mombasa hinterland. Later they became a corporation identified with a range of economic activities that included agricultural production, cattlekeeping, rubber and copal tapping, and trade. These endeavors led to expansion and prosperity. Giriama moved to occupy an area that stretched along the coastal hinterland from Mombasa northward beyond the Sabaki River and formed it into a dynamic society and economy. The old political system proved inappropriate to the new conditions and was modified at the local level, but although it had not been replaced or adapted into a new, single system by the end of the century, in 1913 the Giriama were able to respond to colonial pressure with open confrontation.

*Cf. the Kamba and the Taita, who often lost considerable portions of their population in times of famine: Robert Cummings, "Aspects of Human Porterage with Special Reference to the Akamba of Kenya: Towards an Economic History, 1820-1920" (Ph.D. dissertation, University of California, Los Angeles, 1975), pp. 335-36; Hollis Merritt, "A History of the Taita of Kenya to 1900" (Ph.D. dissertation, Indiana University, 1975), pp. 103-4. The famine in the hinterland in 1836 sparked a permanent refugee community of Kamba at Mariakani, near the Rabai: Lamphear, "The Kamba and the Northern Mrima Coast," in *Pre-Colonial African Trade: Essays on Trade in Central and Eastern Africa before 1900*, ed. R. Gray and D. Birmingham (London, 1970), p. 83.

4

Britain and the
Coastal Economy, 1900-1912

The Giriama, whom early twentieth-century administrative departments regarded as shiftless, lazy, and unintelligent, became the most dynamic element
in the recovery of the coastal economy during the first twelve years of the
twentieth century. Had the British not intervened, they might have continued
in this rôle. Prior to 1912, when administrative interference was launched
suddenly and intensely, the Giriama added new dimensions to their economic
system.

THE EARLY COLONIAL PERIOD

The Giriama achievement occurred at the coast at the time that the British
were setting up the foundations of the Protectorate economy up-country.
This Protectorate economy relegated most Africans to the rôle of wage-
laborer, and it set up structures that would eventually undermine the economic system, based upon Africans as producers, which the Giriama had
demonstrated to be viable at the coast. Moreover, the British expanded their
administrative forces to incorporate all Africans in the Protectorate into this
system. The goals of this system, conflicting with Giriama goals, served to
hinder Giriama expansion. Although it may have seemed to the Giriama that
the coastal economy had developed independently, it was actually at the
periphery of the Protectorate economy and would eventually be incorporated
into it through institutionalized changes. Caught up in the growth of this far-
reaching Protectorate economy, the coastal economy and Giriama expansion
eventually succumbed to colonial priorities.

The completion of the railway in 1902 established British control over the
route to Buganda and dominance over peoples along the way, but it left a
huge debt that biased the development of the Protectorate's economy toward

paying for the railway. At first, there were serious questions to consider about the designs of the Protectorate. How could it best fulfill its economic potential? The hoped-for minerals that had bolstered the economies of South Africa and Rhodesia had not been found, so the British East Africa Protectorate had to fall back on the same income-producing source that had supported most of the rest of Britain's tropical empire: export agriculture. They then had to decide on the kind of agriculture and the agents who were to manage it. It was not automatically assumed that mainland Europeans were to be these agents. In fact, the Foreign Office explored the possibility of using Finns, Zionists, or various businessmen and merchants, while the Senior Commissioner was encouraging Indians to come to the Protectorate. But the few European settlers who had come to live in the Protectorate managed to persuade the commissioner that Europeans were best prepared to become the colonial developers.[1]

Why were the Africans living in the Protectorate excluded from the competition? British inability to understand noncentralized African systems of government left them dubious about the production capabilities of these Africans. To some extent this view was a result of British experiences in Buganda, where the highly bureaucratic Buganda had impressed British officers with their ability to fight, their receptivity to Christianity, and their early successful experiments in the production of cotton. The British were also influenced by their belief that African slaves were idle and degenerate. This view was derived partly from British experiences on the coast; more significantly, many people representing Britain at the time had racist and class-based prejudices. Finally, British officers were confused about the leadership—or lack of it—among the Africans. In order to use Africans as production agents, the British felt that they would have to understand them better. That would take research, and the government did not want to delay.

The result of the decision to use European settlers and companies rather than Africans as producers was that the Africans were expected to be laborers in this agricultural venture. It soon became clear that if Africans continued to work their own land, they would not have to work for wages, so the British adopted a policy of systematic exclusion of Africans as productive agents in a cash-crop economy, except when they were allowed to grow food for African workers or to kill animals for their hides.[2]

The first major problem was land. Alienating land from Africans was no easy task, as the British East Africa Company had found in 1891 and 1894. To attract settlers, however, a method of alienating land had to be devised. One of the first tactics was to declare all unoccupied land to be crown or government-owned land. In 1897 the Foreign Office first issued twenty-one-year leases and then ninety-nine-year leases. In 1902 the Crown Lands Ordinance was passed, allowing the commissioner, Eliot, to dispense lands as he chose. Settlers pushed for extensions on their ninety-nine-year leases; they induced the government to reduce the requirements for improvements.[3] The most attractive and potentially profitable area was the highlands area recently vacated by the Kikuyu, who had been forced to retreat as a result of warfare and a number of natural disasters. Then in 1904 the Maasai were required to move from the Rift Valley onto the Laikipia plateau.* The Land Committee, a settler-appointed body which significantly influenced official decisions, reported in 1905 that the administration was to provide an optimum economic environment for settlers. If they were to be the developers of the Protectorate, then they needed access to good land, general assistance, and assured labor. The settlers and concessionaires were overseers, not farmers, and they were therefore dependent on African labor.[4]

Labor had never been abundant in the East African Protectorate. When caravans went up-country in the early years, they needed porters and guides. Usually coastal peoples, many of them ex-slaves, were willing to perform this job, but sometimes replacement porters were hard to acquire along the way and coercion was used. The railroad construction was the first large labor-intensive project in the Protectorate; since there were too few African workers, the railway was built primarily by indentured workers from India. That difficulty should have signaled the problem for the future, but apparently it did not, for the development plan up-country was designed to be totally dependent on African labor.[5]

Complaints from settlers about the lack of adequate labor began in 1903. Africans had had virtually no experience in the kind of work Europeans wanted them to perform. Europeans wanted Africans to work for designated periods at specific tasks, so many days a week, on a contractual basis. Africans wanted to be target workers, for very short periods. Often, once a man had earned enough to pay his taxes he quit his job. For the settlers and concessionaires, this was inefficient: workers required training, and, too often, they left after training. The Africans wanted to continue to work their own lands and help with the harvest there, a practice that came into conflict with the demands of agricultural wage-labor.[6]

Several tactics were used to encourage Africans to serve as laborers. The Hut Tax Ordinance was passed in 1903, and a three-rupee tax was levied. The theory was that if the Africans were taxed, they would be forced to work for the money to pay the tax. If the government appointed chiefs and headmen to collect the tax and to encourage people in their area to offer themselves up for labor, perhaps personal persuasion would send workers into the labor market. And if Africans were relegated to reserve areas where the supply of land was limited, surely they would soon work out of economic necessity.† This strategy worked among many of the Kikuyu, whose rich land the settlers

*Despite assurances that this move was final, in 1911 they were moved again to the area south of the railway, in order to open up land coveted by settlers. The policy was thus set of establishing separate areas for European occupation and African occupation, the latter being relegated to "reserves."

†The 1905 Land Committee argued that Africans should be limited to reserves of the minimum area required by any group, allowing no provisions for population increase.

had taken. Some of them chose to become squatters on land they had once worked themselves, so that they would at least be allowed to grow food and sometimes to keep cattle.[7]

All these means of manipulation of the Africans, however, required a full administration and thorough vigilance in enforcement. To set up an administrative system for the entire Protectorate was a difficult task.* In the British view, the key agents were to be the headmen or chiefs, but designating chiefs became a critical problem among peoples who did not have indigenous chiefs. Among the peoples in the Protectorate, only the Wanga Luyia and some Luo had leaders who represented full bodies of people. Most of the others ruled themselves by councils of elders, or leaders emerged to meet the tasks at hand. Appointing permanent agents was contrary to African tradition, and these agents only rarely had the authority or the responsibilities that the British needed for their own administrative purposes. The British had been especially impressed with the king of Buganda and his bureaucratic system, and many officers were exasperated at what seemed to them disorder among the Africans of the Protectorate. When they had needed allies to assist their protection of the caravan route to Buganda, they had designated spokesmen among each of the peoples with whom they allied, and they extended this procedure throughout the Protectorate by simply appointing chiefs.

To solidify the position of local chiefs, in November 1902 the government passed the Village Headmen Ordinance, which gave headmen legal responsibility but failed to give them legal power. Their main task was the collection of tax.[8] Most of the first set of headmen appointed were men of local influence who had already proven their allegiance. Mumia of the Wanga, Olenana of the Maasai, Kitoto of the Luo, Kinyanjui and Karuri of the Kikuyu, and Ombata of the Gusii had all discovered that they could derive special benefits from their alliance with the British, although few of these men had the traditional authority to exercise responsibility in as wide a sphere as the British wanted.

The British needed many more headmen in the areas they had not already administered. British officers were still not convinced that "chiefs" were non-

---

*By 1902, the Protectorate had been divided into seven provinces. Three were on the coast: Seyyidie, with headquarters at Mombasa; Tanaland, administered from Lamu; and Jubaland, administered from Kismayu. Three others were designated along the railway route: Ukamba, with headquarters at Machakos, Navaisha, with headquarters at Eldama Ravine; and Kisumu, administered from Kisumu. There was also a designated Northern Territory that extended to the borders of Ethiopia, but few officers were committed to this area. Within these provinces there were twenty-four administrative stations, each with a small body of district soldiers. The administrative stations were Mombasa, Lamu, Kipini, Malindi, Takaungu, Shimoni, Rabai, and Mwatate along the coast; Ndi, Taveta, Machakos, Kitui, Nairobi, Dagoretti, Mumias, Eldama Ravine, Nandi, Kericho, Kisumu and Karungu along the main interior route; and two to the north, at Sobat and Barengo: W. Robert Foran, *The Kenya Police, 1887-1960* (London, 1962), p. 14. The seven provinces were subdivided into districts, and within districts the smallest unit was the location. It was at this level that the government wanted to use headmen and chiefs: G. H. Mungeam, *British Rule in Kenya, 1895-1912* (Oxford, 1966) chap. 5.

existent. The Secretary for Native Affairs noted in 1902 that "this system [of headmen] need not in any way affect the position of the great chiefs. They would still be the leaders of tribes: the Headmen would work under their orders and we should have a regular chain of responsibility throughout."[9] But the "chain of responsibility" alluded to in such memoranda was also non-existent in most instances; it had to be created. Most headmen could not possibly serve the government as effectively as the government wished. Locally, administrators had been allowed to work out their own system, which usually entailed the appointment of a headman, but headmen almost always derived their authority from the government, not from any legitimate traditional source.

While the government was trying in most of the Protectorate to set up an administration based on African units, settlers who wanted Africans to serve only in the capacity of wage-laborers were opposed to the idea of indigenous rule (which they felt to be nonexistent in any case) and preferred the government to set up its own model and put the Africans in it.[10] Settlers questioned the British government's stated obligation to protect the interests of the Africans. It was hard to reconcile this view with the economic aim of self-sufficiency for the Protectorate, which assumed that to expand the settlers' capital and to make use of their skills a supply of inexpensive labor would be forthcoming. Moreover, as settlers demanded increased political representation at the expense of Africans, they defined the problem as one of Africans versus settlers. Confident in their own superior ability to convince the government of the primacy of their needs, the settlers forced the Africans to direct their efforts to staving off the immediate demands, rather than looking out for African interests in the larger framework.

The key to achieving these mutually conflicting goals of African and settler interests lay with the officers who were entrusted to implement them. Governors and commissioners came and went, but a few of the officers who had begun work with the IBEAC continued in the British service in the early colonial period. Men like John Ainsworth, Frederick Jackson, Francis Hall, and C. W. Hobley advocated the African position at the expense of settler's interests. These men often argued that local African law should be administered whenever possible, although they were opposed by the opinions of the High Court, whose justices argued that a single native administrative system should be determined and applied.[11]

These old company officers were exceptional. Most officers had minimal concern for Africans. "The majority . . . saw their administrative work as a job to be done to secure their own salary and promotion, and had not greatly interested themselves in the lives and aspirations of the people around them."[12] Lack of a fixed African policy would eventually create a breach between the officers, who had managed so long without one, and the governor, who felt pressure from the settlers to pursue settler interests at the Africans' expense.

The main goal, both for settlers and administrators, was to develop the economic potential of the highlands. Although the goal had been to produce cash crops, the Protectorate economy could not finance the planting of rubber, cotton, or coffee trees, let alone the several profitless years before the first crops could be harvested. Moreover, during the exploratory phase, when planters set out to study the kind of soil available and the best varieties of crops to plant, they discovered that the most successful crops were the very ones local Africans grew in mixed farming—maize, beans, and potatoes. These were not what Britain needed: Britain needed coffee, cotton, wheat, sisal, and rubber. The government demanded the new crops, but Europeans looking for a profit produced large quantities of maize for the local market.[13]

Most of the cash crops, except for coffee, might have grown as well along the coast as up-country, but to employ the expensive railway the primary place of development had to be up-country. This decision fell in with the European preference for highland climate as opposed to coastal climate, and the fact that there were many more potential laborers among the Africans in the highlands than at the coast:

The choice of what and where to produce in the East African protectorate resulted from interaction between the needs felt by private interests and government circles in London, on the one hand, and the conditions of soil, climate, transport, protectorate finances, and so forth, under which European settlers functioned, on the other. The colonial administration acted as the intermediary between the needs of the empire and those of the local immigrants.[14]

Few administrators considered the needs of the Africans.

For the settlers, the local administration offered aid in many forms. It provided military security to protect them from African unrest. Punitive expeditions opened up new land for settlement and provided livestock that had been captured from the Africans. Settlers and concessionaires had the use of government veterinary, agricultural, forestry, and trade services, and they received subsidized rates on the railway for both exports and imports. The government established experimental farms; distributed seeds, seedlings, and stud animals; and provided grading, supervision, and certification for export crops. Despite all this assistance, however, the economy was still shaky by 1912—and one of the basic elements in this precariousness was the lack of sufficient labor.[15]

Undoubtedly, the direction of the colonial economy and administration brought Africans and Europeans into conflict primarily because the latter came to be dependent upon the labor of the former. The conflict between the economic needs and social preferences of Europeans and of Africans had existed from the very beginning of the European presence in Africa, and as time went by Europeans found their prejudices reinforced. Europeans coming to live and work in the East African Protectorate not only assumed their institutions and ethics to be superior to those of the Africans, they expected that Africans could be improved only through the "dignity of labor."[16] They believed that idleness was wrong. Because the economic system devised for the Protectorate depended on African wage-labor, both settlers and administrative officers came to believe that Africans were suited for nothing else. In a famous passage, Elspeth Huxley wrote:

The idea that the interests of an assortment of barbaric, idealless and untutored tribesmen, clothed in sheep's fat, castor oil or rancid butter—men who smelt out witches, drank blood warm from the throats of living cattle and believed that rainfall depended on the arrangements of a goat's intestines—should be exalted above those of the educated European would have seemed to them fantastic.[17]

Despite their ability to persuade officials that they were the ones to develop the colony, the first Europeans did not perform well. They were allowed to stay on a temporary basis, however, and were ultimately successful at becoming the permanent residents. They had vested interests in the new scheme, and they were willing to work for those interests. If the railway initially led the government into the interior, it was the settlers, with their ability to pressure, that kept it there.[18]

THE GIRIAMA EXPERIENCE

As the twentieth century opened, the Giriama were in by far the best position to work the land that remained after the Afro-Arab plantations were abandoned. This land offered the possibility of expanding Giriama agricultural holdings and continuing the migration that had begun in the middle of the previous century. The faltering Afro-Arab coastal economy, linked to a regional Indian Ocean trade, had long been bolstered significantly by Giriama grain sent from the hinterland for export. This process was to continue during the early years of the twentieth century, and year by year, as Afro-Arab production and trade declined, Giriama families moved into the coastal region to become squatters on this rich and unused land. Along with some of the ex-slaves, who also remained as squatters along the coastal strip and who often joined Giriama clans in order to change their identity, the Giriama combined their hinterland and squatter production, thus becoming the most dynamic element in the decaying coastal economy.

The coast had always been attractive: the land was more fertile and rainfall more plentiful than in the Giriama hinterland, and it was closer to trading outlets such as Takaungu and Malindi. For the Giriama, the coast had a special appeal in that it had a suitable environment for coconut trees, which could be tapped for fresh fermented palm wine (*tembo*); the Giriama used palm wine for all political occasions, as well as for entertainment. Giriama were anxious to move into the coastal strip as squatters on Afro-Arab lands in the hopes of tapping some of the coconut trees and planting grain under better circumstances than before. This linked Giriama fortunes to the fate of the Afro-Arabs, whose fate, in turn, was to a large extent in the hands of the British.

The Giriama understood that the Afro-Arabs would be unable to restore the production of their coastal plantations unless they found substitute labor. The runaways and other ex-slaves had been given permission by the British to settle in various communities along the coastal strip, the Afro-Arabs were relying mainly on their slaves (until 1907, when by decree they were all freed) and the markets were only shadows of what they had been, with many being conducted exclusively by Indian traders. The temptation for the Giriama to try to use the land on the fertile coastal strip was irresistible.

The exact basis on which Giriama chose where to live within the coastal strip remains unclear. Some joined Giriama mahaji who, through their conversion to Islam and their clientage to an Afro-Arab patron, had been allowed rights to work land in the coastal strip. Others joined communities of ex-slaves in such numbers that they dominated those small populations: in the villages of Shauri Moyo and Goshi near Malindi, nearly two-thirds of the families were Giriama.[19] Still others grew maize on the land of some Afro-Arab friend, or on the land of an Indian agent-creditor with whom they had previously worked. Some, apparently, merely occupied land that seemed to be unused, and hoped that they might be able to claim it through occupation. The Giriama began to dominate the Sabaki River valley and the Malindi interior at the expense of the resettled runaway slaves, many of whom became subservient people within the growing Giriama communities. One official claimed that the main ex-slave center at Pumwani was used by northern Giriama—especially by Ngonyo, who had renewed his prosperity in the Mambrui hinterland—to coordinate inland trade.[20]

Most Afro-Arab owners were pleased to have squatters on their land. Squatters offered owners a chance to gain some income from the land, either in rents or in produce, and owners were glad to have someone watch their coconut trees; the nuts were so easy to steal that owners were often unable to export any copra at all. The owners were even willing for Giriama to tap the trees for tembo, for then they would watch and tend the trees and handle the sale and distribution of the tembo. Since the tembo was tapped twice daily and could not be stored, only a local marketing system was effective. Few Afro-Arabs wanted to be bothered with this kind of work even to make a profit from their land. Some owners never knew the squatters were there, but more often the connection was explicit and mutually profitable. The Afro-Arab could remain in the town and still gain some income from his land; he knew that the land was being tended, and having squatters living on his land supported his ownership claims.

Before the abolition of slavery in 1907, Afro-Arabs had the right to all the produce that their slaves grew, but few bothered to demand the grain and to organize its export. Often they let the slaves grow whatever they could and then demanded a portion of the income. After slavery was abolished, almost all slaves remained on their owners' land as squatters until they were forced to leave. At first, Mazrui Afro-Arabs used their compensation money to assist their freed slaves, but eventually the land was sold and the ex-slaves had to move.[21]

Unlike the Giriama, who could always return to the hinterland and presumably still had some claims to land through family members who were cultivating there, ex-slaves had no source of income and, often, no experience beyond agricultural labor.* There were few advantages to retaining one's identity as ex-slave, as compared to becoming either Swahili or Mijikenda in order to benefit from the economic change. As Arthur Champion described it in 1914, it was fairly simple for an ex-slave to join a Giriama clan, and the process assured him of progeny and gave him a claim, ultimately, to communal land.[22] In Rabai, where Fred Morton recently documented the process, an ex-slave would establish blood-brotherhood (*tsoga*) with a male whose clan he would then adopt. If he then paid fees to the clan elders, he was given the privileges of other clan members. He could marry within that social group, and his children became full members of the new society without the stigma attached to one whose parent had been a slave.[23] As a result the marked increase in Giriama population was described in one administrative report as "one of the most remarkable signs of the time" in Malindi District.[24]

Just as in the second half of the nineteenth century Giriama society incorporated people who wanted to participate in the various economic forms of cattlekeeping, trading, and grain production, they continued to incorporate a vast number of ex-slaves in the earlier part of the twentieth century. It should be noted that the Giriama economy was attractive in both of these periods. In the late nineteenth century, the Giriama supplemented plantation agriculture with trade and production of their own. In the early twentieth century, they were best able to capitalize on the resources of the hinterland and the coast. Their rights to the land in the hinterland, their practice in trade, their experience with cultivation for export, and their willingness to risk being squatters provided a design for transforming the coastal economy with new means of production.

After slavery was abolished in 1907, all exported grain came from Giriama and other Mijikenda and the remaining ex-slaves. In 1909/11, for example, Malindi exported 49,742 cwt. of grain, worth 135,462 rupees.[25] Moreover, much of the grain crop was not exported. Although some rice was brought into the coastal towns from the sea, Giriama grain fed the inhabitants of Malindi, Mambrui, and Takaungu, as well as workers on European plantations along the coast.[26] It was not all smooth sailing, however. The lack of transport facilities led Indians to set up trading centers at various points on the hinterland borders, so that the Giriama had less opportunity to bargain than if transport had been provided; the Indian agents also often charged high interest, or became creditors to Giriama who were thus kept in debt.[27] Nevertheless, the Giriama economy remained prosperous.

The cultivation of maize was successful, but the use of coconut trees to produce tembo instead of copra caused the British officials considerable consternation. Copra came from the dried meat of the nuts, which was pressed for oil. If a tree was tapped for tembo, the nuts did not mature, so the decision to use a tree for its wine was irreversible. Copra was a legitimate cash crop which, theoretically, would bring income into the community, whereas

*Theoretically, the British offered protection and made land available to ex-slaves, but in reality few ex-slaves benefited.

tembo was only a means of redistributing wealth within the Giriama community. The Afro-Arabs who owned the trees stood to gain more from copra than tembo; however, laborers to tend and harvest the trees and protect them from theft were hard to find, and the Giriama were exceptionally willing to do all the work for tembo, so it proved to be the most secure way for owners to get produce from the coconut trees. Furthermore, copra as a cash crop did not bring particularly high profits; although it was a steady market, it was slow.[28]

Use of coconut trees for tembo also encouraged inebriation—a serious drawback, from the viewpoint of British officers. As early as 1902 the government passed a Liquor Ordinance that prohibited anyone from supplying Africans with liquor except for medical or sacrificial use. This was aimed at limiting the sale of tembo and discouraging Afro-Arabs from participating in the tembo trade, but to be effective it would have required much more policing than was available.[29]

The Giriama, though they were squatters on the land, did not themselves plant trees. There were a number of reasons for this. Trees were considered to be the personal property of the owner. As long as land rights were tenuous, the investment was too great: one had to wait five years for a tree to produce, only to risk losing its produce because the land had been reclaimed. The owner, on the other hand, discouraged the squatter from planting trees, because it might give him a basis for a later claim to the land. Thus, despite British encouragement to produce coconuts as a cash crop, conflict over land ownership prevented the expansion of copra in the coastal economy.[30]

When Giriama encountered financial difficulties, as they occasionally did, they worked for wages on Afro-Arab plantations—much to the frustration of local British officials and local European planters. The wages were lower than those paid by Europeans for comparable work, but the conditions of work were much more favorable. On Afro-Arab plantations, Giriama often worked on a daily basis, choosing their own hours. Europeans required month-long contracts, with payment at the end—a much less appealing offer. Usually, workers on Afro-Arab plantations were young men who did not have to go far from their families to do the work and who could return home on short notice. This was target work, usually undertaken during hard times, and it lasted only as long as the hard times prevailed.[31] For the most part, the Giriama were able to develop a profitable form of agriculture even without land rights because they provided their own labor. Using fertile coastal lands to grow grain and tembo for trade, they attracted newcomers who wished to identify with them as Giriama and to participate in this expanding profitable economy.

The Protectorate administration and economy was to deal the deathblow to this Giriama development. The final stage came in 1913 when the British administration tried to force the Giriama into the wage-labor market and to restrict them to a reserve that denied them access to coastal land, but the framework for restricting the Giriama was set up in the early years.

By its very existence the Protectorate economy redirected trade from a regional, Indian Ocean economy that was receiving maize, millet, sesame, and coconuts from Malindi, Takaungu, Mombasa, and Zanzibar to a colonial economy linked to international economic units well beyond the Indian Ocean. The center of the colonial economy resided not along the coast, which had long been the center of the East African economy, but in the highlands. The use of the railway as the link to the interior transformed Mombasa into the single major port on the coast. By isolating the coast from the developing economy and by forcing coastal trade to focus on Mombasa at the expense of other coastal towns that had been primary outlets, the coast was relegated to a secondary position in relation to the rich highlands. The normal patterns of production and exchange were disrupted; the direction of trade became modified, and the nature of the products to be traded changed. All this caused struggles between internal trade patterns and those fostered by the colonial economy. British goals prevailed over local preference; the African people's choices came to be severely limited. In contrast to the dynamic and expansive situation that had prevailed at the end of the nineteenth century, the colonial period crystallized people into rigidly defined ethnic groups, economic roles, and social classes.

COLONIAL COASTAL DEVELOPMENT

In the early twentieth century the British found the situation at the coast extremely confusing. For many years, British officials had identified with the Afro-Arabs who, as overseers for the huge plantations, had been the elite of the coast. Moreover, the British had used many of these Afro-Arabs in administrative capacities to assist with the dismantling of the slave trade and slavery. But in the process the Afro-Arabs lost their chance to continue trading in caravans and small stores up-country. New game regulations, restrictions on ivory trade, and controls over the exploitation of wild rubber undercut the bases for Afro-Arab production economy.[32] Discredited, their trade in ruins, the Afro-Arabs were useless to the British as economic agents to rebuild the coast.

The Afro-Arabs themselves contributed to this attitude. Having lived lives of leisure in a slave system, they were uninterested in working the land themselves, and a plantation system based on wage labor was much less attractive than the former system. Moreover, the insistence that they prove claims to their land at a time of land speculation encouraged them to maintain themselves as a landowning elite rather than a planting elite. Once the abolition of slavery was effected in 1907, there was little need to maintain the Afro-Arabs in their prominent position on the coast. It was the European officers and European planters upon whom the future of the coastal economy was expected to rest.[33]

Having witnessed the remarkable productive capacity of the rich coastal lowlands, the British anticipated developing them on the same basis as the highlands. The British vision for the revival of the coast was straightforward: European plantations, using African wage-labor, would produce cash crops—most likely rubber, cotton, and sisal. But the vision was confounded by the reality. Most of the land was claimed by Afro-Arabs, and until the unclaimed or crown lands could be registered and made available for leasehold, or until Afro-Arabs registered their titles and sold land to Europeans, land-holding was tenuous and the development of plantations a serious risk. When Europeans did get land they acquired more acreage than they immediately put under cultivation, but more investment ventures would surely have been launched had land been readily available.[34]

In 1895, immediately after the Protectorate was declared, the British narrowly defined the region in which the government was willing to acknowledge Afro-Arab land rights. This was done in order to reserve forest lands, especially those containing rubber, for the British. In 1903 they began registration of deeds, but a deed could not be registered until a claim had been proved, and many claims had to be settled in court.[35]

Land litigation was a slow process. As early as 1905 the Land Commission recognized that large numbers of African squatters were moving into coast lands. Unless they were required to prove title, they would be able to claim the land by right of occupation. The commissioner also recognized that the potential of the coast, in terms of capitalist development, would remain retarded until land could be sold outright. This was impossible so long as the Afro-Arabs did not hold individual title to their land: "Title allocation . . . set up the legal prerequisites of a capitalist economy."[36]

Not until after the slaves were freed did the Legislative Council pass a Coast Titles Ordinance. By this 1908 ordinance, the Land Titles Court was to investigate all private titles, district by district, and to register all those found to be valid according to the Torrens system of land registration. The residue was to be crown land, available for alienation to Europeans. In Mombasa, where the claims court began its work, most claims were not settled until 1912. In all the coastal towns, the claims were complicated and conflicting. When the court decided on a claim, a survey had to be made in order to register the title; only then could land be sold. This procedure caused both costs and delay. Land came to be regarded as a valuable commodity to be purchased for speculation rather than for production, particularly in the area around Mombasa, where land near the rapidly growing town became commercial property.[37]

To establish a boundary between Afro-Arab lands and those of the Giriama, and to set up the framework of a reserve that would limit the Giriama to the hinterland beyond the original ten-mile coastal strip, in 1908 a boundary called the Baratum Line was designated behind Malindi. It was an artificial line, since many Afro-Arabs had claims beyond it and many Giriama were occupying land east of it, but in this way the British government tried to halt Giriama squatting on coastal lands. Although people were encouraged to move to their own sides of the Baratum Line, no positive action was taken until 1914.[38]

Despite the delay caused by land litigation, by about 1904 Europeans began to claim land on the coast. Whereas many land grants given in the highlands and in the Rift Valley up-country went to individual settler families and only a few to corporations for extensive agricultural works, the coast attracted almost no private settlers. The alienated land went to corporations represented by local managers. The lobbying to Nairobi-based administrators that had been so successful a move for settlers could not be matched by coastal corporations, whose main pressure potential was in London. The investors' primary interest was profit-making; unlike the up-country settlers, who had a vested interest in remaining in the Protectorate, the coastal investors simply threatened that if they did not succeed they would move elsewhere.

Information on European plantation ventures along the East African coast is sparse and uneven; a full exploration of their develoment and decline is sorely needed.[39] Still, the fragmented evidence provides a picture of those estates that were nearest to Giriama territory, in the area of Malindi and Mambrui and in the Takaungu-Kilifi-Sekoke region. The first planters, who arrived in the Malindi area around 1904, came to experiment with cotton. Others, after 1906, came to plant rubber in order to take advantage of the rising demand for and increased profits from this product.

By 1912 there were nine plantations under cultivation in the Malindi area; most of these were eventually subsumed under the Malindi Planters Association. Six individuals had registered claims, but it is unclear whether they planted any of their acreage. The total acreage held by the estates was over 15,000 acres, but fewer than 4,000 acres were cultivated.* Since cotton had only limited success in the Malindi area,[40] most planting was in rubber. In 1910, 1,500 acres were planted in rubber; in 1912/13, there were 3,556 acres. Cotton was interplanted with rubber on 430 acres, and 110 acres were planted in coconuts. Only 35 acres were planted with other crops.[41]

In the Takaungu-Kilifi-Sekoke region, there were six estates by 1912. Most of these were growing rubber, with the exception of Nyali and Powysland, which were sisal estates; Mr. Powys Cobb had purchased 2,174 acres from the liwali of Takaungu and by 1910 had planted 750 acres in sisal.[42]

CONCERN FOR LABOR

Whenever European investors acquired rights to land, their major concern was labor. In contrast to the European estates near the densely populated highlands where the Kikuyu lived, in the Malindi and Takaungu regions the three main sources of labor for estates were Swahili, ex-slaves, and Mijikenda, mainly Giriama. Because of their Muslim tradition, few Swahili were interested in becoming agricultural laborers for wages. Ex-slaves were willing to work on plantations, but their numbers were insufficient to supply Euro-

*See David Miller, "The Failure of European Plantations on the Coast of Kenya to 1914: A Case of Competing Economic Systems" (Department of African Studies, Syracuse University, n.d.) (mimeo.).

pean labor requirements. The Giriama were the major indigenous population in the territory; their population probably totaled 70,000 during this time. The majority of the Giriama lived at least ten miles, and sometimes forty miles, from the plantations.

The Giriama found work on European estates unappealing for a number of reasons. They had long had strong feelings against working as laborers for others. The Portuguese and the Arabs had both tried without success to use Giriama laborers. The plantation economy had originally been based on slave labor, and Giriama therefore linked outside labor with the low position of slaves and remembered the period when Giriama were kidnapped to work as slaves. Moreover, most agricultural work was considered women's work or slaves' work. Men traditionally tended the hearth, offered protection, and did the first clearing for cultivation. They built houses and storage huts. A normal schedule for Giriama men was three days of work and a day of rest. Wage-labor, particularly when it was based on a month-long contract, offered an unacceptable working schedule.

Giriama worked on Afro-Arab estates or for other Mijikenda, but they did this as a short-term measure when in drastic economic straits, and as soon as they recovered economically they returned home. The Giriama opposed wage-labor because it took them away from their homes; Giriama women, in particular, did not want their young men to leave home to work. They remembered sons who had been lost to slavery. Others had become Moslems after going to the coast to live, and were then lost to their Giriama families, because they took new ways and new forms of dress and enjoyed the prestige of being a part of Swahili society. Most important was the fact that the Giriama were producers and had cash, so they had no need of wages. The taxes that had been imposed in 1902 could be paid with rupees earned by selling their grain to Indian merchants. From the profits of their grain sales they could buy all the cows, palm wine, and cloth they needed, and they could accumulate a sufficient number of cows or other merchandise to pay bride-wealth which, for them, was the most useful investment in the future, as it provided labor from wives and children.

The refusal of the Giriama to work for wages was most disconcerting to the Europeans. They persisted in regarding the Giriama men as lazy, although Giriama supervision of agricultural production, though on a smaller scale, was not very different from that of the Afro-Arab. J. E. Jones, the manager of the Malindi Magarini plantation, had had twenty-five Giriama working for him during the drought of 1912, but he found that "it was not possible to rely on the local supply [of labor] to any large extent," so he had developed a network with Kikuyu. He even had a Giriama village on his estate, but the men there refused to work for him. Although Jones recognized that the Giriama were rich in sheep and goats and that they exported "thousands of tons of maize annually," he stated that Giriama women did all the work except for breaking the ground and clearing the bush. In requesting greater government participation in labor recruiting he argued that there was a "very strong chance of their coming out to work if strong moral suasion were brought to bear on them."[43]

Some Giriama worked for Indians, who, according to various European officials, tended to cheat them. This made it difficult for Europeans to understand why Giriama would not work for the higher wages they offered.[44] The assistant liwali of Mombasa argued that Giriama preferred to work for Indians and Arabs because "apart from the difference of colour" they were better acquainted with the local language and were less strict supervisors.[45]

Since the Giriama were unwilling to serve as plantation laborers, all European plantations at the coast had to draw on the labor pool used by the Europeans up-country—Kikuyu, Kavirondo (mainly Luyia and Luo), and a few Kamba. Wages were higher at the coast, to encourage workers to travel the greater distance from their homes. Sometimes Kikuyu came to the coast on their own looking for work, and sometimes coastal plantations sent recruiters up-country, but once workers had been hired they usually returned or sent someone else the next year. Up-country laborers, however, were unaccustomed to the coastal climate and tended to contract malaria and other diseases which limited their ability to work in the fields.[46]

Ex-slaves and Swahili added to the labor force on coastal plantations, and several of the coastal plantations were worked by Somali laborers who had lost their homes in British-Somali conflicts. This was, however, hardly a permanent source of labor, and refugees were not in a particularly good position to work effectively. In addition, fighting broke out among them during their tenure of work, and much time had to be spent in dealing with the disruptions.[47] Several coastal planters suggested that indentured workers be brought from India, but many objections were raised to this proposal. It was feared that indentured laborers would not want to return to India, that their higher wages would disrupt the local wage-scale, and that they would have a "deteriorating" influence on local laborers.[48]

Not only European plantations but all agencies on the coast supplied their needs with up-country workers. The Public Works Department, the director of government transport, shipping agents such as Smith, McKenzie and Company, and even some Arab planters used this source of labor. One planter even hired 200 Ganda.[49]

Land and labor were not the only problems for coastal European planters. The first European ventures of any size around Malindi were cotton experiments. At first the government gave credits to companies to encourage cotton-growing, but by 1906 the government had given the coastal companies full responsibility. In addition to trying to plant cotton on a plantationwide basis, the companies passed out free seed of Egyptian staple cotton and encouraged the Giriama to plant small plots of ground. This first European venture continued in the tradition of W. W. A. FitzGerald of the IBEAC, who in 1892 had encouraged the Giriama to diversify their economy and to grow cash crops. The Giriama brought their cotton into Malindi, and by 1910 cotton was being ginned on the local gin and sold in the Malindi area. As it turned out, efforts to grow cotton were deemed unsuccessful, even on a plantation basis, because the soil requirements of cotton are so specific that it was a productive crop in only a few areas. The Giriama produced enough cotton to provide the seeds for future experimentation in 1910, but the credits and government aid ended and soon thereafter the cotton scheme apparently failed.[50]

The cotton experiment had hardly persuaded the Giriama to work on other plantations as wage laborers, since they could stay at home, grow on their own land, and experiment with cotton at minimal risk. The end of cotton-growing brought no financial distress to the Giriama, but the demonstration of the failure of a European venture probably made the Giriama around Malindi even more cautious.

Rubber was the crop that held the greatest promise for plantation agriculture on the coast. As early as 1879, wild rubber had replaced ivory as the major export from Zanzibar. The demand continued to be high in the first years of the twentieth century, and the potential profits from cultivated rubber were extremely promising. The international rubber boom in the early part of the century and the high prices brought by wild rubber from the Sekoke forest encouraged Europeans to plant rubber. In 1906, Europeans planted the first *Ceara* rubber trees around Malindi. The trees first produced in 1910, when Malindi exported its first and only hundredweight of *Ceara* rubber at the same time that over 4,000 cwt. of wild rubber was exported.[51]

The expansion of rubber plantations brought the lack of labor home to European planters on the coast. Prior to that time, despite complaints of shortages, almost all labor on the coast had been comprised of ex-slaves and up-country workers, but in 1908 there was a Protectorate-wide labor shortage, and the coastal plantations felt the repercussions. Agricultural ventures throughout the Protectorate were attempting to expand. In Kavirondo, administrators were apparently encouraging men to stay and grow their own crops rather than leave their district to work as laborers elsewhere. To make the problem worse, the secretary of state for the colonies, Lord Crewe, sent a letter to the governor arguing that government officials should not participate in labor recruitment.* But the planters used whatever labor they could get. By 1910 coastal planters had put in 1,500 acres of rubber trees. By 1911 they had planted almost 3,700 acres, but only 54 cwt. of *Ceara* rubber was exported, while the largest export of wild rubber in this same year was 5,108 cwt. Anticipating a sharp rise in their demand for labor to plant more rubber and to tap the now-maturing trees, planters began to put pressure on the government.[52]

The other crop in which Europeans placed hope was sisal. The first sisal

*Lord Crewe's official notice restricted government recruiting of labor for private purposes, stressing that the government's only role was to offer regulations for proper treatment of workers. But the Legislative Council tabled both the Colonial Office's dispatch and the governor's circular on the matter; with the exception of the correction of abuses, the situation remained the same: Crewe to Sadler, 27 August 1908 (PRO: CO 533/44).

was planted experimentally in 1904, and the largest plantation was begun by Powys Cobb between Kilifi and Takaungu on land he purchased from the liwali of Takaungu. But the Giriama vehemently disliked the task of cutting sisal, and almost never worked on sisal plantations, so the labor situation remained the same.[53]

From the perspective of the European planters, labor conditions were highly unsatisfactory. Even with the inauguration of a three-rupee tax in 1901 and the appointment of headmen in 1902, neither financial persuasion nor political coercion could move the Giriama to work. Encouraging the Giriama to grow cotton was at the same time discouraging them from working for wages. The Europeans often blamed the Afro-Arabs for the labor shortage, arguing that if the Afro-Arabs had refused to allow the Giriama to squat on their land, then the Giriama would have had to work for wages, but the situation was actually more complicated than that.

One might ask why, in the light of the Afro-Arab experience, Europeans did not perceive the difficulties of production in the coastal strip. They knew that the plantations had failed because of lack of labor, and they knew that the Afro-Arabs had not employed the hinterland peoples, but they attributed failure to a "degenerate" slave system and success to capitalist development with wage labor.

THE EARLY ADMINISTRATIVE SYSTEM

Given the fact that the European planters complained annually about the shortage of labor, it is necessary to ask what sort of administrative assistance was being offered for this capitalist venture. Because the headquarters of the Coast Province was in Mombasa, the provincial commissioner concentrated his efforts on the problems specific to Mombasa as a crossroads for the entire protectorate, rather than on the development of the coast in general. Officers were also stationed at Malindi and Takaungu, but in the first years the problems of land litigation and the abolition of slavery demanded their attention, and they were in any case far from the hinterland regions of the Giriama. Many of them were actually better attuned to the problems of Mombasa and of labor sources up-country than to those of the people in their own districts.

Moreover, local officers lacked the administrative structure which had affected the tactics used up-country to obtain labor. When the annual requests for taxes were made—usually by an Afro-Arab agent who came in from the coast for the purpose—the Giriama paid only haphazardly, and no one returned to punish them for nonpayment. The headmen delegated to collect the tax were rarely punished if they were derelict in their duties, and the British officers on the coast were replaced so often that headmen were seldom accountable to any particular individual. The presence of administrative officers was minimal, whereas most up-country Kikuyu were likely to see and deal frequently with an administrative officer, since the main officers for the Protectorate were stationed in Nairobi. In addition, Giriama headmen, unlike Kikuyu "chiefs," had little incentive to encourage their own people to work, for they got no rewards. In fact, the headmen agreed with the rest of the Giriama in objecting to wage-labor for the young men.

In the early years, neither tax nor headmen were taken very seriously by the Giriama. When in 1901 the government set up the first tax, of one rupee, and arranged for the appointment of local headmen through the village Headmen's Ordinance of 1902, Giriama did not fully understand these actions as an extension of British rule, because the implementation of the tax for the Giriama had come about as a result of British arbitration to end a conflict between the Giriama and the Kamba. In 1901, Giriama were fighting in the southern area against the Mariakani Kamba, who after the lengthy famine of 1899/1900 had disrupted a Giriama trade route to the coast. Ndungu wa Marai, the spokesman for the kaya, had convened the kaya council, which decided to call upon warriors to fight. He also asked the British district commissioner at Malindi, G. H. L. Murray, to negotiate a settlement. Murray arrived in the midst of the fighting, stopped the conflict, ordered all bows and arrows to be piled before him, and burned the weapons. The Giriama, by custom, offered to pay for Murray's assistance. When they asked his fee, he placed a cloth on the ground and asked everyone to pay one rupee. He then asked them to choose representatives from their respective areas to be government elders to collect one rupee from each person who was not present. The Giriama say they selected *mwitsi mwitsi*—men who were raw, blown by the wind, not really weak but not strong—in short, second-rate men.[54]

The conclusion of the Kamba war, with a fine and chosen representatives, coincided so closely with the official determination of a one-rupee tax and the formalization of the first headmen that Giriama thought their own request had created them. Significantly, they had received something in return for their rupees—peace negotiation—and they did not comprehend that the tax, but not the benefits, would continue. The call for representatives to collect the tax was hardly a prestigious offer, so the Giriama had carefully chosen men they could easily spare.

The African administration among the Giriama, installed by the British in 1902, by 1912 consisted of only twenty-eight appointed headmen who had been designated as tax collectors and around whom would be formed twenty-eight administrative "locations." Headmen's duties were limited to collecting taxes (and, it was hoped, extorting labor from those who could not pay), but when neither was forthcoming, the penalties for Giriama headmen had been minimal.[55]

The Giriama headmen were old, and their generation was due for retirement. The men the Giriama had selected in 1901 had been junior elders in an installed ruling generation. By Giriama custom, the ruling generation had a predetermined life-span. The Giriama did not choose their top-ranking senior elders: they were too old, too few, and worthy of better than the task of tax-collecting. Collection of fees had been a traditional job for youths who then presented the money to the elders. For the next decade, British officers continued to enlist Giriama of this junior-elder rank into their service, unaware of their junior position and unwilling to back them with police support.[56]

The headmen's authority was limited in other ways as well. They did not have power over all the people in their designated location; their personal authority rarely extended beyond their own village. Many headmen were spokesmen for councils and could convene councils, but they could not impose rules or regulations on the councils—no one could. Any attempt to amalgamate councils brought about a conflict of authority. Younger men who were due to become senior elders in the next-initiated ruling generation were not prepared to take orders from headmen simply because these headmen derived their authority from the British.[57]

By 1908 some "chiefs" (who received 15 rupees in salary) and other headmen (who got only 2 percent of the tax they collected) had been appointed for all areas of the Giriama plateau, but the Giriama still did not like paying tax, and they avoided it whenever possible. Headmen had no basis for coercion unless they brought in government police—who were, however, never offered. Consequently, the headmen found their position to be a difficult one. Moreover, in 1901 their duties had been restricted to tax collection, but by 1908 headmen were charged with many responsibilities: to maintain law and order; to collect the hut tax from all people in their area; to assist police in locating offenders; to use every influence to encourage, maintain, and supply labor; and to maintain the roads.[58] Some attempts were made to persuade the headmen to fulfill these new responsibilities, but with little result. The preoccupation of British officers with other questions and the preference of the Giriama for remaining isolated from administrative activities combined to soften the impact of the colonial presence.

IMPACT OF THE EARLY COLONIAL YEARS

Dissimilarities in land, labor, crops, and administrative situation meant that the European development of the coast was undertaken on a very different basis from the development of the highlands. The participants in the venture were companies, not settlers. Land had been difficult to acquire; it became available late, and not necessarily in the choicest locations. Labor had to be recruited in competition with the settlers and administrative needs up-country. And the administrative framework, which had assisted the settlers so effectively, was of minimal help to coastal planters. Moreover, they were isolated, with little communication with each other, with the central administration, or with their composite investors in London. Coastal planters began to demand greater administrative support to prevent the loss of coastal investors, and the Protectorate administrative and economic framework began to bear down on the coast.

Part of the reason the government had not yet concentrated its energies at the coast was that settler agriculture, despite the money and efforts invested, had by 1912 been only mildly successful. Exports from the Protectorate consisted primarily of maize and miscellaneous items that were grown in both settler and African areas, rather than the cash crops Britain desired. The next largest export, 21 percent of the total, was of African-collected hides and skins. Three percent of the exports was of African-grown cotton from Buganda. The settlers provided an additional three percent from coffee and two percent from dairy products. If up-country progress was limited, then coastal development had fallen much short of the anticipated goals, despite British policy intended to create the legal framework for capitalist agriculture.

The delay in land settlements coincided with improvements in the condition of the Giriama and ex-slaves as squatters, and made them even less willing to serve in the capacity of laborers. From the Giriama viewpoint, delay in the capitalist development of the coast offered distinct advantages. The Giriama were able to exploit coastal lands by squatting; they were systematically able to refuse to work for Europeans on the grounds that they objected to the conditions of contractual labor and that their grain production brought them sufficient wealth. But the British also placed restrictions on the Giriama that hampered their economic expansion. They prevented Giriama claims upon coastal lands by transforming land-holding patterns to individual ownership; they established regulations that cut into the tembo trade, one of the most lucrative local enterprises; and they pressured the Giriama to become wage-laborers instead of recognizing their performance as producers and facilitating a market economy that would have allowed a coastal export economy to thrive.

Through their control over land-holding, communications, and administration the British prevented the Giriama from exploiting the land to make it productive on a secure and permanent basis, and they discouraged Giriama squatting on coastal land. At the same time, through the incompetence of British administrators and sometimes through fortuitous circumstances, the Giriama were able to exploit the coastal strip contiguous with European plantations to a degree unmatched by most other African peoples at this time. The British development of a capitalist model that relegated Africans to a wage class, with the use of an artificial indigenous administration comprised of chiefs and headmen, labeled people as belonging to distinct classes and geographical regions, fostered stratification, and pitted the coastal economy against up-country settler communities. All of this created tension and warned the Africans to be wary of administrative and economic changes wrought by the colonial government.

5

Giriama Opposition, 1913

Giriama dominance in the coastal economy came to an abrupt end in 1912, when the first officer was assigned to the Giriama interior. Unlike other African areas where the British goal was to achieve general African compliance, British officers came to the Giriama with a specific and almost desperate demand: they needed Giriama as wage-laborers. The decision to bring the Giriama under close administration was a direct result of the 1912 labor shortage throughout the Protectorate and of the specific labor demands of coastal plantations and government projects in Mombasa.

The attempt to accomplish two things at once—administrative control and acquisition of labor—distorted working arrangements between Giriama and British agents. British officers at every level made unfounded assumptions about government power. Ultimately, the question was not whether the Giriama would provide labor, but whether the government could bring the Giriama under control. To the embarrassment of most of the administrators involved, this ostensibly poor and powerless society proved to be both rich and powerful.

LABOR DEMANDS

From the outset, the overriding demand for laborers throughout the Protectorate prevented stabilization of British administration among the Giriama. The labor question so dominated the political and economic dynamics of the Protectorate that the Native Labour Commission appointed in 1912 "took evidence and made recommendations on almost every aspect of the territory's affairs."[1] Before Girouard, the governor, left the Protectorate in 1912, he made several proposals on land and labor that were strongly influenced by South African practices and were designed to assist the settler community; in

74

them Girouard named the Giriama as the greatest untapped labor source in the Protectorate.*

In 1912, labor was more than ever in demand. Work on Kilindini Harbor and the construction of a water system were under way in Mombasa, and the government was extending the railway from Nairobi to Thika.[2] The coastal estates, in particular, reported a number of reversals resulting from the perennial lack of labor and a drought which severely limited production in 1912. They claimed that all capital flow into the coast would stop unless the government supplied laborers for their plantations. The failure of coastal Africans to provide coastal labor drew many complaints, and up-country estate owners objected strenuously to the higher wages at the coast, which were drawing off highland laborers.[3]

At this time the already limited supply of labor had been further reduced. In Kikuyuland an epidemic of cerebrospinal fever had broken out, and in Kavirondo local men were being encouraged by their administrators to produce cash crops at home rather than to work away from home.[4] Moreover, as the volume of laborers increased, unregulated transport, feeding, housing, and health care created complex problems. Labor demands grew, and labor recruiters competed for workers.

Coastal planters argued that they had special problems. Too many of the local Giriama were drinking excessive amounts of tembo. The lack of administration within Giriama district made it difficult for government officials to put pressure upon the Giriama to become wage-laborers. Taxes were low enough that most Giriama could pay them without resorting to wage-labor. Government headmen were of no assistance; many of them actually hindered recruiting efforts. Giriama who acquired wealth bought cattle, tembo, or wives, not European goods. The Giriama disliked regular, long-term employment, and objected to leaving their homes in order to work. Some planters did observe the increasing wealth of the Giriama, but either they attributed it to the "immunity from raids" resulting from the Pax Britannica or they considered it an insignificant factor in limiting Giriama interest in working for wages.[5]

Attempts at counteracting African reluctance to serve as wage-laborers followed a standard formula. If administrative presence was intensified and standardized and if government regulations were instituted, if taxes were increased and access to land limited, if restrictions against desertion were enforced, if government encouraged and facilitated labor recruiting, then the labor problem would be solved. But all this took extensive administrative effort.

The new governor, Henry Belfield, argued on 25 November 1912, in the

*When the provincial commissioner of the Coast, S. L. Hinde, recommended in 1911 that a special officer be assigned to Giriama, Girouard gave him enthusiastic support: "Coast Province Quarterly Report," 31 March 1911 (KNA: DC/KFI/113).

opening session of the legislative council, that some peoples were "disinclined to come out to work." He specifically referred to the Giriama, who instead of providing work for the coastal plantations refused "to come out of their country and do a hand's turn for anybody." One remedy for this, according to Belfield, was to send to Giriama territory officers with the administrative authority to conscript Giriama into the labor market.[6]

BRITISH ADMINISTRATION

By 1912, the Giriama perspective on the coastal economic situation differed widely from that of most British representatives. Giriama had rarely seen European officers and planters. Their taxes were usually paid (if they were paid at all) to Afro-Arab agents. Their headmen often assisted with tax collection, but rarely did any other work for the government. As producers, Giriama had been so successful that they survived the 1912 famine. They had watched the dismantling of the machinery of slavery and had incorporated many of the ex-slaves into Giriama society, thereby increasing both population and productivity. They had observed European plantations along the coast, refused requests to work, and recognized that the plantations had been adequately maintained without Giriama labor. By squatting on fertile coastal lands and by developing an internal trade in palm wine, they had successfully adjusted to the reduction of their grain markets. Threats to their economic equilibrium seemed to be minimal. Certainly the British presence had scarcely been felt in the years since the Protectorate was declared in 1895, and there were few signs to indicate that conditions would change.

British agents regarded the Giriama solely as a means to the economic stability of the Protectorate; their goal was to develop cash crops in the highlands and along the coast. Since the Giriama lacked an administrative advocate, few British agents knew anything about them. Officers came and went from the stations at the coast and at Rabai, and the few who understood the historical situation of the Giriama no longer worked on the coast.

By 1912 the British had carried out seventeen years of administration up-country, and they anticipated few problems with the quiet Giriama of the coast. It never occurred to them that they might have to make a military conquest of the Giriama.[7] The Giriama were hardly a warlike people in the way that the Nandi, the Sotik, the Maasai, and the Kikuyu were known to be.[8] The Giriama warrior's responsibility was exclusively defensive. The Giriama had supported the British against the Mazrui; there were friendly Giriama around Jilore; and the administration at Rabai had worked intermittently with southern Giriama over the years. Moreover, two new missions had been established—at Kaloleni, by the CMS, and at Mwabayanyundo, by the Catholic White Fathers. All this suggested an amicable relationship, even support for the British government. It was assumed that the Giriama, like the rest of the people at the coast, were struggling to survive. The emphasis on

Giriama as potential laborers led administrators to overlook evidence of Giriama prosperity.

The major responsibility for providing Giriama laborers to meet the demands of coastal planters fell to Charles W. Hobley, who was appointed as coast provincial commissioner in November 1912. Hobley had begun his East African career in 1890, as a young geologist and the first administrator of the Luyia of Nyanza, and he was now one of the most senior officers in the Protectorate.

Hobley prided himself on being an amateur anthropologist and he had always vehemently pursued African interests. When asked by the Labour Committee in 1912 why the Giriama had thus far failed to serve the coast as workers, he attributed it to "the lack of internal authority, based on a 'Kambi' or Village Council," since these elders had asserted that young men simply refused to come to work for wages. He hoped to "ameliorate" the problem by reviving the power of the council. Officially, Hobley was adverse both to raising taxes to encourage labor and to interfering with the "Reserves" "in any way," pointing out that "various tribes had very definite rights to certain areas."[9]

Hobley had previously risked his career and been denied promotions for his strong defense of African rights against those claimed by the settlers. In 1910 Governor Girouard had concluded that Hobley would never work well with a white community and suggested that he should be retired or transferred to a purely African province in Uganda.[10] Hobley began his term on the coast in the belief that he was working in the Africans' interests. Hobley was, however, determined that this new position was to be the crown of his career. Therefore, when the Protectorate administration decided to force the Giriama into the labor market, Hobley became committed to coastal development. Giriama laborers would be the key to his success—or his failure.* To persuade Giriama to become wage-laborers, Hobley intended to apply the up-country system of using government-appointed headmen as agents. He failed to realize that the Giriama experience was extremely dissimilar to that of their fellow Africans up-country, who had known years of British presence in the form of settlers, administrators, and labor recruiters.

A month before Hobley's appointment, Arthur Champion had been appointed as the first assistant district commissioner to administer the Giriama interior. He was told to "press for taxes, and to send all the young men who could not pay to work outside their area, on estates or for public works." Africans acclimatized to the coast were especially needed, because up-country laborers who were brought to the coast not only disliked the climate intensely but were likely to fall ill there. Champion took this task seriously and anticipated cooperation from the Giriama.[11] At 29, he had already worked among

---

*See Charles Hobley, *Kenya: From Chartered Company to Crown Colony* (London, 1970); note that he has little to say on the period of his career spent among the Giriama.

both the Kamba and the Kikuyu, but neither experience prepared him well for his confrontation with the Giriama. Champion began his tour among the Giriama with great enthusiasm but under what the British termed "rough safari conditions."[12] The plan called for a permanent station to be built in a central locality and a reserve to be marked off to limit land-holding. Champion was to take a census, collect taxes, designate the location boundaries, and verify which appointed headmen should continue to serve. He was to set up official Native Councils and obtain labor to clear the roads, to build council houses, and to construct his temporary stations. He was to put a stop to all illicit trade in ivory and, most importantly, he was to encourage the Giriama to become workers for the Mombasa waterworks or for European planters.[13]

Champion chose northern Giriama territory as his first location, because although the majority of the population resided there, the area had hardly been touched by British administration. People living in southern Giriama were theoretically under the jurisdiction of the government station at Rabai, and were aware that British officials could reach them quickly by railway. The CMS mission at Jilore in the north had been abandoned due to high mortality from fever,[14] but missionaries in the south at Kaloleni and Mwabayanyundo were preaching religion, education, and hard work. Champion had no northern mediators. When he built his temporary station beyond Jilore on the southern banks of the Sabaki River, he had to acquire his own allies there. This area came to be called Mangea, after his station, and the area north of the river came to be known as the Trans-Sabaki. It is no accident that the area in which Champion built his station became the core area for the Giriama rebellion two years later.[15]

GIRIAMA RESPONSE

With a few exceptions, the Giriama population responded negatively to Champion's efforts. His requests cut at their economic core and disrupted their political balance.

The economic basis of Giriama society might well be undermined if the young men left to become wage-laborers: these men cleared new land as the Giriama expanded across the Sabaki River, and they were the ones who took their families to the coastal strip to plant grain. Stringent tax collection would undercut Giriama hard-earned profits, while British discouragement of the tembo trade and abolition of all ivory trade (and confiscation of ivory) cut into Giriama secondary sources of revenue.

A new political balance had developed: Giriama, in an area that was now 150 miles long and 50 miles wide, had become dependent on local councils, and they had granted status to young men who had acquired wealth through trade and to men who had become assimilated into Giriama clans. Ngonyo wa Mwavuo, whose father had joined a Giriama clan from the Digo and who had never been initiated into an age set, was perhaps the most wealthy

Giriama in 1912, and he was extremely influential among the Giriama, both because he had been directly acquainted with British attitudes and expectations as early as 1895 and because a number of Giriama were in debt to him.

Administering a society with a noncentralized political system had always been difficult for the British. The problem of using headmen was particularly serious in Giriama. In the first place, Giriama had years earlier chosen headmen to be tax collectors, a job they hardly considered to be prestigious. Moreover, most of the headmen were chosen from among the juniors in the ruling generation. Their seniors had advantages over them, including the privilege of settling disputes that were unresolved on the local level, the right to collection of personal fees for such arbitration, and access to a number of highly valued oaths, especially the medicines of Fisi, which were believed to have the power to kill. Headmen could act only so long as they did not infringe upon the areas of responsibility and privilege of their seniors.

The ruling generation which had been installed around 1870 had lost all its members of the first rank through death, but three members of the second rank were still alive. Pembe wa Mrimi, though extremely old and feeble, remained in the kaya with his family and a few retainers. He was the acknowledged spokesman for the Giriama as a whole. Bogosho wa Menza was a cattle trader in Biryaa, and Wanje wa Mwadorikola lived just north of the Sabaki River at Masendeni. Critically, these three men had authority through Fisi.[16]

The fact that in 1912 only three seniors were left showed that initiation of a new ruling generation was overdue. Had the internal Giriama political process been uninterrupted, the senior and junior elders of the present ruling generation would have been forced into retirement, to be replaced by a ruling generation of younger men. The Giriama had let the transition process atrophy, mainly because a ruling generation served for approximately forty years and the Giriama had experienced considerable change in the previous forty years, but anticipation of a new installation had not died with the old men who were keepers of the ritual secrets. Younger men claimed legitimate leadership rights.

The headmen were caught in the middle. Most should already have retired. Their status as elders by age was undercut by their lack of status by rank. British officials were thus supporting overage headmen, who were losing legitimacy, against younger men who had legitimate rights to power, who had no means of claiming those rights without the traditional sanctions of initiation ritual, and who were dependent upon the retiring elders to install them.[17]

In other areas of Kenya, unofficial chiefs had been successful either through personal police forces renowned for their brutality, through command of their clans, or through the offer of attractive personal rewards—particularly land—that made it in their interest to go against their own people in order to support British administrative goals. Giriama headmen lacked all of these incentives and sources of power. The animosity between elders and youth made the demand for youthful laborers difficult for headmen to meet. Since the Giriama had not settled in their homestead clusters according to clan, the clan could not be used as a personal support group. The headmen, who had often been chosen because they were regarded as "yes men," could claim little respect in the community. Their rôle on councils was as conveners and spokesmen, not directors; they could not control councils nor could they persuade the Giriama that ultimate authority in all judicial cases was to be removed from the council and the medicine men (who used oaths) and turned over to the district officer. Moreover, when Champion reduced the number of administrative locations from twenty-eight to fifteen, headmen could no longer even pretend to carry out their duties over such a wide area.[18] The rewards were in any case minimal. Headmen were paid a small fee for their duties, but were not offered access to new land such as Ngonyo had been given in 1896 for his collaboration with the British, and they lost more by the British takeover of the ivory trade than they gained in fees.

Although Champion expected assistance from the headmen, he discovered that they often agreed to cooperate but failed to perform. Having found four sympathetic headmen whom he judged to be effective, he appointed them presidents of Native Councils: Ziro wa Luganje (of Mwangudo in Mangea South), Tsumu wa Iha (of Vitengeni in Mangea North), Baya wa Kadidi (of Jilore)—all from south of the river—and Mkowa wa Gobwe (Garashi) of the Trans-Sabaki. On these men fell the greatest responsibility for collecting taxes and assisting with the work involved in setting up an administration. They reluctantly supplied food, water, porters, and laborers. Without their help Champion could never have succeeded, for with only four constables he was expected to impose government authority and win its acceptance.* Even the local headman, Tsumu, could not get enough porters and had to rely heavily upon his own family.[19] Most headmen, trying to set a middle course between the people and the government, failed to serve either. They made excuses of ill health or old age; some disappeared when they heard Champion was coming; others made wild promises but did nothing.

Champion encountered difficulties at every turn. At Jilore, where there had long been a mission, a previous district officer had insulted the African minister Lugo Gore, a slight the Jilore population remembered bitterly.† In Garashi, in spite of the enthusiasm of Mkowa, the headman, the elders said that they could not allow their young men to work without the permission

*Champion had a list of sixteen gazetted headmen and eight more who were on probation. See Map 4, showing loyal and disloyal headmen and the location of their authority in relation to Champion's headquarters at Mangea.

†On 22 March 1912, Aubyn Rogers, secretary, CMS, sent a letter to H.R. Tate, D.C. Malindi. This letter covered complaint letters from the Reverend Lugo Gore and Wazee wa Ashofu. This matter went to the CMS bishop and to the governor and resulted in a reprimand for Hemmant. He refused to apologize, however: E.V. Hemmant, "Letter regarding the Mission Complaint against Him," 26 March 1912 (KNA: CP 2/101); "Reverend H. Binns to CMS," 12 July 1912 (CMS: G3 A5/1912/71), par. 10 (I am grateful to Jocelyn Murray for this latter citation).

and advice of the kaya.[20] Champion was often told that any headman too ardent in carrying out his duties would be threatened with witchcraft.[21]

Champion was personally disliked by many Giriama. His youth worked against him with a people who traditionally equated power with age, and his police, interpreters, and house-boys were even younger than he. Since they had seen other British officers leave, never to return, Giriama suspected the officers of collecting taxes for their own use.[22] Champion became a personal enemy of the headmen when he started confiscating ivory, since headmen were often the principals in this illicit trade. People refused to sell him food, and one headman and his Kambi council tried to kill one of Champion's interpreters by witchcraft.*

Giriama went to extremes to avoid paying taxes. They moved to distant places such as Kademu and Ndigiria near the Taru Desert. Many produced a receipt with a relative's name and insisted it was their own, an assertion Champion could not disprove, since many people had the same name.[23] Sometimes his police were attacked, and Champion discovered stores of arrows, a sign of increased Giriama hostility.[24]

The harder Champion worked, the less support he got. He became exasperated when the Giriama showed him little respect and when they dismissed what he had to say "as if he were a missionary."[25] Unlike the Kamba and Kikuyu, among whom he had previously worked, the Giriama, Champion felt, failed to express respect, let alone enthusiasm for government: "Direct insolence [was] by no means exceptional."[26]

Yet Champion was sympathetic to the Giriama. After eight months of work among them he argued against the basic colonial policy for labor: "It is not possible to succeed by any means that are at present legal. The MGiriama will never be of much use as a labourer: he is too conservative and independent. Increased taxation would throw more onto the already heavily laden shoulders of the women."[27] Instead, he proposed that the government assist the Giriama to expand their production in the Sabaki Valley. He suggested irrigation of the valley, construction of two major roads linking the far interior with Malindi, and establishment of trading centers along the new roads.[28] Giriama had demonstrated their capacity for production. They needed good seed, markets, and encouragement to grow cotton and rubber, which would be accepted in payment of the tax. Their wealth was indicated by the tax collection: although the Giriama were unwilling to pay, they clearly had the money, and no laborers had been produced through tax pressure.

H. R. Tate, the district commissioner at Malindi, agreed with Champion's plan. He suggested that the administration encourage Giriama economic development by providing good seed, roads, dams, and reservoirs.[29] Champion and Tate both recognized Giriama agricultural ability and concluded that to recruit them as laborers was virtually impossible.

*This was Tsumu of Vitengeni, who eventually became one of the most trusted headmen.

This could have been a turning point in Giriama-British relations. Champion had followed Hobley's philosophical approach, but evidence from Giriama conditions indicated that the Giriama should be supported in their own efforts at production, not demanded as wage-laborers. Although Champion did not understand fully why the Giriama were adamant in their refusal to work, he understood that implementation of the labor policy would be extremely difficult.

THREAT

For reasons not quite clear, Hobley either ignored or rejected the recommendations of Champion and Tate. His decision not to act on Champion's suggestions most probably stemmed from his disillusionment with junior officers in the civil service in general, and not from any specific opinion of Champion's abilities.[30] The Giriama were unaware that Champion was arguing against the labor policy he was trying to implement, since Hobley toured the Sabaki Valley in June to argue vehemently for the labor policy. He planned his trip to lend his weight to a tax collection in July (before the harvest) that was intended to force young men to work.

To the Giriama who heard him, Hobley's message was extremely threatening. He stressed that the "Native Councils" were no longer simply Giriama councils, but were to serve government in executive and judicial functions. This was intended to leave no doubt that the British government was permanent and powerful. He told the Giriama that if they failed to obey, he would send a military patrol to ensure obedience, and that he proposed to "acknowledge their tenure of the country north of the Sabaki River only as tenants at will of the government"—a clear suggestion that the Giriama were on the verge of losing their Trans-Sabaki lands, where over a quarter of the population resided. (Hobley added, in his report to the governor, that he "would be glad to hear if H. E. [the governor] confirms my view.")[31] Hobley carefully opened his report of this June safari with the argument that the Giriama had only recently occupied the land north of the Sabaki. His authority was the Reverend W. E. Taylor, who wrote in 1887 that the northern boundary of Giriamaland touched the river at Jilore. From this Hobley established that Giriama occupation of the land postdated the IBEAC's administration, which began in 1888. He was presenting a strong claim that this Giriama-occupied land belonged to the British.[32] Hobley had apparently changed his mind: rather than reviving the traditional council, he was transforming it into new councils. And he was not respecting Giriama "rights to certain areas"; he was proposing a serious reduction in their holdings.[33]

If any single incident sparked the organization of a full-scale Giriama response to intensified British demands, it was this visit by the provincial commissioner in late June of 1913. The Giriama had many grievances: taxes, the presence of nearby government stations, incessant demands for labor, usurpation of Giriama councils for the purposes of British administration, and loss of the ivory and tembo trade. Hobley intended to rouse the Giriama to more enthusiastic support for the British, but he did not acknowledge their grievances. Moreover, two things that he did discuss with the Giriama discouraged their support.

The first was his appeal for widespread participation in large government councils as a sure means of successful defiance against the medicine men, whom he thought to be warlocks. His purpose, naturally, was to displace the elders' fear of witchcraft by a belief that British power was stronger than the medicine of the *waganga*. However, since the power of senior elders and that of Fisi medicine men were integrated he was, in fact, encouraging usurpation of power from senior elders—particularly from the three remaining leaders, Pembe, Bogosho, and Wanje, whose major responsibility was judicial.

Second, Hobley stressed those duties of the councils which were being expanded to include executive as well as judicial functions. He wanted the councils to assist in hut-tax collecting, building roads, digging wells, improving agriculture, and suppressing drunkenness among the young men.[34] They were also to help the government by catching murderers and escaped criminals.* Giriama support, or lack of it, was being put to a test.

Hobley was a paternalist. He wanted to take care of the Giriama; he thought he knew what was best for them. He expected headmen to lead their people into civilization, with the indispensable help of government agents. The Giriama, however, viewed Hobley's visit as a threat. His mere presence had greater impact than his words. Once the provincial commissioner had visited them and had called upon forces even greater than himself in his cause, Giriama could no longer doubt that their relationship with the British had developed from one of casual encounter to one in which they were being increasingly threatened by an alien government.†

RESISTANCE

People in northern Giriama who had heard of Hobley's visit became extremely agitated. They had two basic responses: one came directly from the young men, and the other was stimulated by women.

The Chakama Incident

Young men, feeling intensified pressure to leave their homes and become laborers, became much bolder in their opposition to recruiting—toward their headmen, toward police, and toward Champion himself. This finally culminated in an incident at Chakama in early August.

*He stressed this and reiterated the other points when he addressed the elders at the baraza in November 1913: C. W. Hobley, "Giriama District Report on Political Situation and Evidence," Mombasa, 19 November 1913 (KNA: CP 5/336-I).

†Champion actually argues this point in his "October Report on the Present Condition of the Administration of the Wagiriama and Kindred Wanyika Tribes," 28 October 1913 (KNA: CP 5/336-I).

On 10 August, Champion detained nine young men who had "displayed a most defiant attitude" when he suggested they go to work to earn money to pay their taxes. He "exercised pressure" by having them carry stones for the station at Mangea. On 13 August, some thirty armed men appeared. They attacked the camp, and a nervous police officer fired without orders, killing one man.[35]

The attack had been made to free the prisoners, but it was also the culmination of growing hostility over the labor demands and Champion's persistent confiscation of ivory. He later learned that because a Baluchi ivory trader had been concealed in a nearby village, the people thought Champion was baiting them when he repeatedly warned that traders in ivory would be punished. The young men hoped that by a show of arms they could frighten Champion away.[36]

The Chakama incident reflects several critical aspects of the deteriorating British-Giriama relationship. Although it was a Giriama man who had been killed, most British officers thought in terms of punishment. Champion held that the loss of a life was sufficient penalty and that the matter should be dropped. The Giriama expected blood-money to be paid to the dead man's family. Hobley, however, wired from Mombasa that Champion was to demand the "ringleaders" for punishment or force the people to hand over 100 men for three months of paid labor in Mombasa. If they refused, they would be visited by a forty-man patrol.[37] He was, perhaps, reacting to his own helplessness in the face of the current epidemic, which had cut off the source of up-country labor, but it was a strong reaction. Champion went to Malindi on medical leave until 28 September; the district commissioner in Malindi therefore worked to settle the matter. He arrested several young men and collected a fine of sixty goats from the extremely disgruntled Giriama.[38]

From the point of view of the Giriama, it was they who had lost a man and the government soldier who should have been punished. Under Giriama law, kore (blood-money) was to be paid to the family of the dead man by the man who killed him. The matter was complicated by the fact that the dead man's nearest relative was Ngonyo: Champion had indeed offered to pay kore, but Ngonyo refused to accept it, arguing that according to European law, if one man kills another, then the killer must die. Champion of course rejected this solution. Ngonyo still refused kore; furthermore, he refused to pay his taxes. The D.C. reacted by forcing Ngonyo's people to work at jobs around the station. Eventually Ngonyo capitulated and sent people to carry stones as tax payment, probably because he did not want the growing friction to reach the point of explosion.[39]

This incident stirred up Giriama in all regions. They heard that the Europeans had killed a Giriama and had not paid kore. For them, the matter was far from settled. They were more certain than ever that the British were the ones in error; they attributed their difficulties to the British; and they were dedicated to preventing headmen from carrying out their duties.

Mekatalili and a Return to Tradition

The second and more widespread response to the British demands found focus through the actions of Mekatalili, a woman in Gallana. She had heard Hobley speak at Garashi in June, and she was determined to respond. She wanted to prevent Giriama men from laboring for the British as well as to "restore the country to its old condition." She began by gathering women and assessing their grievances; they then consulted both Wanje and Ngonyo and directly accused headmen of being traitors to the Giriama in order to get rewards; Mkowa, one of the headmen, denied having received any reward, but Mekatalili promised revenge. When Ngonyo heard the accusations, he suggested that the women go to the kaya to propitiate the ancestors.*

Champion's later report of these activities interpreted the gathering as much more subversive than it really was:

[Mekatalili and Wanje] collected a following under the guise of making harmless enquiries into the question of the rains (always a draw). The curious soon came to see what was happening, and in no time the witch Katilili got their attention and told them that the Government headmen had received each 1,000 R to sell young men to the Europeans, that the Europeans would send them over the sea and they would be sold as slaves and never see their native land again. That now was the time to resist for the Europeans had no power.[40]

The Giriama had formerly lost many of their young men to slavery in this fashion. They had no way of knowing that the British would never behave as the Afro-Arabs had. The young men argued that laborers had gone to the coast and never returned, and that the call for labor was a government bluff: "If the government had wanted laborers, then government would not have bought off Arab slaves and removed all obligations to work against their will."[41]

Mekatalili and Wanje encouraged many people from the Gallana and Godoma areas to travel to the kaya to consult with the elders, propitiate the ancestors, air their grievances, and restore Giriama government. Although compared to the number from Godoma, Mangea, and Gallana, few people from the Weruni and Biryaa areas in the south participated, the meetings at the kaya in early August did draw crowds from throughout Giriamaland.†

*Ziro wa Luganje, "Statement," 4 October 1913 (KNA: CP 5/336-I); Mkowa wa Gobwe, "Statement," 15 November 1913 (KNA: CP 9/403). Ngonyo told them, "You have left your kaya. You must return and consult spirits (*koma*) there" (quoted by Mekatalili in "Statement," 14 November 1913 [KNA: CP 9/403]. Wanje said he had not been consulted before she called her meeting (Wanje wa Mwadorikola, "Statement," 15 November 1913 [KNA: CP 9/403]). People from Ziro's location at Vitengeni did not participate. They remembered British punishment they had experienced in 1908 when young Giriama had tortured some of the elders in order to end the drought. Wanting no part of further British punishment, they chose to remain aloof from this controversy (Ziro wa Luganje, "Statement," 15 November 1913 [KNA: CP 9/403]).

†Few Giriama of Weruni participated because there the mission offerings of good land, medical care, and education had gained some support (Kitu wa Syria, "Statement Made before Pearson outside *Kaya Giriama*," 14 November 1913 [KNA: CP 9/403]). In addition, the aban-

Those speaking at the kaya had several major concerns. They forbade any Giriama to agree to labor demands, tax collection, headmen's councils, or the construction of government roads or buildings. They forbade headmen to continue their support for the British and insisted that they pay back any money they had received for recruiting laborers. They reconstituted their traditional kambi councils under the senior elders: Wanje was designated the chief judge of Gallana, and Pembe and Bogosho were to share duties in the south. They wanted to restore the power of the kaya, and encouraged many elders to return there to live. They demonstrated concern for their economic conditions by praying for rain, cursing people who bewitched goats or caused crops to fail, and denouncing anyone who divulged information about ivory. They cursed anyone who gave a daughter in marriage to a Duruma,* and anyone who wore European clothes, used soap instead of castor oil for cleansing, or washed at drinking places. Much of this was aimed at Giriama who had gone to the missions and who were wearing shirts and trousers and assisting the British administration to disrupt Giriama society.[42]

This endeavor to regenerate traditional Giriama customs was made effective through the use of several oaths, in particular Mukushekushe and Fisi (the women swore the former and the men the latter). According to Kadidi wa Bembere, one of the women of Biryaa who "laid" the Mukushekushe: "Mekatalili's business was to gather the people to checkmate the government's request for labour. She was not however at the oath, nor is she one of our chief women. She was in the kaya, but her grade is too low to permit of her taking part in the oath."[43]

Oaths were commonly used among the Giriama; often the mere threat of an oath was sufficient to change a person's behavior.[44] The Mukushekushe oath cursed every person in a family, wherever he might be. Cast as a revenge against children who had behaved in such a way as to dishonor their parents, and resulting in the discreditation of the entire family line, this curse was never taken lightly. After this oath was taken at the kaya, the water used in the oath was carried throughout Giriamaland by the women. They sprinkled it in the waterholes of the country as they repeated the oath.[45]

The Fisi oath worked somewhat differently. The secret oath of the hyena

---

doned Kaya Kidzini was not very far away and Kitu wa Sirya, the headman representing its immediate surroundings, maintained that his Kidzini clan was fully independent of Kaya Giriama. Finally, those living in Weruni were aware that troops could reach them quickly by the railway ("Statement of Some Giriama Elders before Hobley at Waa [Mombasa])," 4 November 1913 [KNA: CP 5/336-I]; GHT: Joshua Gohu wa Uyombo [Mavueni], 15 February 1971).

*The Duruma preferred Giriama wives to their own because taking a non-Duruma wife allowed them to break away from the restraints of matrilineage and to amass greater personal wealth, which their sons could inherit directly. This was obviously the same problem Giriama faced in the north, where Giriama women were marrying Afro-Arabs, but it may also have been an excuse Mekatalili used to make the women of Biryaa and Weruni receptive to her objections against the British: "Notes from Baraza at Biryaa," 11 November through 13 November 1913 (KNA: CP 5/336-I) and Hobley, "Report on Political Situation," 19 November 1913.

cult, it had long been regarded by the British as the most powerful Giriama oath. This probably reflected the respect the Giriama themselves demonstrated for it. The Fisi had been used periodically throughout Giriamaland to forbid washing in vital waterholes during drought, and to cleanse areas of witches. After the Giriama left the kaya, this oath was used to proscribe other forms of unacceptable behavior. When the medicine had been buried, the entire water supply was considered to be contaminated and anyone who broke the terms of the oath and drank from the source was expected to die. During the famine of Magunia in 1899/1900, all the waterholes of Giriamaland were put under the protection of the Fisi oath.[46]

Fisi and Mukushekushe oaths had so long been used to regulate proper behavior that a rumor that they had been sworn was generally sufficient to cause their proscriptions to be followed. In any case, most of the Giriama were predisposed to opposing the British taxes, labor demands, and judicial system, and to supporting a revival of traditional Giriama government. Since they had left their kaya residences, traditional Giriama government had grown increasingly weak. Particularly at this time, when the installation of a new ruling generation was due, the Giriama faced difficulties in coping with the threat of the British. Perhaps the Giriama were wondering if they could afford *not* to strengthen their government. The dual aim of the oaths was to provide this strength and, at the same time, to keep government servants from performing their duties. Of course, there was also the wild hope that the British, failing in their goals, would become discouraged and go away, leaving the Giriama alone.

The British gave more credence to the efficacy of the oaths as directly anti-British than did the Giriama themselves. Still, the few people who were likely to continue helping the British were those who had some vested interest in doing so. Some headmen saw this as a way to escape the forces of the British; others feared both sides, knowing that British strength was greater than that of the Giriama.

The oaths legitimized behavior that most Giriama had previously been conducting independently. It also made the likelihood of witchcraft against anyone who continued to assist the British much more believable for the people in general and the headmen in particular. The aim of oaths taken at the kaya was not to fight the British but to try to win back those Giriama who had transferred their loyalties to the British—in short, to subvert the British efforts, in favor of Giriama government, culture, and independence.

It is odd, in a society where government resided exclusively in the hands of men, that this campaign should have been led by a woman, and one who was not even a clan leader or prominent elder. It might have been expected that Mekatalili would have drawn her authority among the Giriama from either the women's kambi or the Kifudu secret society, but it was, instead, her anguish over the growing disintegration of Giriama society that led her to try to convince others to do something about it. She has been called both a prophetess and a witch, but it seems she was neither.[47] Her legitimacy must have emerged entirely from her charisma. She was an effective and emotional public speaker, and as she began to publicize the injustices she felt, she found many Giriama who agreed with her. Although her legitimacy was nontraditional, her plea appealed to tradition. She wanted a revival of the kaya and the traditional kambi, a return to the many customs which had been "spoiled," and an absolute rejection of British demands for Giriama labor. How much of her campaign she thought to be expounding truth and how much she felt to be good propaganda will never be known. In any case, her impact was immense: this was the beginning of a formal attempt by Giriama to regain their political independence.

Mekatalili was successful for several reasons. She recognized that the requests for young men as laborers were opposed by the female as well as the male population. Too, it worked to her advantage to be outside the formal structure of Giriama government while at the same time receiving support from some of its members.* The growing freedom of the Giriama from their pattern of government a century before had become so strong that had one of the clan elders suggested returning to greater control by authentic Giriama councils, many men who held positions of importance due to their wealth or achievements would have opposed the suggestion, fearing loss of their independence. Since it was Mekatalili, however, who pointed out the need for a revitalization of tradition (which the Giriama had been feeling increasingly ever since the British began their active administration) she was able to provide a sense of unity of purpose the Giriama had not had for over a century, in a form that was not threatening. Finally, since she was far removed from both the traditional and the British co-opted administrative network, and because she was a woman, British officers and headmen initially dismissed the reports of her actions as "old wives' tales."[48]

Mekatalili's energy and powers of oratory had provided a focus for Giriama grievances, but she had no control over the oaths sworn in the name of Giriama independence. It would therefore be wrong to regard the meeting at the kaya and the proscriptions that emerged from the oaths sworn there as a well-planned, tightly organized campaign. Mekatalili almost certainly did not originate all the actions that eventually transpired in the kaya, nor did Bogosho, Wanje, and Pembe apparently work in conjunction or try to control the outcome of the movement. The women were behaving independently. The people brought grievances to the kaya; there they were heard by the elders and supported by oaths. This was not a situation calling for war, but a campaign for Giriama unity.[49]

*The exact relationship between Mekatalili and Wanje has become extremely unclear. In some reports he was called her "male helper," in others, her "son-in-law." These two people were not related by marriage or blood. Long before her campaign, Mekatalili had married a man whose home was Masendeni, so she and Wanje had been neighbors. Later, after they were imprisoned together up-country, they cared for each other as man and wife. The use of the relationship terms is a reflection of this as well as of their experience after their return to Giriamaland in 1924, when they lived in the kaya as head of the newly established men's and women's kambi (Champion, "October Report," and responses from oral interviews with Giriama).

A THREAT TO GOVERNMENT EFFECTIVENESS

Unaware of the meetings at the kaya or the oaths, Champion returned from medical leave in late September with renewed enthusiasm for collecting back taxes and building his new station at Njalo. He received no cooperation from the Giriama; even loyal headmen were afraid. He could not obtain porters; headmen's councils were not meeting; no one paid taxes. No laborers were forthcoming to build his new station. Ziro wrote from Vitengeni on 4 October that neither elders nor nyere had come to his council for more than two months, and he mentioned the kaya meetings. Mkowa said his people at Garashi were so set against providing labor that some were migrating northward into Waata country at Ndebute. They replied to his summons: "Even you, Mkowa, we can shoot you with arrows because of this business of the Wazungu."[50] He advised Champion in another letter: "Sir, think about this matter seriously. I, Mkowa, in my heart, very much fear for the government."[51] Champion started on safari and found villages empty, his station at Vitengeni robbed, roads overgrown, and council houses unfinished and dilapidated. Headman Kombi wa Yeri wrote from Shakadulu that government councils were now nonexistent and the Giriama were holding "little councils in the bushes at which a few elders meet and give judgment secretly and eat the fees."* At Kirwitu, Nduria's nephew, who had asked to replace his uncle as headman, refused Champion's offer of the office because of the oath: "I am a Nyika, and I shall be killed by it."[52]

The headmen were caught in the middle. It was they whom the British officers blamed for Giriama lack of cooperation. And it was they, along with clerks and mission converts, who had most reason to fear the oaths. The headmen knew that the medicine men would not hesitate to poison them if they did not meet the terms of the oaths. Mekatalili's campaign was working: headman were unable to perform their duties.

Angry and frustrated, Champion pursued Mekatalili until finally, on 17 October, with the help of Mkowa and his deputy, he arrested her near Garashi. She signed a statement in Champion's presence, but did not admit to any wrongdoing.[53] Later that same day Champion arrested Wanje (probably at his nearby home in Masendeni). In his October report, Champion conceded that Mekatalili's campaign had been effective: "Every Giriama is much more afraid of the kiraho (oath) than of the government; the WaGiriama boast openly that the government are afraid to fight them and for that very reason have never done so."[54]

Although Champion did not openly confess that the government had lost all control over the Giriama, his recommendations for restrictions and force indicate how completely the year of dedicated efforts on the part of the British government had failed:

---

*Kombi wa Yeri, "Statement," 7 October 1913 (KNA: CP 5/336-I). Champion had originally heard about the Marafa meeting from Kombi, a Christian headman of Shakadulu. He dismissed the report as "women's gossip."

The time has come for firm action and the placing of the administration on a sound basis. The tribe will then, and not until then, realize its position with regard to Govt. The WaNyika are no exception to the rule and ours must be asserted if it is to receive the respect which is so essential in the successful government of a black race.[55]

The Giriama who cooperated in the effort to foil British colonialism and to restore Giriama autonomy were from all regions of Giriamaland. Their resistance was harder for the British to handle than open warfare would have been. Champion was insulted and frustrated—and more determined than ever to surmount the embarrassing Giriama challenge. The accusation that payment to headmen was intended to "buy" young Giriama workers was incomprehensible to British officers whose co-workers had put an end to the slave trade. To have their administration halted by an oath which threatened their most trusted servants with witchcraft was humiliating. Champion and Hobley honestly believed that the changes they were proposing were in the interests of the Giriama. They had ample knowledge of the direction of the colony's economy. No Africans in Kenya would be able to behave independently of the economic and political design that had emerged.

As a result, Giriama defiance could not be permitted. Now Champion reversed the position he had taken in May when he urged the government to drop the labor policy. He made general recommendations for stringent action, couched in such terms that it seemed they were to serve both as punishment for Giriama misdeeds and to ensure the promised labor. In reality, they were desperate measures, a last-ditch attempt to gain administrative control. The deportation of Mekatalili and Wanje could not possible soothe Giriama discontent. The challenge now was to overcome Giriama resistance. British officers were no longer primarily looking for laborers; they were struggling to retain administrative control.

6
British Punishment,
1913-1914

The Giriama situation produced an administrative problem unmatched else-where in the Protectorate. In most cases, British officers concentrated their efforts on gaining administrative control over an African group before mak-ing specific economic demands upon the people. The Kamba, Kikuyu, Luyia, Gusii, and even the Nandi had first been brought under control and after-ward suffered restrictions on their land and demands for their labor.

By October 1913 the lack of British administrative control over the Giri-ama had been conclusively demonstrated. In their attempt to respond under pressure Hobley and his officers then used two tactics that had been success-ful under other circumstances but which, when combined in this Giriama situation, produced devastating results. To gain control, in the name of punishment for Giriama misdeeds they threatened military action. At the same time, they decided to reduce Giriama landholdings—a successful tactic for obtaining taxes and wage-laborers under conditions of secure administra-tive control, but potentially disastrous as a tactic against a people over whom the administration lacked control.

COLONIAL REPORTS AND COASTAL PRESSURES

Unfortunately, the Giriama resistance campaign coincided with outside pres-sures for laborers which obscured the uniqueness of the Giriama situation. At Mombasa, the interpretation of Giriama action in the hinterland was dis-torted by criticisms and pressures brought to bear on the provincial commis-sioner by London and Nairobi.

In London, the East African Coast Planters Association was formed in June 1913 to cooperate with the local Coast Planters Association in Malindi. Its main purpose was to "secure . . . a fair share of the benefits of the British

government in those parts [of East Africa]."[1] In an August letter to the
secretary of state for the colonies, the planters noted the negligence of the
coastal administration compared to that of the highlands:

There is an entire lack of administration in the native countries immediately behind
the Coast line, such as the Wagiriama country. . . . More government officials . . .
would do much to bring the natives into touch with plantation life, and to help
mitigate the difficulty of obtaining adequate and suitable labour.[2]

Having spent the previous year arranging for laborers to be imported from
Aden and Somaliland, their major concern was for labor. They decried the
fact that the problems of land tenure and title were still delaying the initiation
of new plantations, and they urged the "immediate delimitation of native
rights." To encourage local Africans to become laborers, they suggested
curtailing both the tembo trade and the "usurious" practices of the Indian
traders, and raising the standard of the "coast natives generally" by schools
and education.[3]

But they went much further than these standard suggestions for assistance
with the task of capitalist development. They insisted that the situation at the
coast was so different from that in the highlands that a special lieutenant-
governor should be appointed to reside in Mombasa and to take charge of
the coastal development of the mainland and of Zanzibar and the Pemba
Islands, recently acquired by the Colonial Office. Moreover, they were em-
phatic that the coastal belt needed improvements in health conditions, particularly control of the malarial mosquito.

They blamed the fact that the coastal belt had been retarded to an "incal-
culable degree" on land-tenure problems and "settlement of native rights,"
and reminded the colonial secretary:

Future development of this rich Coastal belt is mainly dependent on a wise and
sympathetic policy of administration. . . . It is felt by us that only some such radical
administrative reform will reestablish the confidence of investors, which is absolutely
essential for the development of this valuable British possession.[4]

Hobley was criticized for the laxness of the administration, but he received
assurances that the coastal belt under his charge was to be the most significant place of development in the Protectorate. This was his chance to make
his mark.

A second source of pressure on Hobley was the report, also made available
in August, of the year-long investigations of the Native Labour Commission.
Using evidence taken from many witnesses, including Hobley, coast planters,
and other agents, the committee placed the blame for the shortage of labor—
"The Coast tribes are not supplying labour, and local requirements are filled
as far as possible by these two up-country tribes [Kikuyu and Kavirondo]"[5]—
and suggested a remedy: "As a general recommendation it is agreed that
Government as very large suppliers of labour direct its attention especially to
the Kamba and Giriama tribes."[6]

The Labour Commission report gave several reasons for the shortage of labor. Primarily, most Africans were uninterested in working because they had a secure economic base. They had ample fertile land, large quantities of stock, and trade profits:

It is clearly recognized that there are practically no natives who need to work for wages in order to live, and those who do work are, broadly speaking, animated by a desire to accumulate stock for the purchase of wives, who are again a potentially more productive form of wealth.[7]

The report also stated that some district officers failed to encourage Africans to become wage-laborers—a position fully in keeping with London's directives. The evidence indicated the Giriama to be unpromising as labor recruits, but the urgency of the need obscured the obstacles. The coastal shortage of laborers was so critical that the commission approved the importation of indentured laborers; most members thought restrictions should be maintained, but a minority report even rejected levying restrictions.[8]

The report specifically charged administrative officials to arrange for "the demarcation of undemarcated Reserves with a view to reserving sufficient land for the present population and the prevention of encroachments on to Crown or alienated lands." Moreover, the report argued that Giriama "squatting" (paying rent or a portion of crops grown on a farmer's land) was "wrong in principle and detrimental to the labour supply," whereas families working on a farm as wage-laborers were to be encouraged.[9] This report of the Native Labour Commission gave Hobley the authority and encouragement to move at full speed to bring the Giriama into line.

To add to the Labour Commission report and the pressure from the Coast Planters' representatives, Champion's interpretation of the situation in his October report reflected the common official attitude toward Giriama labor. His report contained a complete reversal of his position of the previous May. Now he was angry and he wanted the Giriama punished into compliance.

Champion implied that the situation had changed since May. Now the Giriama could be coerced into the labor market—if the government demonstrated its military power, if the agitators were deported, if the oaths were removed, if the elders were punished, and if the kaya, "a hotbed of sedition," was destroyed. More than that, to prevent Giriama "escaping into the bush" and to give him better control, Champion now suggested that the Giriama be restricted to a reserve south of the Sabaki River and west of the ten-mile coastal strip, thus opening up the Trans-Sabaki to Europeans. He was now agreeing with the suggestions Hobley had made earlier in June. The degree of Champion's desperation is evident from the tone of his memo:

The loss of their fertile plain of Modunguni and that of Garashi would be a punishment certainly felt by the most unmanageable section of the tribe and one that would not be forgotten for a long time to come. At present it is a crying shame to see the rich black cotton soil of the valleys over-grown with rank grass and tangled with reeds and grass, where enough rice would be grown to suffice half the wants of the coast, if in the hands of intelligent people. . . . I am of the opinion that European planters being thus right alongside the reserve would soon get their labour and they should be encouraged to offer WaNyika small plots on signing contracts of labour for a stated period of time during the year.[10]

Champion argued, as before, that any increase in the hut tax would merely overburden the women and still not produce men as laborers. Since he had failed up to this time to collect the tax, however, he now urged that permission be granted to destroy all huts on which taxes had not been paid by the appointed time.

The October report that Champion sent to Hobley demonstrated Champion's extensive knowledge of the Giriama after almost a year of working among them, and, for the most part, expressed sympathy with the Giriama position, but it concluded in frustrated anger. Champion's suggestions, however unrealistic, were intended to ensure that he could accomplish the task he had been assigned to do even though the facts suggested that his task might be an impossible one.

THE NOVEMBER REPRISAL

Champion's report only inflamed the situation. Hobley ignored all the sympathetic portions, but used Champion's accounts as evidence that Giriama had committed criminal acts. He welcomed Champion's recommendations as seconding his own suggested solution: to punish the Giriama severely, to force them into active participation in the administrative network, and to free land for European use.[11] As a result of these three reports—from the Coast Planters representatives, from the Labour Commission, and from Champion—the charge to Hobley was clear. The coast was designated a crucial area for development and the Giriama earmarked as the potential laborers. Hobley's task was to facilitate the change. As a result, he probably responded with greater force to the Giriama resistance of August 1914 than he might otherwise have done.

Hobley had received other reports, reinforcing Champion's, that trouble was brewing in Giriama. Local missionaries and district commissioners at Takaungu and Rabai passed on whatever they heard and sent out their faithful servants either to confirm the reports or to discredit them as baseless rumors. The accounts they sent back were contradictory. Some claimed that people were rushing to Weruni from Gallana after hearing that a government war on the Giriama was to begin near the river.[12] Others reported that the Giriama were preparing arrows, forming companies, and conspiring with the Somali to fight the British.[13] Giriama anger against the British was aimed at Champion, the man who had been actively annoying them.[14]

Hobley asked Ralph Skene, the district commissioner of Malindi, to give him full details of the situation around Malindi. At the end of October Skene reported a standstill in Giriama cooperation. He encountered problems in getting the necessary loads of material to Mangea to build the station. The labor agreement he had forced from the elders at Chakama had been received with great disfavor by the nyere, and some elders there had been threatened with violence and witchcraft.*

Meanwhile, the district commissioner of Mombasa was sent to Kaya Giriama. He returned to Mombasa from the kaya neighborhood with eight elders whom Hobley proceeded to interview, at first with no success. After several interviews that elicited only denials, the Afro-Arab Mudir of Tiwi was asked to intervene. He finally "succeeded in winning their confidence, and they admitted with great trepidation that there was an organized agitation in the country against the Government."[15]

Out of fear combined with pressure, these Giriama elders provided a picture for the British administration that erroneously attributed to Mekatalili's kaya sessions the organization of war against the British. The elders were quick to state that they did not approve and that the "plot broke down" as a result of their refusal to comply.[16]

However, they also offered an explanation for their own preparations for war. When Champion returned to upper Gallana after his medical leave in Malindi in late September, the rumor spread that he

had gone to organize an expedition against the Giriama. The Giriama became very frightened and made such preparation as they could to protect themselves, driving off their cattle, burying their food, and sharpening their weapons. They are merely frightened and we have no reason to think they contemplate any attack either on the ADC [Champion] personally or his police.[17]

This was enough to confirm Hobley's growing belief that the situation demanded administrative action. He requested and received permission from the governor to "investigate matters on the spot," meaning that he would go to the kaya. However, Hobley's actions indicate that he always intended to go beyond mere investigation to settle the matter conclusively.[18]

The British were never in danger of being expelled from Giriamaland. The Giriama had not been preparing organized parties of armed warriors to begin an offensive. The few groups of armed men Champion encountered were acting to protect what was being threatened at the moment. However, Champion and Hobley were in danger of being humiliated, and their efforts to develop the coast had already experienced a severe setback. It is no wonder, then, that the British officers on the coast were in the mood for severe punishment and stringent restrictions: they were indignant and angry.

Hobley ensured the outcome of his expedition before it began. He found very useful the interpretation that the Giriama campaign at the kaya had

---

*"I am told that the young men consider this call to labour as a piece of bluff on the part of the local officials. They state that if the Government wished the people to work, the slaves of the Arabs would not have been bought off by the Government and given their liberty and all obligation to work against their will, entirely removed": Skene to Hobley, 31 October 1913 (KNA: CP 5/336-I).

been organized to wage war against the British. He intended to force the
Giriama to confess this. He planned to remove opposition completely by
gaining the confessions of the traditional leaders (particularly Bogosho and
Pembe) and by obtaining accusations naming Wanje wa Mwadorikola and
Mekatalili, who were already British prisoners, as the "ringleaders." The
district commissioner of Malindi had been holding the two since Champion
had captured them in mid-October. They were to be brought to the kaya and
formally charged while Hobley was there. He wanted to have the oaths
removed, the kaya closed, and a fine assessed on the Giriama sufficient to pay
for his expedition, which he viewed as having been made necessary by their
misdeeds. Hobley wanted to demonstrate the government's strength and at
the same time to discredit the traditional leadership and the activities they
supported.[19]

On this occasion, British officers, who frequently accused the Giriama of
"cunning," were guilty of the same technique. Hobley ensured that his forces
would appear stronger than they were. He was accompanied by Captain
Eustace and twenty-four police, four of the "confessed" Giriama from the
kaya neighborhood, Champion, J. M. Pearson (the assistant district commissioner at Rabai), and fifty-three Gallana elders. He instructed the elders in his
party as to their role in the formal encounter and pitted his government
"friendlies" against the traditional government's "antagonists."[20]

He began at Bogosho's in Biryaa. Hobley told the assembly that he knew
all about what had happened and that he intended to stay until they had
given him a full report. Three times Hobley confronted them with accusations, and each time all the elders, including those from Gallana (led by
Mkowa, Tsumu, Ziro, and Kombi) went into *njama* (private council). Each
time, after returning, they admitted a little more.

By the time the third report had been given Bogosho refused to talk, and a
man from headman Tsumu's location in Mangea became the spokesman.
Bogosho insisted that he knew little about the opposition except in connection with the council fees he had been denied. He assured Hobley that his
family had always paid their taxes on time. The situation must have been a
difficult one for him, as he was confronted with the combined power of the
British administration and their Giriama supporters. He bore the brunt of the
accusations, and during the course of the day he was relieved of his position
of leadership.[21]

Under pressure, the elders named Mekatalili and Wanje as the "agitators,"
they removed the oaths, and they agreed to make a new oath as soon as the
crops were harvested.[22] They balked at the suggestion that the kaya should be
removed to a position more central to the Giriama population, however,
because they lacked the authority to make that decision.[23]

The next day, Hobley moved his party to the kaya to confront Pembe. He
forced four of the accused elders to accompany him, and Mekatalili and
Wanje were present as prisoners in Hobley's camp. Pembe virtually ignored

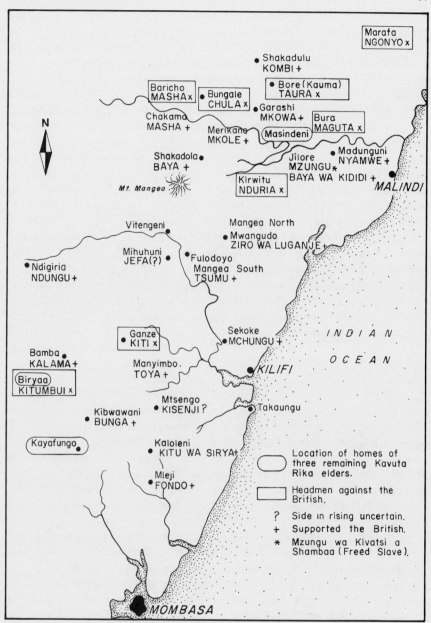

Map 4.   Headmen's role in the rising, 1914.

Hobley and "obstinately plaited a mat" from palm leaves. Fondo wa Nyama, a young government supporter, emerged as spokesman for this palaver, speaking for all but Pembe.[24]

Finally Hobley was satisfied. He forced the elders to pledge to move the kaya to a place that better suited the needs of government, and he told them that Kaya Giriama would be closed. The Giriama would have to pay 1,500 rupees for the expenses of his expedition. He then took Pembe, three Biryaa elders, Wanje, and Mekatalili with him to Mombasa as prisoners so that the governor could meet with them and approve Hobley's actions.[25]

On 1 December 1913 Pembe wa Mrimi and his family moved from the kaya to Kadunguni. From that day forward the kaya was closed.[26] Mekatalili and Wanje arrived on 18 December as prisoners at Kisii, where they were to be detained for five years. They were allowed a hut, ten cents a day for food, and a blanket apiece to protect them from the cold.[27]

Years later, Hobley was to write proudly in his memoirs of this November reprisal against "the tribe [which] was on the verge of open rebellion. It was, however, averted by a stupendous effort at a memorable durbar in the center of the district." In 1913, however, he probably would not have openly admitted what he then went on to say. "Matters thus quieted down for a time, but the undercurrent of opposition was always there and ready to crop up again at a favourable opportunity."[28]

RESULTS OF REPRISAL

What had Hobley's November actions actually accomplished among the Giriama? He assumed that the November reprisals had reversed the situation in Giriama so that government headmen would thereafter hold the positions of power. He had discredited the last of the traditional elders: Bogosho through humiliation, Pembe through his forced evacuation of the kaya and loss of his primary place among the Giriama, and Wanje through deportation. He had rid the countryside of Mekatalili, to whom he referred as the "witch" who stirred up the trouble, and he had demonstrated government support for his headmen.[29]

To the British it looked as if they had gained support from new Giriama areas, particularly Weruni, outside Champion's sphere of influence. Those who had most helped the British were duly rewarded. Since the people of Kaloleni under Kitu wa Sirya had refused to join Mekatalili's campaign, they were exempted from the fine.[30] Kitu emerged as the leader of all Weruni. Fondo wa Nyama, who had impressed the British officers at the baraza by giving them a cow to slaughter, was appointed headman in one of the Weruni locations. Gunga wa Baya replaced Pembe wa Mrimi as headman for Kaya-fungo Location. The combined zeal of these three men encouraged British officers to think that their administrative problems would be solved.

Those headmen who from the beginning had been considered "loyal servants" had proven their loyalty now, but they were still only a small percentage of the twenty-eight headmen. Mkowa and Ziro, who had accompanied Hobley to Mombasa to speak to the governor against their own people, were exempted from the fine.[31] Mkowa returned to Garashi as the most influential headman in Gallana. Ngonyo, now extremely old, had remained quietly at Marafa throughout the affair. He seemed unlikely to do otherwise now. Marafa had about 700 people, whereas Garashi had over 4,000. With the support of Mkowa and Kombi wa Yeri of Shakadulu, Hobley mistakenly assumed that the administration was in control of the majority of the Gallana population.

The people in Biryaa were generally discounted. Having barely escaped prison, Bogosho and his companions returned to Biryaa, wishing only to remain as inconspicuous as possible.[32] The Biryaa headman, Kitumbui, never gave trouble—nor did he work actively for the British. This was the area where most of the clan heads still lived, yet British officers gave the people there almost no attention.

In Mangea, the loyalty of Ziro and Tsumu led the government to ignore Nduria of Kirwitu, who had not been punished either for his role in the Chakama incident or for his presence at one of the oath-takings. He still opposed the government. In Godoma, the support of Mchungu of Sekoke, Baya wa Gunga of Manyimbo, and Kalama wa Sada of Bamba overshadowed the notorious disloyalty of Kiti wa Mwiswa of Ganze, who lived in their midst.

The majority of the headmen continued to serve in name only. Finding replacements for some of these ineffective headmen would have been a difficult task, but by allowing them, including a few who were actively hostile, to remain, British officers were running the risk that dissident headmen might become focal points of resistance.

In addition to the fact that not all of the headmen were loyal, Hobley and his officers assumed, mistakenly, that their headmen had real authority over the Giriama, while they had actually been divided even further from their people, and their traditional authority, from which they had derived whatever legitimacy they could claim, had been undercut by the British. Headmen had almost no power to enforce government demands; they could only threaten that the British would send a military force.

Thus, instead of ending animosity toward Giriama headmen, Hobley's actions in November widened the gap between government representatives and the Giriama population. It had been the younger Giriama who had been the most defiant, but they were not participants in the oath-taking. Hobley's actions unwittingly brought together the most conservative elders and the defiant young men in a nontraditional coalition against the headmen, who were mostly junior elders. What Hobley failed to understand was that the elders had not *initiated* the opposition; they had merely responded to other Giriama and used their positions to shape an effective, unified opposition to British demands. The majority of the elders, the youth, and the women were still unwilling to comply with British administrative demands.

With the fracturing of leadership and the closing of the kaya, dissatisfied Giriama could work only in local groups. For the moment, active Giriama opposition, if any remained, was powerless. The government had shown that it would, as promised, support its headmen. Outwardly, the Giriama ended their noncooperation. They attended government barazas; they provided porters; they helped to clear roads. But none of the problems had truly been solved. Only their options had been reduced. The main issue, labor, remained untouched.

Although Hobley wrote to the governor in November that "the present crisis has taught us a great deal and the knowledge acquired will be of great value for future administration," he had not dealt fully with the determination of the majority of the Giriama to maintain their dominant economic position.[33]

THE TRANS-SABAKI LANDS

It is apparent from his reports that Hobley had a hidden agenda. He had not mentioned labor recruitment during the meetings, presumably because his main goals were to reestablish government control, to discredit the traditional elders, and to uphold the authority of government headmen. He also failed to mention proposals for evacuation of the Trans-Sabaki lands. However, he stressed in his report that the policy of removing Giriama from the Trans-Sabaki had been approved by the governor, and that it should be persistently pursued. He gave three reasons why the move should be made now. Ngonyo should be moved because of his participation in the illicit ivory trade. The "recent" Giriama migration meant that they had left behind them in the south large areas of formerly cultivated land which had "reverted to jungle." Contrary to any available evidence, he argued that "although the rainfall is better in the S. half of the district and the soil equally good, the African belief in cutting down virgin bush and forest for purposes of cultivation outweighs these considerations," and he asserted that "full value can only be got out of the Sabaki valley by irrigation works carried out by European capital."[34] Hobley did not mention the Trans-Sabaki evacuation as part of the punishment, but he clearly regarded it as such.

The British Plan

On 22 November 1913 the governor agreed to all the terms of Hobley's requests, including the recommendation that the Sabaki River become the northern boundary of the Giriama. "Those of them who are settled to the North of the River shall move to the South bank as soon as practicable."[35] This gave Hobley the permission he needed to begin evacuation of the Trans-Sabaki.

Hobley was apparently less sure of government's control than he led others to believe. On 21 November, five days after his return from the kaya, Hobley produced a "Plan of Campaign in the Event Punitive Measures Become

Necessary." In it, he suggested that the government would have to anticipate opposition in the form of "guerrilla operations" and he calculated the procedures to effect the most damage without leaving starving people whom the government would then be forced to feed. He estimated the best time for an expedition as December, June, or July and calculated the routes that four columns of the King's African Rifles should take to concentrate the Giriama away from coastal peoples (who might be their allies) on the edge of "an inhospitable, foodless country" where they "should quickly come to terms."[36]

Given the difficulty of a large-scale evacuation and the potential costs of military assistance in the event of resistance, why did Hobley emphasize evacuation? The evidence offers only suggestions. Presumably he felt intense pressure from investors. Coastal agriculture had been developed by investment firms whose owners were concerned with business profits rather than with family success. Few of the coastal planters were settlers in the sense that people had been settlers up-country. Hobley was not just trying to meet the labor needs of existing plantations; he and the investors envisioned sufficient labor to entice more European planters to come to the coast to participate in its renaissance—an incredibly tall order.

Hobley's belief in capitalist development overrode his belief in African traditional rights. He and Skene shared a basic philosophy: "[The Trans-Sabaki] is very valuable agricultural land which could undoubtedly be made to produce far richer returns if worked by enlightened European planters than at present in the possession of savages."[37] This was the prevailing attitude. Many officials considered the Giriama incapable of producing cash crops because they lacked capital and were thought to be of low intelligence. Skene defended the evacuation as a wise administrative move for progress:

It is not intended by this [evacuation] to enunciate a principle to the effect that one is justified in taking from another what one can make better use of oneself. But it is obvious that native crops do not require the special kinds of soil that certain economic products do, and it is therefore no hardship to the native to require him to cultivate land which is less suitable for such economic products.[38]

Hobley and Skene were arguing that the Trans-Sabaki lands were more suitable for rubber and cotton than was the land south of the river, but the facts do not bear them out. There was ample evidence of failure of the proposed "European crops" on the Trans-Sabaki land. In September 1913, J.E. Jones, the manager of the Magarini Syndicate, requested permission from the commissioner of lands to trade 5,000 acres of his land north of the Sabaki for 5,000 acres occupied by the Giriama south of the Sabaki. He wanted the Giriama land because his land had "proved unsuitable for cotton and rubber production."*

*"Letters 16 September 1913 through 5 March 1914, Sabaki Rubber-Cotton Company and the Magarini Syndicate, Ltd." (KNA: CP 4/294). Later, in an action inconsistent with his support for the evacuation of the Trans-Sabaki, the governor, Belfield, overruled the commissioner's denial and granted Jones's request.

Earlier, Hobley had recorded European difficulties with rubber production: "Ceara rubber has been a commercial failure on the coast up to date. Unless coconut and sisal cultivation can restore the fortune of those interested, nearly all the money invested must be lost."[39] This rubber failure, noted *before* the drop in the world-market price, suggested that coastal plantations could fail even when supplied with Giriama labor. Hobley apparently chose to ignore this evidence in proceeding with his plan for evacuation.

If European cash-crop experiments failed, the Giriama agricultural system clearly succeeded. In June 1913 the district commissioner of Malindi had praised Giriama efforts:

Of the nationalities and tribes which make up the non-official population of this district, Europeans, British, Indians, Arabs, Africans and the native of Giryama, the only tribe which may be said to have held its own during the bad times resulting from two years' shortage of rainfall are the Wa-Giryama. European planters have been very hard hit; Arabs are certainly poorer than when I was in charge before; Indian firms in Malindi and Mambrui are with a few exceptions in a far from satisfactory condition and Swahili cultivators especially those who are past middle age have been having very hard times for the last 6 months and there is nothing edible in the shambas until the beginning of July.[40]

As a part of his "Proposal for the Development of the Coastal Zone" in July 1913, and to stress the potential of the Sabaki Valley, Hobley indirectly confirmed this view:

In places the Giriama have large shambas and produce great quantities of maize which is sold at the coast either at Malindi or Mambrui, laboriously carried coastward by the women and the trade is capable of great expansion with the improvement of communications and some organization and support. Giriama grain feeds Malindi, Mambrui and native labour employed on the plantations.[41]

The Giriama were thriving even under adverse circumstances; they had overcome the initial deprivation of tax demands. It would take more than persuasion to get them into the wage-labor market. Perhaps Hobley's reasoning was that they would never become wage laborers unless they were deprived of their granary.

When Arabs and Indians resident at Mambrui, north of Malindi, wrote to Hobley in May protesting the move of the Giriama ["WaNykia" of Mijikenda] to the south of the river, they argued that the "WaNyika" would suffer immensely and that Mambrui was dependent upon them for food and trade.[42] In the previous year Hobley had emphasized the potential use of the Sabaki Valley by remarking that Giriama grain, carried "labouriously" coastward by the women, fed Malindi, Mambrui, and African workers employed on the plantations.[43] Now he responded in a completely different vein: "One can I suppose expect such an appeal from people like those of Mambrui who are merely parasitic as regards a food supply. . . . They must grow it like other people."[44] He assured them that they would benefit from the development which he expected from the coming of Europeans. Hobley seemed to be ignoring the facts and proceeding on the basis of some mythological success.

Even his junior officers questioned the wisdom of the evacuation. Champion, who had exchanged places with Pearson at Rabai, wrote a memorandum advising extreme caution.[45] In early December Pearson wrote to Hobley from Mangea, inquiring whether the evacuation of the Trans-Sabaki was to be an administrative step, as Skene had assumed, or a punitive measure:

In my own mind, there is considerable doubt as to whether the Giriama elders ventured to tell you in your tour all the causes of the recent disquiet in this country, and I am anxious to know and to remove any feelings of animosity which they may have toward us, and to reassure the natives once more from a source of local repute of the good intentions of government towards them. I attach considerable importance to a mission of this character, at the present juncture, and it would be a thousand pities if the administrative move from the Northern bank of the Sabaki and collection of expenses of your mission [to the kaya] were misunderstood.[46]

Pearson also suggested that the government send an Afro-Arab who had served MacDougall in 1895 to explore the Giriama reaction, since he "to this day has enormous influence over those elements which I [Pearson] am most anxious to befriend."[47]

Hobley's reply, via Skene in Malindi, showed his concern about the "appearance" of government, which allowed him to assume that the Giriama fully understood what his own officers had not:

The ADC [Pearson] has adduced no reasons as to why the Giriama should misunderstand the collection of the expenses of my mission and the proposed removal from the North Bank. There is only one explanation and that is that they are intended as punishment for their past attitude toward government. If he [Pearson] has any further information on the subject he should submit it. I am loathe to send an Arab thru the country to stir up any past events and consider that it would be rather a confession on our part that we could not deal with the situation without invoking the assistance of Arabs.[48]

For Hobley, this must have been an untenable situation framed by the colonial context: despite his personal feelings for Africans' rights, he was still a prisoner of the prevailing attitudes of racial superiority and British national honor, and the survival of his own career was threatened. The worst danger of all—the one he had fought so hard to avoid during his earlier years in the colonial service—was that the Africans might win one of these confrontations. That had to be prevented at all costs: there were no reasons sufficient to allow African disobedience on a large scale.

The Giriama Reaction

The Giriama response to the proposed evacuation was not immediately visible, since Skene announced the move in the company of twenty-five police assigned to help collect the fine.* The move was to be completed by 1 August.

*The importance of a demonstration of government's dignity is indicated by the orders: "They will proceed in full marching order viz Fez, Jersey, Shorts, Puttis, Rifle with sling, Belt with Bayonet and brace, 2 pouches, Haversack, waterbottle, great coat and blanket folded and fastened between coat straps onto the braces" (2 February 1914, Commissioner of Police, N.B.I.

H. R. Montgomery, who replaced Skene as D.C. of Malindi, told the head-men to choose an area south of the river for their new residence and promised that they could recross the river to harvest their crops. Although Mont-gomery assumed they would take all the people of their locations with them, without police support the headmen could not effect such a move; however, even the most cooperative headmen were reluctant to admit to Montgomery their lack of power to lead a move of Giriama back south of the Sabaki.[49]

Only Ngonyo openly objected to this move from the start. He had moved to Marafa with Sir Arthur Hardinge's permission and he said he was too old to move again. Montgomery refused his requests for compensation, believing that Ngonyo was actually trying to protect buried ivory.[50] Because they were working through headmen and because they traveled with a police escort, the British officials were getting a false impression of Giriama willingness to move.

Emphasis on the evacuation overshadowed the completion of the Giriama terms of punishment. The fine payments proceeded smoothly, since they were collected under police escort. The pro-government oath was sworn in March at Vitengeni. Montgomery and Pearson met with a "large number of Head-men and Elders representative of the Giriama in the District," but the oath-administering group was not constituted according to Giriama custom. Pear-son, in his account of the ceremony, admitted that he suspected fraud, but became convinced that the Giriama had sworn the authentic hyena oath, since the symbolism seemed appropriate and the elders appeared to be solemn and sincere.[51] Despite Pearson's satisfaction, evidence indicates that the oath-taking was an illegitimate ceremony conducted only for the benefit of the British officials. The best evidence for this is the fact that the oath had absolutely no impact, in contrast to the oath taken the previous August to proscribe support for the government. There is other evidence as well. Friend-ly headmen administered the oath, rather than Bogosho and the other elders designated to administer it; they were not even present. Before proceeding, the group had demanded that Montgomery and Pearson pay a fee to join the Vaya secret society—a highly unusual request in terms of Giriama tradition, according to which the most powerful people became members of the Vaya only after years of participation as councillors. Moreover, the main element in the Fisi oath is the medicine, which must be sprinkled and consumed for the oath to take effect; no medicine was involved in the Vitengeni ceremony. In fact, the whole description of the ceremony contrasts vividly with the eyewitness report Hobley gave of the ceremony which had removed the initial oath the previous November.[52] The facts that Hobley did not attend the oath ceremony nor did he immediately notice from the descriptions given by Montgomery and Pearson that the ceremony was fraudulent suggest that he had very little hope of achieving his goal of Giriama pro-government support through this oath.

---

to D.C. Taveta, in Arthur Champion, "Movement of Wa Giryama from the North to the South Bank of the Sabaki," 11 February 1914 [KNA: CP 5/336-I].

If the British were satisfied with the oath ceremony, they were displeased about the plans for the new kaya. At this same meeting, Montgomery insisted that the Giriama begin operations to build the new kaya near Mt. Mangea. He was offended by the many excuses offered by those present. The only excuse he considered important was their need, in the not-too-distant future, to hold the initiation ceremony at the kaya to install as councillors the final two age-sets of the ruling generation. He compromised, promising that if they started a new kaya, they could return to Kaya Giriama for this special ceremony. The Giriama agreed to begin building as soon as they could assemble the medicine men of each clan, who had to be present when the path to the kaya was cut.[53]

The British officers' request that a new kaya be consecrated required their headmen to give orders to traditional elders, whose authority in this matter was far greater than that of the headmen. The headmen did not wish to confront their superiors with such impudent demands, which in any case they did not support. If the kaya were moved and the government made it into an active center, then their newfound power could be threatened. The headmen therefore insisted that the conservative elders were causing the delay.

The elders they so accused were not simply being obstinate, nor were they all opposed to moving the kaya. Some, of course, objected to the move simply because the British wished it, but the real problem was that no one remembered the necessary rituals. The surviving clan heads were not of the most senior age-set, so they had never been privy to those long-term ritual secrets. Since the Giriama had lived in Kaya Giriama for so long and had celebrated the rituals regularly, the secrets had not been passed down until the ritual took place. Most headmen did not realize that this ritual was lost; the elders wanted to hide the fact of their ignorance from the British and their own juniors.

The issue of the relocation of the kaya was causing increasing tension; as late as May there were few indications that any Giriama were making plans for evacuation. Montgomery sensed that the evacuation was going to be more difficult than he had initially anticipated. He extended the deadline to 1 October to ensure that the final crop would be completely harvested. He requested permission to begin collecting tax in the Trans-Sabaki after 1 October, with the aid of a police force. He announced that anyone still north of the river after October 1914 would be forcibly removed by his police and that he would have all empty dwellings and villages burned as insurance that the people would not return to them.[54]

In the context of such a serious pending event as the Trans-Sabaki evacuation and with indications that there might be unrest, Hobley's decision to go on six months' leave from East Africa on 1 June 1914 seems inexplicable. He had been on the coast since late 1912 and he was certainly due a leave, but his own investment in the Trans-Sabaki evacuation was so great that one would have expected him to stay to see it completed. Perhaps the extension to 1 October of the deadline for the move made it impossible for him to delay his leave any longer. In any case, C. S. Hemsted was appointed acting provincial commissioner; with much less awareness of the history of the Giriama situation, he would be called upon to respond in several emergencies for which Hobley would have been much better prepared.

The same month that Hobley left, Champion returned to Mangea as A.D.C. and Pearson went back to Rabai. Preparations to move the Kaya had bogged down. Few people had moved south of the river; in the north, they were still building new houses and planting new crops. Some people had moved further into the forest, and a few had moved from south of the Sabaki across the river to Garashi.[55]

The attempt to build a new kaya proved to be disastrous. Champion appointed 1 July as the starting date. All headmen and the heads of the six clans were instructed to come to the designated spot with food, tools, and workers to build the kaya. H. L. Hazleriggs, the assistant district commissioner of Malindi, arrived to supervise the work. He was extremely angry to find only a small showing: thirteen headmen and forty elders, but none of the six clan heads, had appeared. Exceeding his authority, Hazleriggs informed those present that if they did not begin a new kaya, Kaya Giriama would be destroyed within a month. This would leave the Giriama without a kaya in which to initiate the incoming councillors. Only afterward did Hazleriggs request approval from the acting provincial commissioner, thus presenting Hemsted with a situation in which a refusal would be a public sign of administrative weakness; Hemsted therefore consented.[56]

At this point it became evident that the Giriama had no intention of evacuating the Trans-Sabaki. While Hazleriggs was struggling to get the new kaya started, Champion reported disturbing news: "If forced, they will resort to armed resistance." Gallana Giriama had organized a plan to burn down Mangea (Njalo) station, in the hope that the British would blame the Mangea Giriama and punish them unjustly. This was expected to cause sufficient resentment to encourage the Mangea Giriama to join the Gallana Giriama in "pushing the government out of the district."[57]

The Giriama of the Trans-Sabaki had not changed their minds about evacuating their land; they had been lying, and now their bluff had been called. They had discovered that agreeing to government requests was easy, even if they had no intention of carrying out the orders. Now, as the time for the move was drawing near, the intention to disobey became obvious—they were burying grain and sending their cattle to the Tana River valley. In addition, Ngonyo, for all his tacit recognition of administrative power, still had no intention of leaving his land. He continued to play for time, hoping that the British would fail to carry out the move. By July, Giriama headmen in the north were expected to be demonstrating their good faith by being well under way with the move. No longer able to pretend that they were going to leave their lands, they made a decision. From their previous experience with the government response to Mekatalili's campaign, Giriama rightly anticipated that the government was planning to force the evacuation by using soldiers. They actively prepared for war by making arrows and by storing arrow poison.[58]

Montgomery had anticipated none of these actions and was unaware that they were being planned. He had depended on his headmen, and he had received their verbal cooperation. This perpetuated the error that had existed prior to Mekatalili's campaign, when the headmen were unwilling to admit their lack of authority. However, by the end of July Montgomery had to admit that the Giriama would not move until forced, and that, if forced, they would put up a fight. Nevertheless, he thought the reports of Giriama activity sent by Champion were greatly exaggerated, particularly in regard to Giriama aggression. After investigations by headman Ziro and an extensive safari by Champion, Montgomery had to confirm the bad news. The headmen still assured Champion that they would move, but this was reminiscent of their promises to provide labor in the previous year. As before, few people attended Champion's meetings. He was struck by the absence of young men in the villages, and at Baricho, Lukole, Marafa, and Garashi the few elders who did come to meet with him were extremely reserved. People were busily clearing bush, planting tobacco, building huts, and storing bows and arrows—hardly proper activities for people planning a major move.[59]

Even Mkowa was losing his influence over the people of Garashi. The elders there, rather than planning to follow him south of the river, were "holding him up to derision as a coward," and were making arrows. They discussed plans to drive the government west of Jilore on the main road and wipe them out at an ambush at Kakoneni, between Jilore and Malindi. This plan was based on the same tactic as Hobley's proposed punitive expedition, except that it would push the British toward the sea instead of the Giriama to the desert. By 29 July the verdict was clear: "The administration north of the river was in a state of complete chaos—passive hostility—needing only a spark to burst into flames." Champion suggested that the government forcibly move Ngonyo, in the hope that the rest of the people would follow him— that act alone would probably have been a sufficient spark to set off the fire.[60]

THE ROOTS OF REBELLION

If Hobley had decided in the previous November only to collect the fine and to hear the government oath, then the Giriama and the British might have reached an enduring compromise in the early months of 1914. Lurking beneath the apparent calm, however, was the proposed evacuation. Why, then, did he try this evacuation as a means of forcing the Giriama into the labor market, against the evidence that they were the only successful producers in the coastal economy at that time, far surpassing both the Afro-Arabs and the Europeans?

The answer is complicated. Hobley's career was on the line, and he was drawing on all of his resources. He had been disappointed in the past by junior officers who lacked the perception and dedication he himself had demonstrated, and he seemed to rely on his own judgment, based on prior experience in other areas, rather than on the information originally accumulated by Champion, who was actually in a better position to assess the situation. Hobley's Nyanza experience was inapplicable to the Giriama situation, yet he treated the Giriama as if they were Nyanza people in conflict in the 1890s, forgetting that the people of Nyanza had been a dense population of multiple ethnic groups squabbling over land and power. To the Nyanza the British government alliance brought protection and economic gain through opportunities to trade food and provide porters for caravans, and there Hobley's role as negotiator had been extremely effective. He was rewarded with prestige for having successfully arbitrated conflicts. The alliance with Mumia of the Wanga Luyia had been real: the Africans and the British had afforded each other mutual protection. The alliance with Giriama headmen was a charade in which the headmen gained almost nothing. The earlier tactics were unlikely to be effective with the Giriama.[61] Exactly why Hobley reversed his position regarding Africans when he came to the coast remains unclear, but because he decided to risk his reputation on the success of the British proposal for development, he took a hard line against the Africans.

Hobley was caught in an untenable position, trying to be all things to all people. He wanted his officers to think the pressure was coming from above; he wanted the governor to believe that matters were fully under control; and he wanted the Giriama to believe that the British government had exclusive power over them. Since he ignored or overrode much of the information he got from Champion, and withheld other information from the governor, the responsibility for the tactics used against the Giriama resided solely with Hobley. Presumably, had Hobley been successful, he would have organized a labor supply on the coast favorable to European expansion and would have ended a long, dedicated career with distinction. Had he not attempted to meet the charge to produce Giriama laborers, on the other hand, he would surely have been evaluated as an administrative failure. His efforts failed, and he was eventually discredited for trying to activate a plan designed in London and unsupported on the local level. Because of the intensity of the pressure from the investors and the Labour Commission, he responded to the Giriama refusal to work by dealing with manifestations of the problem rather than with the problem itself; as a result, he postponed any solution. Either he failed to recognize why the Giriama were refusing labor demands or he chose to proceed despite this evidence. In any case, he underestimated the Giriama reaction to a forced move from their Trans-Sabaki lands.

By August 1914 the Giriama supported the British administration no more fully than they had a year earlier when they gathered at the kaya. By appearing to be compliant, the Giriama had succeeded in warding off British forces and recovering their own position. The conditions in the Trans-Sabaki, accentuated by government pressure to begin the evacuation, had resulted in preparation for open conflict. For the Giriama, it was purely a defensive position: they were preparing to fight should the British bring in the military to force them to move. In addition, some Giriama of the north were suggest-ing tactics to encourage the Giriama of the Southern Sabaki, known for their support of the government, to come to the aid of their threatened northern countrymen. Certainly, the Trans-Sabaki Giriama would rebel rather than move from their lands.

The northern Giriama were not the only concern. At the close of July, Wanje and Mekatalili mysteriously appeared in Biryaa. They had escaped from prison in Kisii on 20 April, but due to their age, no official had expected that they would survive a trip on foot to the coast. Champion received a confirmed report that they were "holding open baraza" and were "levying a toll of fowls and grain," in the south.[62] Ironically, it was to be British demands of another kind in Mangea that would ignite open conflict and thrust the British and the Giriama into full-scale war.

7
Rebellion, 1914

By midsummer of 1914, the goal of obtaining labor had taken a back seat to the need to demonstrate full administrative control over the Giriama. The tactics taken to fulfill the original goal—punishment for noncooperation and plans for a forced evacuation of the Trans-Sabaki—had uncovered the skeletal nature of the government's administration and its ineffectiveness among the Giriama. By 1 August, the situation had become seriously unstable: Giriama in the Trans-Sabaki had balked at the 1 October evacuation deadline, and Mekatalili and Wanje had reappeared in Biryaa. British officials chose this moment to destroy the kaya, thereby unnecessarily antagonizing southern Giriama and setting Giriama in every region on their guard.[1]

Just at this time the First World War spread to East Africa, intensifying pressure on the Giriama situation. The British found themselves exactly where they had been in 1912: they needed Giriama laborers immediately (this time as porters) but lacked the administrative control to force compliance. The pressure from Germans at their back door, the administrative priority of a military campaign, the critical need for porters to support the troops, and Hemsted's lack of experience as acting provincial commissioner all contributed to the events that led to the British-Giriama war.

THE DESTRUCTION OF THE KAYA

The destruction of the kaya, intended as a demonstration of British power, only served to antagonize the young men and elders of the south and to undercut the effectiveness of the loyal headmen there. The threat to destroy Kaya Giriama, made the previous July by Hazleriggs when the elders failed to build a new kaya, was implemented in order to save face. For this reason, the British made a ceremonial occasion of the event. They wanted to teach the Giriama another lesson. A Public Works Department dynamite team accompanied Hemsted and his D.C. of Mombasa, A.J. Bretts, along with Montgomery, Pearson, and Champion, to the still-closed kaya. With them were about fifty loyal elders, including headmen Mkowa, Gunga wa Baya of Kayafungo location, and Fondo wa Nyama, who acted as spokesman for the pro-government Giriama group.[2]

Once again the British listened only to the few loyal headmen, giving local Giriama no chance to express their concerns. Fondo was a particularly bad choice as spokesman, since he had been the target of animosity from his own people for his excessive pro-government zeal. He had been appointed headman after Hobley forced Pembe from the kaya the previous November,[3] and Champion had already received a request for his removal. Petitioners at Rabai accused him of being overbearing in carrying out his duties as headman.[4] When Fondo told the officers that the Giriama were not opposed to the destruction of the kaya, he was speaking without the support of the larger Giriama community.

The elders watched silently as the main trees and gates were blown up, all the dwellings and trees inside the kaya burned, and the entrance dynamited and barricaded. Next day, it was reported, they went away quietly to their homes. British officials thought the matter was closed. Fondo wa Nyama had endorsed their action; other headmen had given tacit consent. But, despite the outward calm, anger was simmering. The nyere of Weruni met to discuss the situation, and decided that the headmen had "sold the land" and conspired with the government to destroy their traditions. Although they did not act at this time, they consulted several elders and placed themselves in readiness for armed conflict.*

WORLD WAR: CHANGE IN PRIORITIES

The war with Germany, which extended to East Africa on 4 August 1914, provided a new context for the Giriama-British relationship. Its suddenness and proximity threw British administrators off balance; their labor effort was transformed from one to get Giriama onto European plantations into a call for porters, interpreters, and guides. The Giriama, hearing the news of Britain's conflict with Germany, realized Britain's sudden weakness and the new dimension to the British need for help.[5]

The Giriama had a German source of information on the war as well. When the British government declared trade in ivory to be illegal, many Giriama traders had simply taken their ivory to be sold in German East

*"Destruction of *Kaya Giriama*," 4 August 1914 (KNA: DC/KFI/13). It must be noted that the potential "ringleaders" Mekatalili and Wanje were recaptured and sent back to Kisii on 7 August, so they played no active part in subsequent events: A.D.C. Rabai to P.C. Mombasa, 7 August 1914 (KNA: CP 9/403).

Africa, to which some of their old Takaungu trading partners had escaped after the Anglo-Mazrui rebellion in 1895. In 1914, German agents approached the Giriama, urging them to fight for their freedom. Several of these agents can be precisely identified as having been in Godoma and Mangea and possibly in the Trans-Sabaki around mid-August. One, a Somali named Haji, came to a village in Tsumu's location and told the inhabitants that he had received a charm from the Germans that would protect them from bullets. He claimed that with his special medicine he could kill Champion and "cut off his head."[6] The villagers were promised assistance from the Germans, but no Giriama left with Haji to kill Champion. Nevertheless, the idea had been planted in the minds of the people, and they now saw that others besides themselves wanted Champion's death. Haji told the Giriama to put a black flag in front of their homesteads as an indication that the inhabitants were pro-German, so that when the Germans came, those villages would not be burned (later, in the uprising, many black flags were indeed found by British troops).[7]

Another report identified as German agents two slaves of sons of Mbaruk bin Rashid, who had fled from the Giriama region to German East Africa after his rebellion against the British in 1895. These agents had been among the German forces who had entered British territory at Taveta. They brought the report that the British troops were being defeated by the Germans, and that the Germans would shortly be able to help the Giriama.[8] The German agents bolstered Giriama belief in British weakness, and offered aid that encouraged resistance.

OPEN CONFLICT

Giriama discontent was widespread and the situation volatile, but open conflict was not yet inevitable. It was the British, through their own actions, who pushed the situation into warfare. There is always the possibility that this was intentional, but more than likely it was a case of administrative bungling. The sequence of events indicates a series of errors and miscommunications.

The Giriama and the British first came into direct conflict in Mangea, when Champion, against his better judgment, responded to recruitment requests for Giriama porters for the war. Just as requests for evacuation in the north had uncovered the headmen's lack of control over their people, so the demand for porters in Mangea spurred direct opposition to headmen and to Champion personally.

Despite his reservations, Champion reacted too quickly to Hemsted's 15 August telegram requesting porters, which read: "1000 men urgently required military purposes Mombasa must be able-bodied capable of carrying heavy loads of sand stones . . . service six months wherever required stop collect in gangs and dispatch to report Watkins Mombasa stop arrive before 25th stop wire progress on morning of the 17th."[9] Champion understood this to mean that he had ten days to collect and send to Mombasa a thousand able-bodied young men. Although the request seemed unreasonable, considering that not one Giriama had yet been recruited as a laborer, Champion, in accordance with his training, tried to obey. Hemsted was later to inform the governor that the telegram was sent to Champion via the D.C. of Malindi only "for his information,"[10] but Champion could not have known this.

Just to get porters for a labor-recruiting mission to Vitengeni Champion found himself compelled to "use force never resorted to before."[11] On the day that he wrote to his superior officer that "any attempt to collect men in gangs will I fear result in bloodshed and quite possibly cause a revolt of the whole tribe which at present it might be inconvenient to have to quell,"[12] he sent patrols out to all headmen in Mangea, Biryaa, and Godoma, asking for fifty laborers from each man's location. He received angry and categorical refusals. Although his superior urged him to "use no such force as in your opinion may be calculated to provoke open resistance [since] your ineffectual orders for labour only tend to diminish your authority,"[13] the caution came too late. On 17 August the long-building hostility between the Giriama and the British administration escalated into open conflict.

One of Champion's men, on a patrol near Vitengeni, gave local Giriama the incentive they needed to fight. Finding only women and children in one village, a policeman raped a woman; he was fired upon by Giriama men hiding in the bush nearby, but he escaped. Champion heard the shots from his camp and went to meet his men. The police reported that they had been fired on but omitted mention of the provocation. Champion assumed the Giriama to be at fault, and took it as an attack upon himself when the offending policeman was killed by an arrow shot from the bush. He wrote to the D.C. of Rabai that "a more unprovoked and dastardly act [could] hardly [have been] imagined."[14]

The Giriama, on the other hand, felt they had good reason to fight. The incident of the rape made it easy to recruit fellow Giriama in the area; the death of the policeman evened the score for the young Giriama who had been killed by a policeman at Chakama the previous year; and Champion became a focus for Giriama hatred.* His demand for laborers had intensified Giriama anger: they feared that a large police force would come to take their young men away. If conflict was inevitable, the Giriama of Mangea had little to lose by initiating it. They were determined never to provide labor voluntarily.

Giriama Organization

A rumor spread that Champion had been killed by Giriama attacking his Mangea station; this, more than anything else, fanned the flame of Giriama rebellion (at no time did the British think Champion had been killed; he had been inconvenienced, but was never in serious danger). Spurred on by their

---

*Rape was not to be taken lightly, and resentment had been simmering for a long time. GHT: Karezi wa Mwasada (Bamba), 22 December 1970; Champion, "Report on Armed Disturbance at Vitengeni," 21 August 1914 (KNA: CP 5/336-III).

knowledge of British vulnerability to the Germans and supported by other fighters who had joined the cause, dissident Giriama in Mangea and Godoma took the offensive, concentrating their energy upon those places which were symbols of British power: Vitengeni camp, Mangea station, headmen's houses, government council houses, and European plantations. Threats were received at two plantations—Sekoke, south of Malindi, and Magarini, west of Mambrui and north of the Sabaki River. The threats were saber-rattling rather than serious aggression, but the European managers sent agitated requests to Malindi and Takaungu for assistance.[15] A few northern Giriama came south of the river to join their Mangea neighbors in the fight.[16]

Upon hearing that Giriama had defeated Champion at Mangea, young men in the south set about trying to get support from the kambi:[17] "The kambi were at first too scared to do anything, but when they saw the courage of their sons, those who were against the Mzungu [Europeans] came forward one by one to take their place of leadership."[18] Traditionally, when Giriama prepared for war, they went to each elder and asked him to contribute a bull for the ritual. Now the group decided that bulls should be brought for slaughter. In this case, the main purpose was to have each headman (not only the elders) contribute a bull, in order to demonstrate their support of their own people and their opposition to the British. It would be, in addition, a tacit recognition that the elders of the kambi sitting in council were superior in leadership to government-appointed headmen. This was also a tax the Giriama were collecting for themselves.[19]

The nyere, grouped into military contingents of about fifty men each, visited the homes of the headmen. They were under instructions from the full group not to hurt anyone unless there was resistance. The headmen were asked to pay goats and cows and to accompany the men to the meeting place. Fondo wa Nyama and Kitu wa Syria escaped the armed parties, but one nyere led almost two hundred men to confront headman Gunga wa Baya. Gunga paid two cows and five goats and then sat through a frightening and humiliating session in which they argued over whether he had made a sufficiently large payment for their purposes:[20]

If you murder him, what do you gain? And they sat there with several nyere pointing arrows at him as though they were waiting to shoot. And . . . [he] sat quietly through the ordeal and waited quietly to see what action they would finally take. He watched them slaughter all the animals and eat everything in [his] presence.[21]

He had purchased his life by demonstrating his intention of no longer working for the British. Before Kitu and Fondo had been captured, word reached Weruni that Champion was, after all, safe, so hostile actions against the headmen apparently ceased. However, the headmen had been served notice that their future was in jeopardy. They had been intimidated by Mekaṭalili's campaign the year before; this time their lives had been threatened. Now both sides in Weruni waited for the next move.[22]

British Response

The blame for the British response to the Giriama actions falls primarily upon Hemsted, who was acting in Hobley's absence, but the conditions of the larger war with Germany gave overriding authority to the military officer commanding the troops of the King's African Rifles. When Hemsted informed Nairobi of the attack on Champion at Vitengeni, the officer commanding troops first instructed Champion to evacuate to the coast. Had that been done, the British might have postponed their dealings with the Giriama until after the war with Germany had ended. But the Giriama were too close to the war front; their dissidence could work for the Germans. Later in the day, therefore, the officer countermanded his own order and insisted that the Mangea station be held at all costs. A patrol was sent from Malindi to assist Champion, and Charles Dundas, who had recently arrived to become the D.C. Rabai, was sent to take over Mangea station. The British were determined to quell Giriama unrest.[23]

In the chaos of the situation and the pressure of the war conditions, Hemsted's response to the next set of messages regarding Giriama unrest was exaggerated and premature. He received multiple reports about the unrest almost simultaneously,* and he wired for troops and had them marching in the field before a true picture of the Giriama situation had emerged.[24] Champion had learned from headmen who came to his station for protection that the dissident Giriama were from widespread villages. He wrote that "quite ninety percent" of the Giriama were "actively hostile to the government" and that should a rising start, "all would join to drive us out of the country," but he was careful to assure his superiors that he himself was safe.[25] The rumors of threats to the plantations at Sekoke and Magarini proved to be not only exaggerated but unfounded. In one case Giriama had merely warned British workers that they would resist anyone who came to recruit them; in another, no Giriama even appeared. This was confirmed by the officers Hemsted sent to investigate the situation, but Hemsted failed to wait for their reports. Most probably it was a telegram sent to Takaungu from Dundas (who had encountered a few restless Giriama in crossing the Rare River on his way from Rabai to Mangea) that increased Hemsted's alarm. Dundas's assessment of the situation had been made in haste, and he had wired "General rising of Giriama and situation very grave."[26] Dundas met no more armed Giriama until he got to Mangea and in his full report, written two days later, he called the Giriama action "more demonstrative than determined."[27] By then the King's African Rifles' offensive was under way.†

*Montgomery to Hemsted, 22 August 1914 (KNA: CP 5/336-III); Montgomery to Hemsted, "Disturbance at Magarini," 25 August 1914 (KNA: CP 5/336-III); Henry to Vidal, 22 August 1914 (KNA: CP 5/336-III). Even Lascelles, acting in Dundas's absence at Rabai, had wanted troops in the area, but rumors that Duruma and Kamba were about to attack Rabai and that German *askaris* (soldiers) were in the neighborhood all proved to be false: Lascelles to Hemsted, 25 August 1914 and 26 August 1914 (KNA: CP 12/222).

†Hemsted, from Mombasa, chose to request troops, out of fear that the administration had

Military Escalation

Without doubt the actions of the military escalated the British-Giriama conflict. Local administrators wanted military support to accomplish a number of goals they had been unable to achieve alone. Almost all of them wanted the Giriama punished and desired a "show of power" for the government.[28] Montgomery wanted the military to evacuate the Trans-Sabaki, and everybody wanted the Giriama to provide porters. Even the governor wanted the Giriama to be given a "sharp lesson."[29]

The British response must be understood in the context of the war with Germany. The proximity of the Giriama to the German East African border and Giriama trading links with their southern neighbors connected Giriama resistance to possible internal German infiltration. Since troops were needed elsewhere, the Giriama situation did call for a quick resolution, but the timetables set to handle the Giriama were unrealistic. In six days, the troops were expected to quell the rising, procure the necessary porters for the Carrier Corps, evacuate the Trans-Sabaki, and return to active service against the forces of German East Africa.[30] Their attempt to accomplish these multiple unrealistic goals served only to bring the war to the general population.

Patrols swept through the northern and southern areas along the Sabaki River, burning villages and attacking every Giriama they met. Twelve Giriama in the north and thirty along the south bank were killed. For the first time, the Trans-Sabaki Giriama were drawn into the fray.[31] Once the KAR arrived, the majority of the Giriama population perceived that they had no alternative but to fight back; they shared a traditional obligation to defend the Giriama against all enemies.

The KAR march through Giriama territory, burning villages all along the way, met with "more or less continuous opposition."[32] Because of Giriama resistance, the KAR commander decided that he needed two full companies and a month's worth of supplies to complete the military task and evacuate the Trans-Sabaki.[33]

The tactics of the military at this juncture gave the Giriama false hope. The six-day blitz affected most of the northern population, and the ten-day lull that followed, before KAR reinforcements arrived at a new camp at Jilore to renew the offensive, gave the Giriama a false sense of success. They renewed attacks on Jilore and on headmen's villages.* On 4 September Giriama from Biryaa joined the hostilities in attacks on Mangea station and on Tsumu's village near Vitengeni.[34]

Even more intense anti-government feeling was demonstrated in Weruni. There, the hostile nyere increased pressure on their headmen. They were

---

suffered nearly total loss of control: Hemsted, "Notebook," 23 August 1914, and Hemsted to Chief Secretary Nairobi, 26 August 1914 (KNA: CP 5/336-III).

*Dundas was to write in his memoirs years later that it was this initially short period of "punishment" that had allowed the rising to spread: Charles Dundas, *African Crossroads* (London, 1955), p. 73.

particularly angry with Fondo wa Nyama, whose loyalty to the British was all too clear. He refused to pay his fee of bulls as a token of unity with the dissidents, and for this his life was forfeit. On 7 September a group of warriors attacked his house while frightened neighbors looked on, and he was killed with a poisoned arrow. Emboldened by his death, the Giriama of Weruni went on to threaten the mission stations at Kaloleni and Mwabaya-nyundo.[35] The death of this loyal headman and threats that caused evacuation of the missions brought the war to Weruni. On 11 September fresh attacks were made on Mangea station by a group which included three hundred Giriama from Kaloleni area.[36]

By this time the King's African Rifles had returned. A camp was established at Jilore on 8 September. Now the whole of Giriamaland was in upheaval. Troops returned to Mangea and the Trans-Sabaki. H.J. Lascelles, assistant district commissioner of Rabai, went with KAR and police to halt the resistance in Weruni and Biryaa. By 13 September many Giriama were gathering at Kaya Giriama, including large numbers from Mangea. Montgomery wrote at this time that there could now be no question of peace; the Giriama must be punished.[37] The war, far from ending, had escalated. The second KAR sweep, begun on 10 September, sent shock waves throughout Giriamaland. The troops fired on all Giriama they met, whether or not they were hostile, and systematically confiscated goats and burned dwellings. The weapons and tactics of the British-led troops surprised and stunned the Giriama, whose only experience with guns had been in the fighting against the Arabs several decades before. Now they were facing repeater rifles. Eleven years before, when they had fought with the Mariakani Kamba, each side had lined up, shot a volley of arrows, and retired to regroup and fire again.[38] Now, when they retired to regroup, the shooting continued. In earlier confrontations there had been few deaths; now they were experiencing major losses.

Some warriors fled to the bush, totally demoralized. Others began to make systematic attacks on the soldiers from their hiding places in the bush. This fighting technique, not new to them, was the only way that men armed with bows and arrows could be a match for troops with rifles. The Giriama were still determined to resist British control, and guerrilla warfare continued sporadically, but the encounters with the King's African Rifles in this second campaign made it obvious to them that they had little chance of defeating the British.

TO END THE FIGHTING

British and Giriama had completely different views on the way to achieve peace. The longer Giriama watched their homes burn and their neighbors and family members killed, the more they wanted the fighting to stop. The Giriama were divided into two groups: those who wanted to fight the British and those who had been drawn into the conflict by the military action. With the return of the troops, the latter group sought a resolution to the conflict, but they had little access to the British and virtually no control over the former group. Therefore, the Giriama, whose opposition to the British had never been organized and unified, were not unified in their efforts for peace.[39]

A conclusive settlement that would ensure peace was not, however, all that the British were seeking. They were also concerned with punishing the Giriama; that could be accomplished more easily by continuing hostilities. They were still planning for a conclusive defeat and the capture of ringleaders. In particular, they wanted Ngonyo's surrender and the capture and trial of the murderer of the Vitengeni policeman. Defecting headmen were also marked out for punishment.[40]

Attempts at Peace

Giriama options to end the fighting were limited by circumstances. The destruction of the kaya had removed the Giriama's only possible organizational center. Their simultaneous military efforts lacked formal intercommunication. As rumors spread and feelings became aroused, the nyere had snatched up bows and poisoned arrows and grouped for an offensive. When heavy casualties occurred, many fled out of Giriama territory into the Taru Desert, north to the Tana River, or south into Duruma country. Under these circumstances, there were no means for the people as a whole to surrender; all that was possible was for individuals to do so.[41]

Despite their search for allies, the British administrators (with the exception of Champion) were suspicious of any Giriama who offered friendship. They could not distinguish between trickery and sincerity. The policy of Dundas, in particular, was to continue reprisals until the Giriama had ceased all hostilities and had promised to begin no more.[42] But the continuing reprisals, together with the lack of unity and poor communications among the Giriama themselves, worked against any such cessation. The uprising had in effect acquired a life of its own, and there seemed to be no way to bring the fighting to an end.

Two separate Giriama attempts for peace were made almost simultaneously, in Weruni and in Mangea/Godoma. In Weruni the dissidents themselves worked for peace. Fondo wa Nyama had been killed and Kitu wa Syria had barely escaped with his life, but despite the rumors of attacks on the missions and on Rabai, the offensive in Weruni had been "a half-hearted effort."[43] Dissident action had been immediately countered by police and by plundering King's African Rifles. The Weruni Giriama had fewer grievances than others, they had little hope of ultimate victory, and they had not placed reliance on German aid. Their main incentive had come from the rumors that Champion had been killed at Mangea. Many of those who had started by fighting had ended by fleeing.

Remaining Giriama dissidents made an apologetic approach to headman Gunga who, a month earlier, had been publicly humiliated and had paid his fine. Now the same men who had led this incident decided that Gunga was their only hope in securing peace. He was a useful liaison because, although a headman and considered loyal, he had not been in that position long. By paying the fine he had given tacit support to the dissidents, but had done nothing active enough to make the British lose confidence in him. Therefore some Giriama asked Gunga to send a letter to the district commissioner requesting an end to the war. His son, Mwinga, who could read and write English (he was a clerk for the district commissioner of Mombasa), was to write the request.[44]

Upon receiving Gunga's letter requesting peace, Lascelles, who was in charge at Rabai, said that headman Kitu would have to join Gunga and some of the rebels in going to Mombasa to talk to the provincial commissioner; Lascelles was acting according to an error in telegraphed instructions which said to "reserve" Kitu instead of to "rescue" him. The delegation appeared in Mombasa without papers, and Hemsted could not understand why they had been sent. He was unsure whether he was supposed to imprison them or to grant them audience. When he did ascertain the purpose of their mission, he rejected their offer. He was still intent upon securing a united bid for peace from all the Giriama, and he wanted the ringleaders of the trouble, not those who had been loyal.[45]

The Giriama of Weruni and Biryaa had little to lose and much to gain by seeking an early surrender. Administered from Rabai and living even further from the station at Mangea, they had not been asked to supply any significant number of laborers, nor was their possession of land in dispute. Their major grievances were the destruction of the kaya and the control being exerted—or attempted—by headmen loyal to the administration. In contrast, the Giriama of the Trans-Sabaki had nothing to gain by surrender. Their homes had been destroyed and their goats confiscated; they had few belongings left; their land was in any case to be requisitioned; and further reprisals against them were certain. The deepest divisions had occurred in the central regions of Mangea and Godoma. Here lived the people who had experienced British control at its closest, who had borne the brunt of labor demands, and who had been expected to lend support to the extension of administrative control. Thus they had the most to gain from success, and they had, moreover, been encouraged by the promise of German support. King's African Rifles expeditions had been frequent in this area, and although this propelled some toward surrender, for others it only intensified the determination to continue fighting.

The problem of securing peace was much harder for the Giriama in Mangea and Godoma than it had been in Weruni. The loyal headmen were scattered. Mkowa and Kombi had paid a fine to the dissidents and then fled for their lives to Waata country. Tsumu and Ziro had been attacked by some of their own people, and although Tsumu had been rescued, Ziro was thought to be dead. In the Trans-Sabaki, Ngonyo had no interest in negotiating for peace. Since the British were willing to recognize as peacemakers only their appointed headmen or those whom Champion had mentioned as leaders in

his report on the first attack at Mangea, the possibilities of useful and recip-
rocally trusting communication were extremely limited. Those who had been
totally loyal to the British, such as headmen Mchunga of Sekoke, Nyamwe of
Madunguni, and Msaga of Jilore, were totally distrusted by the Giriama.
Nduria of Kirwitu had sided with his people against the British, and was now
in hiding. No headman was a mediator acceptable to both sides. As a result,
the peace feelers from the Giriama of this region came through a coastal
Arab, Sheik Fathili bin Omar. Long a friend of the Giriama, he had worked
for the British as Mudir of Arabuko (Sekoke). Those seeking peace here,
unlike those in Weruni, were not the dissidents themselves but elders who
were tired of hiding in the bush and were frightened by the threats from
British on the one hand and hostile Giriama on the other.[46]

Montgomery's reply to the peace offers negotiated by bin Omar was the
same as Hemsted's in the south: "Partial submission will not be accepted."
Dundas was of the same mind. He sent Champion to Marafa to check on the
rumor that Ngonyo was ready to surrender, and when it proved to be false, he
replied, "I propose to make no attempts to solicit their submission."[47] The
political and military officers working in the north had almost no knowledge
of or interest in what was happening in the south, beyond the fact that the
rising had spread to that area. To them, the real trouble was in the north, and
that was where the solution lay. Thus, without consultation, the expectation
of a unified surrender was maintained.

British Reversal: Search for Peace

Circumstances outside the control of either the administrative officers or
the Giriama intervened to change the British tactics. The war with Germany
had intensified and the King's African Rifles were desperately needed elsewhere. The use of troops to control the uprising could be justified but their
use for inflicting punishment could not. This situation was sufficient to change
the minds of Hemsted, Montgomery, and Dundas at the end of September,
when the Giriama approaches in themselves had failed.[48] British officers now
worked for peace.

Hemsted, in the south, reconsidered and accepted the peace offer, setting as
punishment a fine and a levy of men to serve as porters. At about the same
time, Dundas and Montgomery agreed to meet the elders from the north in a
separate negotiation. A meeting was held at Jilore on 5 October and the terms
were announced. Who was present remains a mystery, but evidently a sufficient number of village elders were there to convince the officials that the
Giriama were serious about ending hostilities. These elders agreed to the terms
proposed by the British, despite their inability to fulfill those terms. The five
specific conditions were: one, all persons wanted on capital charges for two
years prior to the beginning of punitive measures were to be handed over to the
administration; two, the Giriama were to secure the formal submission of the
heads of the tribe and of the leaders of the rebellion; three, one thousand men
were to be handed over to serve as porters in the Carrier Corps; four, the

Giriama were to pay a fine of 100,000 rupees as damages, with the whole fine to be paid in cash (this equaled 6 rupees per head per adult male); and, five, the Giriama were to agree to the evacuation of the Trans-Sabaki (although none of those negotiating lived there).

The Giriama agreed that all the conditions were to be complied with within seven days, failing which British hostilities would recommence.[49] In addition, Dundas required all arrows to be surrendered to the government. On the part of the British, this was a compromise: they had ceased to demand that all the Giriama should sue for peace together. Even so, the terms of this peace, particularly the seven-day time limit, were totally unrealistic. Families were scattered, loyalties were being questioned, homesteads and food supplies had been burned, and few Giriama could influence the actions of their fellows, some of whom were by no means ready to end their aggression.

Nor were some of the British military officers content to wait out the peace period. A particularly severe action against a man named Solomon Kadzitza made him a martyr and the only hero of the Giriama war. Kadzitza, remembered by the Giriama as a tax collector in Tsumu's area, was caught between the opposing forces solely because he could read English. In an act of good faith, two of the dissidents of the south agreed to take a message from the King's African Rifles captain at Rabai to his counterpart with the armed forces in Mangea. The message told of the agreement for peace in the south, indicating that this should assist the attempts to make peace in the north. When the two messengers arrived near Tsumu's at Vitengeni, they were confronted by a group of warriors returning from a fighting expedition. The warriors demanded to see the letter, and since none of them could read they took it to Fuladoyo for Solomon Kadzitza to read. When they learned that the letter was requesting peace from the Giriama on the northern side, they forced Kadzitza to destroy it. When the two messengers returned to Rabai and told what had happened, the officer then in charge, Captain Rose, set off on a patrol, with one of the messengers as guide, to identify Kadzitza for punishment.[50] He decided that even if Kadzitza had been forced to tear up the letter, he had read the contents and should have gone on to deliver the message himself. The severity of punishment he decreed far exceeded any guilt incurred: Kadzitza was allowed to go into his house for his Bible and to say goodbye to his family, and then he was tied to a tree and shot.[51]

This action and others committed by Rose immediately after the terms of peace had been accepted (Kadzitza was killed about 11 October) were enough to convince those Giriama who still wanted to fight that the British were insincere in their offer of peace. Rose, who knew of the terms of settlement in north and south, went on to kill seven Giriama who were running away at Magogeni, and seven others at various villages. He captured four hundred goats and burned several villages after two arrows had been fired at his troops.[52] Those Giriama seeking peace could not justify such actions to their fellow Giriama.

What, then, had the 5 October meeting at Jilore achieved? It failed to bring about an immediate end to hostilities or total capitulation on either side, but it did show that the British were willing to discuss a settlement, and it indicated to many Giriama that the British would eventually prevail. British officers, for their part, regarded Giriama resistance to be over; they imposed harsh punishments on those Giriama who were refusing to fulfill the peace conditions.

The Giriama of the Trans-Sabaki and the anti-government forces of Mangea and Godoma, however, had not participated in the meeting to discuss peace conditions. These were the Giriama whose situation had initially provoked open hostility. They remained as intransigent as ever, for both the physical and the psychological environment encouraged continued resistance. They could hide in the bush and continue resistance for an unlimited period, and in so doing they would be leaving their more compliant kinsfolk to pay the fine. Moreover, since the British regarded all Giriama as guilty, there was little advantage to be gained from cooperation. Even headmen had to pay because those under them had not been fully controlled. In fact, the greatest impetus for surrender was the fact that Giriama became tired of life in the bush.

PEACE AS PUNISHMENT

Since the British had yet to demonstrate their power incontrovertibly, implementation of the peace terms took on added importance as punishment for resistance. Through this mechanism the Giriama were to be totally subdued. Officers believed that any weakening on the part of the British would award the Giriama the victory they had failed to win by active resistance.

Just as they had promised the Giriama that they would destroy their kaya as punishment for failing to build a new one, the British promised to resume attacks on the Giriama if the peace terms were not met in seven days. Charles Dundas, who was about to leave his post in Giriama, urged continuation of punitive measures if necessary, even if this resulted in "ruin for the tribe." He went so far as to contemplate bringing in a troop of Maasai, whom, as he pointed out, the Giriama dreaded. Dundas believed that the Giriama had attacked the British without provocation, taking advantage of the German war crisis. They had shown ingratitude for the help given to them in famines. "We have therefore no reason to show consideration for them and may consult only our own interests."[53]

It was upon Dundas's successor, Francis Traill, that the responsibility fell for resolving the Giriama situation with patience and skill. Traill arrived at the KAR camp at Jilore on 26 October. A British officer of the old school who had served at Malindi in 1910, he had written one of the few favorable reports on the Giriama.[54] Traill chose Jilore—convenient to Malindi, with ample water, in an area of good arable land, and close to the Sabaki—as the temporary administrative headquarters. It became a center for friendly Giriama and their families, as well as a prison camp for those awaiting special punishment.*

Following his predecessor's recommendations, Traill again sent the KAR on active duty on 31 October. At this stage, the KAR could accomplish very little, but the situation was too risky to let them go back to the war front. A false rumor, spread by German agents, that 3,000 Giriama were advancing northward on the town of Witu unnecessarily diverted a full company of KAR. The demand for almost instantaneous Giriama compliance was directly connected with the fact that British troops were needed to confront the German enemy elsewhere, but Traill became convinced that the Giriama could not comply with the terms of the peace quickly.[55]

Traill continued his pressure on the Giriama, but soon came to agree with many earlier officials that the Giriama would do anything rather than work for the government. In one village twenty-two young men had paid an average of sixteen goats each, saying they would rather die than work for a couple of months: "Government should be realistic. If this is the Giriama attitude, then attempts to get labour are self-defeating. . . . Since August things have been upset, the Giriama have lived in the bush like animals, lost huts, stock and friends. Still they refuse to work."[56] It became clear that punishment would have to be spread over a long period of time. When Hobley returned to Mombasa in late November to resume his post as provincial commissioner, it was generally agreed that the uprising was over; however, much opposition continued.

Hobley heard various interpretations of events from his officers. Champion was the most sympathetic to the Giriama position. He argued that the duties and responsibilities of headmen had been extremely difficult for them to fulfill, and from his years of experience among the Giriama he suggested that government policy had been "too rapid" in the two years preceding the uprising. He understood that the Giriama felt justified in behaving as they did; he pointed out that Giriama who wanted to help the government had no

---

*The prisoners included Makaziro wa Ikombe, alleged to have killed the policeman who had raped Makaziro's wife; Sirya wa Jefa, who had escaped from Champion's camp at Vitengeni after shooting at a labor recruiter on 16 August; two men who supposedly incited the attack against Mangea on 22 August; and several headmen, including Ngonyo, Maguta of Bura, and Nduria of Kirwitu. Traill had the names of three others who had led the burning party against the CMS Mission and government station at Jilore, but they had not yet been arrested: Traill (from Vitengeni) to Hobley, 16 March 1915 and 10 April 1915 (KNA: CP 5/336-V).

Tsumu and Ziro, who had been forced to hide because they did not join the dissidents, eventually stayed at Jilore with their families for a time, but finally returned to their homes and their duties as location headmen. Kombi and Mkowa, who had saved their lives by paying a fine and fleeing to Waata country, sent word to Traill that they did not wish to return to government service to collect the fine and find porters. They said that they would come forward upon completion of the terms of settlement. Kombi remained in the north, but Mkowa went first to Weruni and then to Merikano, just south of the river. He, like Ngonyo, wanted no part in the settlement. Both men argued that they had never at any time participated in the hostilities: "Memo," anonymous, n.d., apparently in Traill's handwriting (KNA: CP 5/336-IV).

choice but to flee from their own war parties and hide in the bush; and he disagreed with the government policy of treating all Giriama as equally guilty. Dundas held much more severe views, and his opinions ultimately overruled those of Champion. Hobley concluded that there had been no justification for the uprising. He was angry that the affair had gotten so far out of hand during his absence, when now he was responsible for the recovery. He left punishment to Traill, however, as his own attention was focused increasingly on the war effort.[57]

By the close of 1914 the British administrators accepted, however reluctantly, that their peace terms had not brought the disturbances to an end. Almost three months had passed since the Giriama elders at Jilore had agreed to the terms, but scarcely any of the conditions had been fulfilled. Only 141 laborers out of the quota of 1,000 had been produced, and of these 43 had run away. Of a fine of 100,000 rupees only 30,000 had been collected. The Giriama had suffered severely. During the fighting the British had burned at least 5,000 houses, captured over 3,000 goats, and killed over 150 Giriama, while they themselves had lost no men and had only a few wounded. British officers still argued, however, that the Giriama needed to be punished. As always, the Giriama were resisting the evacuation of the Trans-Sabaki.[58] Few people were moving south of the river. Some had scattered north to the Tana River to join the Pokomo, some had gone up the Sabaki River and over to Taveta, some had taken refuge along the coast, and some had simply hidden in the bush. Hemsted recognized that the situation was serious when, at Hobley's request, he toured the area in late December. Collection of the Giriama into a reserve was no longer desirable simply because it would allow for more efficient administration; it was necessary if there was to be any administration at all: "If hostilities (initiated by the British) are re-opened and protracted as they must be from the nature of the country pending full compliance with our terms, there appears the gravest danger that the tribe will disperse [completely, leaving Giriamaland empty]."[59]

The actual fighting had lasted just over a month. The Giriama knew they had not rid themselves of the British, and the British on their side recognized that the Giriama dissidents were less demonstrative but still determined. The situation for both sides was, if anything, more unpleasant than it had been before the uprising. People were scattered, resources were limited, and famine threatened. More and more Giriama were leaving their territory. If this trend continued, the British efforts would have been in vain and their hopes for laborers quashed, so British officers were to focus their energy once again on bringing the Giriama into the administrative fold.

8
Aftermath, 1915-1920

The five years that followed the Giriama rebellion were years of hardship and frustration for both the Giriama and the British. At first the situation was critical. The administration suffered from divided leadership and lack of experience, while the Giriama had become a dispirited and divided people who had lost homes and possessions and hope, many of whom had become fugitives, and who, above all, had no leaders to mediate for them. The entire year of 1915 was spent in a methodical campaign to meet the terms of the punishment. Subsequent events show that though the Giriama were cowed, nobody emerged victorious. Modified conditions and a sequence of unusual developments served to confuse the Giriama-British colonial relationship even further.

PUNISHMENT

The terms of the punishment—evacuation of the Trans-Sabaki, a fine of 100,000 rupees, and enrollment of 1,000 laborers—should by rights have been fulfilled by *dissident* Giriama. Instead, it was those who had been neutral in the conflict and who wanted to see their country return to a stable condition who paid the highest price and assisted the administration to collect the fine and obtain the labor. In addition, these people had to accept into their communities those who had been forced out of the Trans-Sabaki.

British officers considered the headmen, with the exception of those few who had demonstrated their loyalty beyond question, to be among the leaders of the rising and marked them for punishment accordingly. Yet, at the same time, they needed assistance from the headmen in order to implement the punishment. The headmen had little basis or incentive to help the British in this difficult task. Those who had been headment in the north were expected

125

to settle their people between well-established villages in Mangea and Weruni. They had the least to gain by supporting the British, for they were not only losing their land but moving into locations of other headmen, with whom they had to compete; consequently, many of them led their people in opposing the government.* Even Mkowa and Kombi, who had been especially supportive, escaped, sending word that they would return after the fine had been collected. In Mangea, only Tsumu was willing to assist, and he had little effectiveness. In Weruni, headmen were less frightened of their own people and more willing to cooperate with the British than they had been, but they were still concerned that the wartime situation might suddenly change conditions.

Useful though the troops had been in facilitating evacuation of the Trans-Sabaki and collecting portions of the fine from the residents there, the KAR was desperately needed for the immediate war effort. In January 1915 the KAR patrols made their last marches into the Trans-Sabaki to force people in Baricho, Shakahola, Garashi, and part of Mangea to contribute their "fair share" of the fine.[1] One patrol burned 400 homes, captured 1,800 goats, and killed 19 Giriama. The other burned 200 homes, captured 1,200 goats and 55 head of cattle, and killed 4 Giriama. Neither met with any resistance.

At the end of January the KAR was officially withdrawn. They were replaced by an expanded police force of eighty-five men.[2] At the same time an additional A.D.C., E. R. Thompson, was sent to assist Traill and Champion until the latter took long leave in March. Champion, who had worked so closely with the Giriama and who had been their most sympathetic advocate despite their antagonism toward him, did not return to Giriama. None of the remaining officers shared his vested interest in developing the administrative framework or his historical perspective of the Giriama situation.

The evacuation and the fine collection caused the British to work at cross-purposes. Every Giriama was supposed to pay his portion of the fine, but enforced evacuation created hardship and made it impossible for collectors either to locate those who refused or to maintain good records. The KAR sweeps through the Trans-Sabaki had been designed to herd the whole population south of the river. In fact, this had not happened. A large proportion had moved to the south bank of the river, and some had scattered north and south beyond Giriama territory, but a number had hidden when the patrols went through and then had come out to build temporary shelters to replace the huts that had been burned. As late as July, some Giriama began moving back to the Trans-Sabaki to join those still living north of the river.† Thus,

*Traill, "List," n.d. (KNA: CP 5/336-IV). Ngonyo, Masha wa Lugatzi of Baricho, Maguta of Bura, Chula wa Dzala of Bungale, and Taura wa Bau of Bore (who was a Kauma) all led their people in opposing the government.

†Many of Ngonyo's people remained at Marafa; Chula wa Dzala remained at Bungale; Masha wa Lugatzi had moved south of the river, but some of his people stayed at Baricho. A large number of people at Gandi were openly hostile and kept sentries posted to look out for patrols. Another stronghold, at Konoda Kacha, was led by a brother or cousin of the late Pembe wa Mrimi. This man said that he possessed medicine that would prevent the Europeans coming into the area.

despite almost nine months of military patrols, the Trans-Sabaki remained well-populated.

The turning point came when Giriama elders living around Jilore and the kaya decided to help Traill fulfill the terms of the punishment. They realized that nine months of upheaval constituted a disaster for an agricultural people, and some agreed to work with Traill to assist in the evacuation and in collection of the fine. Traill began to work with the old headmen, whom he no longer regarded as dissidents.* Mkowa came back to Jilore, where Ngonyo was being held as prisoner, and the two offered their assistance as leaders of a large group of elders. They told Traill they realized that the condition of their country was most unsatisfactory. Fresh crops had to be planted soon if famine was to be prevented, and many people were still moving northward to the Tana River. They felt that if the elders lent their support to the administration to complete the peace terms, their troubles would be ended and normal life could resume. In addition, the fine and labor quota had been based on the total population, but it was being met only by those who had stayed within reach of the administration. Those who had fled to the Tana, to Waata country, to the coast around Malindi, to Duruma, or to Taita or Taveta had paid nothing. The elders proposed sending delegations to these places to make them contribute their share of the fine and the labor quota.[3]

Initially, Traill was extremely suspicious of the Giriama overtures. He regarded the Giriama as "past masters in the art of creating false impressions favourable to themselves," but the situation made him anxious to give them a try.[4] At first, he insisted that they prove their power to obtain compliance within the reserve before going outside. Although this sounded reasonable, in fact it was not, for any influence Ngonyo and Mkowa possessed was not over the neutral and friendly Giriama in the reserve but over those who had fled. Their good intentions and their willingness to cooperate, however, signaled a change of attitude that had taken place none too soon, for Hobley, worried, was arguing that Maasai spearmen should be brought in to bring the Giriama to terms.[5]

Evacuation of the Trans-Sabaki became connected directly with the payment of the fine. The fine of 100,000 rupees required an average payment of 6 rupees per adult male, to be paid in cash, not in kind. This was, as before, intended to force Giriama men into the labor market to obtain the necessary cash. The administrators made no allowance for the facts that Giriama houses had been burned and their goats captured and that water was in short supply. Since the Giriama refused to meet the demand by accepting wage-labor, the

*Traill had been forced to rely on the former headmen to continue in office as he set up locations again, not because they had been particularly effective but because he had no alternative. Maringa of Jilore and Nduria of Kirwitu, who had opposed the administration, had been allowed to retain office. Ziro, one of the headmen who had attempted to remain loyal to the administration, proved of little use at this stage. More effective were Tsumu and Ndungu of Ndigiria (a location west of Mangea where people had remained comparatively aloof from the conflict). Ngonyo and Maguta had been headmen in the evacuated area, and therefore there was no possibility of their returning to office at this time; they remained prisoners at Jilore.

cash could not be found.[6] The pressure exerted by the local administrators was in part a response to pressures from the Colonial Office: the cost of the punitive expeditions must be met. Overshadowing humanitarian and even administrative concerns was the necessity to punish the Giriama in full and to collect funds that would balance the budget.

But even these pressures could not produce nonexistent cash, so Traill resorted to compromise efforts. The administration agreed to accept goats—such as were left to the Giriama—in lieu of cash. Much administrative effort was diverted from major duties as assistants collected, fed, watered, and transported goats to feed the KAR.* One of the many ironies of the rising was the situation of British officers feeding goats and staving off epidemics of goat disease while the Giriama around them were homeless and hungry. Traill, with his available police, obtained assistance from nearly six hundred Giriama helpers and made three excursions north of the river. They captured prisoners at Ganze and Bungale, burned villages there and at Konoda Kacha, and reaped the ripe maize (about 150 loads) which was sold at Malindi to contribute to the fine payment. In all, the parties passed through and destroyed about twenty villages, and about sixty-seven people taken prisoner on the north bank were brought back to Jilore.[7]

With this Giriama assistance, the evacuation was considered to be accomplished by the end of August 1915. Since without patrols the British could not control the people's reentry into the Trans-Sabaki lands, and since additional police were not forthcoming, officials simply had to shut their eyes and declare the evacuation to be complete.

But the fine was still outstanding. Traill got additional money by raiding cattle, especially in Biryaa, to be sold to pay the fine unless the owners redeemed them with cash within two weeks. In desperation, some Giriama brought forth ivory they had kept hidden for years. By means of Traill's diligent efforts and extensive cooperative assistance from Giriama who worked to bring the long period of instability to an end, the entire fine was collected by 24 October 1915, almost a year to the day from the date of Traill's arrival at Jilore.

Through Giriama cooperation, the labor quota of 1,000 porters was also met. In spite of great reluctance on the part of the Giriama and great difficulty on Traill's part, laborers were sent to Mombasa as promised, to serve for a period limited to six months. Unlike the years of prosperity, when fathers had little control over sons who moved easily to new lands to begin their own homesteads and who could pay their own brideprice, now, in a time of deprivation, fathers had enough control over their sons to be able to send them for service. As in the case of the fine, however, the Giriama nearest the administrative centers and those who had opted to be cooperative paid a disproportionate share of the costs.[8] Those who were willing to live as refugees

*The British files are filled with telegrams concerning the care of the goats. Cf. Traill to Hobley, 26 February 1915, and Dundas, D.C. Mombasa, to Hobley, 8 April 1915 (KNA: CP 5/336-V).

in the forest suffered only lightly; sons who opted to stay at home were sent into service.

Traill made certain that the requirement of 1,000 porters was not circumvented. He repeatedly entered villages and found young men who had deserted their positions. He always sent them back, and he replaced any men found to be medically unfit.[9] Traill praised the Giriama for providing porters locally and for clearing over a hundred miles of paths: "These may be only small accomplishments compared with the work done for Government by natives in other Districts but for Giriama it is a distinct advance."[10] His reports stressed that the completion of the payments was a great accomplishment. It was, for him, "the end of the second stage of the Giriama Rising."[11]

Two conditions—punishment of the leaders and unconditional surrender of the headmen—remained outstanding and, in fact, never could have been met. With the exception of those from the Trans-Sabaki, the headmen had kept their posts. Punishment of individuals proved difficult. The most important prisoner, Makaziro wa Ikombe, who was accused of killing the policeman at the start of the rebellion, had been tried by a military court under Traill and Thompson in March 1915, found guilty, and condemned to death, but the decision was overruled by the officer commanding troops on the grounds that the court had been improperly constituted. Traill then urged deportation, certain from all the evidence that Makaziro was indeed guilty; indeed, Makaziro's father had admitted his son's guilt and paid a fine of three cows to the kambi. But deportation was also disallowed, and Traill did not have judicial power to try Makaziro in a civil court. The matter finally was settled when Makaziro was found to have leprosy and was sent to Mzizima Leper Camp.[12]

This took care of the only prisoner who had committed a criminal act. As for all the other prisoners in the camp, Traill decided that to keep them in Jilore as political detainees was punishment enough. In the end, even Ngonyo was absolved of responsibility. He remained in Jilore for some time, a blind man who promised to refrain from further opposition and further intrigue.* It was clear that many of Traill's captives had acted against the government, but so had others in almost every location in Giriama. Traill had come in the end to agree with Champion's view that there had been no ringleaders of the rising: "The more I learn of the Rising the more I am convinced that it was the concerted act of the whole tribe, and it hardly seems fair to deport the old men unless we are going to recommend deportations on a wholesale scale."[13]

A spontaneous and leaderless rising had seemed inconceivable, and yet this was in fact what had happened. The Giriama, with varying motives and in varying degrees, had involved themselves in a conflict with the British, and what leadership had emerged came out of the local groups of fighting men, or

---

*Traill, "Handing-Over Report," 12 November 1915 (KNA: CP 20/136). Before his death in November 1920 Ngonyo was once more to come into prominence over the question of Giriama rights to land, by giving evidence at the Malindi Inquiry in 1917: "Handing-Over Report, Nyika Reserve, Rabai," 1 December 1920 (KNA: CP 21/168).

from headmen turning against the administration. Even when their ultimate powerlessness had become apparent, they had had no kaya elders to mediate a peace. Traill concluded: "It is impossible to single out any particular member of the tribe as having taken any pre-eminent part in inciting others to revolt or in directing the operations."[14]

Traill's accomplishments allowed the British officials to consider that the Giriama had been duly punished. Under extremely difficult circumstances, they had met almost all the terms of the peace agreement:

I regard the spirit of active opposition among the Giriama as completely crushed now. The Rising has taught them several things of which they had no conception before, and I do not think the lesson will soon be forgotten. They cannot be described as a loyal or amenable tribe now but that, remembering their characteristics or past behaviour, can hardly be expected. A certain amount of passive resistance must always be looked for from them.[15]

When he left in November 1915, Traill pointed out the importance of effective Giriama leadership for the future: "The lack of organization, and [lack of] obedience to recognized leaders which has always been so marked a feature of the tribal life of the Giriama in peace time, was again apparent in the war and no doubt accounted to a large extent for their failure to accomplish greater results [in the rebellion]."[16]

At the successful completion of the terms of the punishment, Pearson wrote a memorandum pointing out that the government had been fortunate. In the first place, the large percentage of the fine paid in silver was a comment on the previous prosperity of the Giriama and a sign that they had borrowed against the next year's crops. These crops would have to be raised outside the Trans-Sabaki, on which they had previously depended.* Second, the part of the fine that was paid in goats would not have been of any value to the government had it not needed meat for the troops and porters involved in the war. Third, it had been fortunate for the government that more Giriama had not left for other parts but had remained in "the miserable strip of country that lies between the Sabaki and the Ndzovuni Rivers." Finally, Pearson stressed the valuable contribution Traill had made. He was an officer "trained in that school where duty pointed to the end and necessity supplied the means."[17] Without Traill's experience, ability, and dedication, the fine might never have been collected. Traill left Giriama district in considerably better condition than he had found it, but the lack of leadership and administrative agents would continue to plague the British relationship with the Giriama.

A BRITISH ADMINISTRATIVE VACUUM

The completion of the punishment left the Giriama and the British with the necessity of salvaging a relationship out of the two years of strife. As provincial

---

*As early as 1910, grain from the Trans-Sabaki had provided a customs export value at Malindi of Rs. 135,000, and must have amounted to Rs. 150,000 if commissions for buying, selling, and transport charges to Indians are taken into account.

commissioner, Hobley still had the major responsibility for recovery, and he felt that the most pressing issue was to get the Giriama settled permanently in proper locations. To meet this need, the Nyika Reserve, restricted to the southern Sabaki, was proclaimed in March 1916.[18] But it was not a simple matter to continue close administrative relations from inside the Giriama reserve. Mangea station had been a bad choice because of the lack of water. Jilore, the site of the temporary station for the duration of the punishment, was too close to Malindi to be of use as an interior station. When Traill left in November, P.L. Deacon took over and the headquarters for the district were transferred from Jilore to Rabai, where there was a permanent station. H.G. Evans, who had replaced Vidal as assistant district commissioner of Takaungu in August 1915, had begun building a temporary station just south of the Sabaki River at Kakoneni, and J.M. Pearson was stationed there after November. The primary purpose of this station was to prevent the Giriama from recrossing the river.[19]

Traill's personality was missed. Pearson was ill most of the time and was finally invalided out to Malindi. Hobley was the only remaining familiar face, and from Mombasa, where he had been primarily concerned with the war effort against Germany, he was unable to handle procedures for effective control. Still, his report after a tour in 1916 sounded optimistic: "Generally speaking the attitude of the Giriama people has improved to a considerable extent during the last year, and the effect of a continuous administration is gradually beginning to be felt."[20]

To support his argument that the Giriama were developing a "spirit of greater obedience" he listed their accomplishments: they had cut roads; they had cleared standing camps; and they had helped to build the Kakoneni station. He attributed this cooperation to continuous administration, the compulsory recruiting for the Carrier Corps, and the character of the present district commissioner. Not only was this dubious reasoning, but the accomplishments in themselves were far from notable, considering the price the British had paid. Hobley wrote as if the Giriama had reversed their opposition to providing labor: "Some 1200 men [had] been collected without any opposition and through the help of the Elders" since the previous March. This obscured the fact that a majority of the 1,200 had been requisitioned as part of the punishment.[21] Traill had written in October 1915 that he had accomplished the required labor fine with a remarkable excess of about 65 men:

The fulfillment of this part of the terms of peace presented far greater difficulties than any of the other conditions. The opposition shown by the Giriama to providing labourers for work outside their own country was, in my experience, unique among agricultural tribes in the Protectorate.[22]

Some Giriama did become porters for the Carrier Corps thereafter, but had Hobley been able to collect 1,200 laborers following Traill's departure he would have been jubilant. With such a reversal of Giriama behavior, he would not merely have said that their attitude had improved "to a considerable extent." He would have expressed himself in much stronger terms. All that he was actually able to state was that they "were now more amenable than they previously were."[23] Giriama porters were still being conscripted at the expense of meeting local labor needs, and Hobley continued to stress to the Giriama that they must provide workers. He told his subordinate officers that "they [the Giriama] can benefit both themselves and the country best . . . by offering themselves as labourers to the Coast plantations."[24] The Giriama labor question remained unresolved: the years of strife had accomplished nothing.

FAMINE

The strength of the Giriama economy had served as an incentive to resist British demands after 1912; now, recovery seemed almost impossible. The rebellion was followed by famine. Drought caused crop failure throughout the coastal hinterland, and the Giriama evacuation from their croplands, lack of sufficient land in the southern Sabaki, where they had been resettled, and the loss of virtually all their goats, chickens, excess cash, cattle, and ivory intensified famine conditions for the Giriama. Moreover, to pay the fine in 1915 they had borrowed 60,000 rupees against the 1916 harvest.[25] The Giriama remember the famine of 1916 as that of the "fine" (*nzala ya faini*). They saw their old granary across the river sit uncultivated while they went hungry. Conditions became so severe that the administration had to bring in food for famine relief. Giriama began escaping into Malindi district and the coastal belt as well as back across the Sabaki. The question of Giriama repatriation to the reserve and of Giriama land use could no longer be avoided. In July 1916 Hobley received approval from the governor, Sir Henry Belfield, to handle repatriation of all Giriama into the reserve, but the movements of the Giriama and their rights to land soon became entangled with the larger question of land rights along the coast.[26]

THE COASTAL LAND QUESTION

The Colonial Office had long aimed to facilitate capitalist development both on the coast and in the Giriama hinterland. To accomplish this it was necessary for local administrators to establish order out of the disruption that followed the failure of Arab plantation agriculture, to clarify the extremely confused land titles, and to provide a steady source of labor. Because of the war with Germany and the need to bring order to the generally disrupted coast and hinterland, the Colonial Office had not objected to the cost of quelling the Giriama disturbances, but the officials in London expected that six months of fighting and an additional year of punishment would suffice to resolve most of the issues. Instead, the coast, which should now have been teeming with new laborers, was more disturbed than ever, and the cost of famine relief was added to the cost of the KAR patrols and the fine collection. These expenses, combined with the continuing war effort, led the secretary of state for the Colonies to suggest a commission on land that became formalized as the Malindi Commission of Inquiry, and a Food Production Committee that was set up to examine agricultural conditions. Both became involved in the Giriama land issue.[27]

DeLacey's Commission of Inquiry

The main stimulus for the Malindi Commission of Inquiry came from the deputy recorder of titles at Malindi, W. E. F. deLacey, whose job it was to assist with the investigation of coastal land claims. The British administration had hoped to achieve three goals by clarifying Afro-Arab land titles: they wanted to individualize land-holding, to free land for purchase by Europeans, and to force ex-slaves, who had no claims to land, into the wage-labor market. DeLacey's principal involvement was with the Afro-Arabs and ex-slaves of the coast and the immediate Malindi hinterland. As early as 1908 the British had separated the coast lands from Giriama lands by means of the Baratum Line, approximately ten miles west of Malindi. To the west of the line were the Giriama lands, and to the east were privately owned and coastal Afro-Arab lands. People were supposed voluntarily to move to the appropriate side, since in fact Afro-Arabs had many claims on the Giriama side and Giriama occupied areas on the coastal side of the line. When in 1914 government officers finally began moving people to their designated areas, the ex-slaves who had been living in the territory all along were denied all rights to land. This Baratum move became the main source of deLacey's protests, but it was impossible to separate this issue from the Trans-Sabaki evacuation that took place over the same period.[28]

When some ex-slaves who had registered their claims with him were evicted, deLacey became angry over the delay this caused in the work of his court. He blamed the ill-treatment of ex-slaves on ineffective British administration and decided to press the issue. His complaint developed into one of personal animosity against Hobley, who considered the matter insignificant. DeLacey eventually took his case against Hobley to the secretary of state for the Colonies. Through deLacey's actions, pressure was put on the governor to explore the land issue, and Hobley finally agreed to the commission of inquiry.[29]

DeLacey made four allegations against the local administration. He argued that the "removals of people from their land were invalid according to Mohammedan [sic] law"; that undue influence was used to induce owners to withdraw their claims before the Land Titles Court; that dwellings were destroyed in the course of the removal; and, generally, that the provincial administration was ineffective.[30]

Although the main purpose of the commission had been to allow deLacey to voice his complaints, the result was to bring into the open the plight of the Giriama with regard to land. Sheikh Fathili bin Omar, former Mudir of Arabuko, who had acted as liaison in the Giriama declaration for peace, had become deLacey's agent. Probably at his urging, Ngonyo and some elders were asked to testify before the commission.[31]

Ngonyo argued that his rights to land at Marafa had been given to him by

Sir Arthur Hardinge before the turn of the century; his sense of grievance was strong, and his goal was to return to Marafa. The Giriama claim that they had been wrongly removed from the Trans-Sabaki lands gained additional support when it became clear that there had been a discrepancy in the communications regarding the total number of Giriama who were to be evacuated. The evidence given at the inquiry indicated that approximately 27 percent of the Giriama population had been living north of the river prior to the evacuation. This amounted to nearly 20,000 people, rather than the 5,000 the governor had originally reported to the secretary of state.[32]

Hobley ultimately bore the blame for this numerical discrepancy. He had first proposed the evacuation of the Trans-Sabaki in June 1913, and had considered it convenient to carry out his plan as punishment for Mekatalili's campaign that same year. In his original proposal he listed the total Giriama population as 60,880, but failed to mention how many of these were then living north of the river. In his 28 October 1913 report Champion, also recommending the move, gave no population estimate, but on 4 December 1913 the D.C. of Malindi used the 1913 census to estimate a population of 15,000—4,765 men, 5,158 women, and 4,855 children—then living north of the river. This was approximately 5,000 *families*. By 4 May 1914, when the evacuation was proposed by the governor, Henry Belfield, to Lewis Harcourt, secretary of state for the Colonies, the total had been reduced to 5,000 *individuals*.[33] Belfield wrote:

In the course of the tour, the PC found "some sections amounting in numbers to some 5,000 in all" taking advantage of the fact that they were entirely free of control and wandered "outside their own country" and scattered over an extensive and fertile area to the North of the Sabaki, a situation which is entirely outside their traditional tribal location.[34]

Hobley reported that there was an "abundance of vacant and suitable land for their occupation" south of the river, and that the Giriama did not object to the move if they were given time to harvest crops and to choose a new site. He must have known that the move involved a large population, but he apparently decided that it did not matter. Even if Hobley gave the figure of 5,000 families in conversation, and if the governor translated it to 5,000 individuals—which is what the acting governor, Bowring, assumed in 1918— it was Hobley who bore the responsibility. He had allowed his superiors to believe that only a small proportion of the Giriama lived in the Trans-Sabaki and that the land to which they could return, south of the river, was suffi- ciently fertile to support the full population.[35]

This major discrepancy, brought to light during the inquiry, meant that the whole of the Giriama land issue had to be reconsidered. In addition, Ngonyo's evidence opened a second part of the British case to Giriama challenge. British officials had been arguing since 1912 that the Giriama were latecomers to the Trans-Sabaki and were there only as a result of the Pax Britannica. They argued that the Giriama were trying to use land on which they had no legitimate claim. The facts did not bear this out. When, after 1850, the Giriama began their migration northward, the Sabaki River was no more considered a boundary of their land than the Ndzovuni River, flowing into Kilifi Creek, had been when they reached it. In all of this area, Giriama paid Oroma for permission to use the land. When the Oroma were no longer present to grant permission, the Waata had replaced them.[36]

When the Imperial British East Africa Company began its administration in 1888, the Giriama had not yet crossed the Sabaki River. In 1896 James Weaver, who had been an IBEAC official and who then became acting district officer in Malindi, wrote that during the previous five years officers in charge of Malindi had exerted themselves to "get the WaNyika from the far Giriama country, a dry, and not very prosperous district, to come and settle on the fruitful lands adjoining the Sabaki River."[37] He was strongly opposed to the Giriama paying the Waata for use of the land, since permission was issued by the British government. The Giriama, then, had not surreptitiously crossed the river; on the contrary, IBEAC and British government officials had encouraged them to do so.[38] This, in effect, bore out Ngonyo's claim.

The 1916 Commission of Inquiry did not settle the Giriama land question. The governor still had to decide whether or not to act on the evidence. Testimony had exposed the confusion of various British officials regarding Giriama rights to the Trans-Sabaki, and it raised the possibility of a government error in the decision to complete the evacuation of the region. When the commission adjourned in December 1916, those Giriama who had attended the sessions left with the impression that the invincible British government might have been mistaken in removing them from their land. This doubt occasioned local British officers much alarm; the fact that nothing was settled immediately at the close of the inquiry resulted in a loss of prestige for the administrators in the Giriama district and a weakening of their authority. At the time, Hobley referred to the unsettled conditions as resulting from "intrigue" on the parts of dissident Giriama and of deLacey, who bore a personal grudge against him.[39]

Although a disappointed deLacey was told that his allegation of mal-administration was unfounded, responsibility for some ineffectiveness in administration was officially attributed to Hobley. The governor admitted that the initial misunderstanding regarding the number of Giriama in the Trans-Sabaki resulted from a misquoted number, but without clarifying the source of the error he blamed Hobley for the hardship that had resulted from failure to give full consideration to the rights of all parties in the Baratum Line transfers as well as the failure to provide clear, written instructions about repatriations from Malindi district in 1916.[40]

Belfield supported the Trans-Sabaki evacuation as a necessary part of the administrative plan. He attributed the confusion to the fact that the war effort complicated the evacuation, but he held Hobley responsible for subsequent repatriation problems. He censured Hobley directly and, in his ire, conveyed to the secretary of state his opinion that the position of provincial commissioner was both unnecessary and detrimental to communication between the central administration and the district administration.[41] Since Belfield retired immediately thereafter, it fell to the acting governor, C. C. Bowring, to reach a final decision on the findings.*

The situation of the officers who were trying to continue administration in Giriamaland was complicated by the failure of the inquiry to settle the matter conclusively. During the interim between the adjournment of the commission in December 1916 and the decision of the governor made public in January 1918, local administrators were virtually powerless. When Ngonyo began to encourage people to return to the Trans-Sabaki, the district commissioner could do nothing. Hobley's attentions remained fixed on the war effort. He became convinced that German agitators were again at work in his district, while deLacey, who had in any case objected to the constitution of the Malindi Commission, was still keeping the subject of land rights high in the people's minds. Furthermore, A. Morrison, a Mombasa barrister who had formerly been engaged by the Maasai to fight their removal from lands by the government, was hired by some Giriama from Marafa to challenge the original order to evacuate the Trans-Sabaki.[42] The threat of court action, which would have prolonged the conflict and continued disruption, was sufficient to force Hobley into conciliation.

Realizing that he could not maintain the Sabaki River as the northern boundary for Giriama occupation, Hobley proposed a compromise: to allow Giriama to go to part of the land on a temporary basis. But he lost. On 3 January 1918 Bowring recommended that the Giriama be allowed to return to the Trans-Sabaki indefinitely or until adequate water was provided in the south. This was a public admission that the government's officials had made a mistake. The decision had precisely the effect that Hobley, Dundas, and Champion had warned would result from such a demonstration of government weakness: the Giriama were confirmed in their passive opposition to British administration.[43]

The Food Production Committee

Not only did the Malindi Commission have a serious impact on the future of the Giriama, but the Food Production Committee, which had been given the power to deal with the problem of food shortages, also intervened. By February 1918, when food had become scarce, the Food Production Committee was responsible for a government policy advocating that the Giriama return to active cultivation of the Trans-Sabaki:

The Food Production Committee arrived in the district armed with the authority to allow anyone who was willing to plant food crops to go and do so on the north bank. On the same evening of the day on which this was made known in Nyika reserve, the

*C. C. (later Sir Charles) Bowring had been chief secretary; when Belfield went on retirement leave, he served as acting governor until Sir Edward Northey took over in February 1919.

Giriama began to cross the river and continued to do so all through the night and the following days, whole locations crossing in a body including their elders and native council and their women and children. Instructions have not yet been received how the people are to be administered. This has increased the population by at least 5,000 souls.[44]

The reversal of the Trans-Sabaki policy came too late to prevent the worst food shortage since the beginning of the century. The administration's efforts were diverted to famine relief. Giriama were no longer restricted to the reserve but, unlike their prosperous condition in 1912, they were now weak and hungry; many left for the coast, where they hoped to find food.

The return to their granary in 1918 brought benefits by the following year. During 1919 a portion of the Trans-Sabaki was added to the Nyika Reserve, and the Giriama gained legal title to the land they had earlier been forced to evacuate. Grain exports from Malindi resumed and more Giriama moved to the Trans-Sabaki.[45] The British traded economic stability for renewal of political disorder. The rush for new land could not fail to disturb the administration of the reserve. Twenty-four locations had been designated prior to the time the Giriama were allowed to recross the river. Each had a kambi council composed of village elders and presided over by the headman, who was also president of the Native Council. This system was dependent upon government-appointed headmen. Now the whole population was in flux. Headmen as well as those under their authority were on the move. It was ironic that the British administrators who had protested so strongly against Giriama migration because it hindered proper administration should, through their vacillating policies from 1915 through 1918, have facilitated intensified migration.

ECONOMIC VITALITY OF THE COAST

The plan to develop coastal plantations, which had been the original goal of the Protectorate, had undergone major modifications since the initial drive to obtain Giriama laborers to work there. The lack of Giriama laborers had been only one difficulty. Owners, managers, and potential investors were facing a number of serious problems simultaneously. The experimental crops had proved to be less successful than had been hoped: cotton did not thrive in most of the soils of the coast and the hinterland; rubber trees were planted, but their output never exceeded that of collected wild rubber, and when output improved, world prices of rubber fell, undercutting the profits from coastal production. Land was generally difficult to acquire. New acquisitions were dependent upon the litigation of land claims along the coast, and even after titles had been cleared it was often difficult to purchase contiguous parcels for a large operation.* And as though the problems of labor, land,

*David Miller argues that the plantation experiments failed not from lack of land (since much went uncultivated) but for lack of labor (though managers had a preference for the nearby Giriama). He concludes that their failure was due to their unwillingness to pay going wages and their desire for the special treatment they interpreted up-country settlers as getting: David Miller,

and crops were insufficient, the nearby war with Germany drew away all surplus labor and administrative attention and discouraged investment from abroad. No administrator had the determination and ability to deal both with the vagaries of warfare on this scale and with an African people whose interests were contrary to administrative economic goals. As a result, the need to administer the Giriama and to provide laborers to the coast—goals that had been interconnected—both lost their significance after the Giriama returned to the Trans-Sabaki.

AN ATTEMPT TO SALVAGE THE ADMINISTRATION

By 1919, both Giriama and administrators were beginning to weary of the unsettled condition of the Giriama. British officials continued in their ambivalence toward the internal administrative framework. Headmen still lacked authority and respect; councils were unreliable in terms of accountability. The original headmen were growing old; some had been discredited; and most had lost so much of their influence with their people that they were no longer of any assistance to the British. The British had no better substitute, however, so headmen were allowed to remain or were only slowly replaced.

The Giriama were also faced with a leadership problem. Headmen had rarely met acceptance as spokesmen. This lack of leadership had been exacerbated by the delay in holding the traditional ceremonies to install a new ruling generation. The problem of an overdue initiation, which Champion had faced in 1912, was even more acute after the rebellion.

The British and the Giriama began to share an interest in reviving the traditional Giriama government as a basis for leadership. As early as 1917, two councils asked the A.D.C. to support the installation of a new kambi council.* This would make a generational hand-over possible and provide a pool for local kambi membership. There was even hope for the revival of a single all-Giriama kambi centered around the traditional kaya. Moreover, the ceremonies would enable some of the younger men to learn the ancient customs. Because kambi installation seemed a potential solution to their administrative problems, British officers in 1919 urged that a new kambi be installed. Many felt that more effective headmen might be acquired by such a bolstering of the traditional system. They did not believe in long-term benefits from the traditional system—they felt that it was dying out—but in the short term it seemed the only way to place younger Giriama men in positions of leadership.[46]

The logistical problems in attaining full installation to kambi were immense. The initiation process had been stopped before the final age-sets of the presiding generation had been installed. Several officers tried to ascertain

---

"The Failure of European Plantations on the Coast of Kenya to 1914: A Case of Competing Economic Systems" (Department of African Studies, Syracuse University, n.d.) (mimeo.).

*The two were Kitu wa Sirya's council at Kaloleni and Birya wa Masha's at Mienzeni.

the proper procedure. They understood that uninitiated nyere wanted legitimate power but had lost interest in most of the traditional customs; they also realized that the few remaining old men would cling to their power and could, by refusing to cooperate in conducting the ceremonies, prevent the transfer. What the officers failed to realize was that the entire process would require four lengthy ceremonies: one to complete the presiding generation's rule; one to retire the members of that generation and install the new ruling generation; and two to elevate Giriama to their proper positions as kambi. They also did not understand that each of the ceremonies was possible only if the crops were good, and, most important, that a breakdown in the process was likely because there were no longer any elders who knew the ritual for installing the new ruling generation. This ritual had last been held in the 1870s; of the men trained, only Wanje wa Mwadorikola was alive. That one man could remember all the details was doubtful. In the past, this ceremony had been conducted by the Giriama only after the neighboring Ribe, Kauma, Chonyi, and Jibana had completed their equivalent ceremonies, but by the second decade of the twentieth century these rituals were in decay among all of the Mijikenda.[47]

The attempt to install a new kambi also had intrinsic complications. The ceremonies demanded the use of the kaya, which the British had formally closed; they would be meaningless unless all Giriama participated; the traditional spirit of cooperation, joy, and friendliness had been marred by the recent events; and the vagaries of the climate made four successive years of prosperity uncertain at best.

Despite these problems, for several years the British and the Giriama attempted to revive the traditional system. Ironically, this attempt received added stimulation from the return, in 1919, of Mekatalili and Wanje wa Mwadorikola. Their original term of deportation had been only a couple of years, but with the uncertainties of the Trans-Sabaki question and the Malindi Inquiry, they had been detained for several years more. Upon their return, they were met at Rabai "with an enthusiasm rare among the Giriama."[48]

For a while it seemed as though the installation would be successful. The governor, Sir Edward Northey, came to the district to announce the reopening of Kaya Giriama, and in September the D.C. at Kakoneni station discussed with a large number of elders, including Ngonyo, the possibility of the return to Kaya Giriama of Wanje wa Mwadorikola and representatives from each of the six clans.* Both these actions were in anticipation of holding the proper ceremonies to bring new blood into the leadership, but they were also a triumph for Giriama who had wanted their kaya reopened. Wanje and Mekatalili went to live in the kaya. Wanje became the official head of the kambi, and a women's kambi was instituted with Mekatalili as its head. They held no position in the administration, but they became de facto leaders for

---

*H. L. Mood, A.D.C., mentions that on 28 September 1919 Lamb discussed this with the elders at Kakoneni: "Safari Diary" (KNA: CP 50/122).

those who still wanted kaya leaders. However, the reopening of the kaya turned out to be only a token action; all attempts to use traditional initiation to legitimize present authorities remained unsuccessful. Both the British and the Giriama were handicapped by this lack of any system for legitimation of Giriama leadership.[49]

By the end of 1919 the British had suffered a decline rather than an increase in their powers of administration. In September 1919, on a long-overdue leave, Hobley left Giriama administration. He was the last of those who had been involved in the early years and who had a vested interest in Giriama administrative success. Before the year was out, the station at Kakoneni had been abandoned. It was no longer of much use, since it had been established to prevent people from recrossing the river, and extreme malarial conditions had developed when the Sabaki River changed course slightly. Since so many of those stationed there had been invalided out, Kakoneni was declared a health hazard.[50]

Thus, after seven years there was no longer an administrative station in the hinterland. Theoretically the Giriama were organized under Native Councils in a reserve that had been extended to include the Trans-Sabaki, but the population was still in flux due to the opening up of this land and increased migration to coastal lands, which had been stimulated by the famine. Headmen still acted as agents of the government and received some degree of acceptance by their own people, but most headmen had learned to be unassertive, doing little for the government: only by favoring neither the administration nor the Giriama could a headman hope to survive. This was little different from the situation in 1912. Kaya Giriama, which six years before Champion had called a "hot bed of sedition," had been reopened under the leadership of those "seditionists."[51] The loss of many young Giriama men to the Carrier Corps as punishment for the uprising had not made the Giriama eager to provide a steady supply of labor for the development of the coast. In any case, the demand for labor had lessened, not because the British had accepted that the Giriama were unwilling to work as wage-laborers but because the war had ended the Carrier Corps demand and the European estates on the coast had failed to achieve their anticipated success.

ASSESSMENT

Many factors contributed to the decline of Giriama prosperity. The personalities of Champion and Hobley, Ngonyo and Mkowa, Mekatalili and Wanje, Gunga wa Baya and Traill had all influenced the turn of events. Famines, a world war, and lobbies in London were beyond the power of colonials and Giriama alike to avoid or control. But it was the British officials' belief in the myth of a single-minded purpose, of the government's "power," and of a "workable policy" that allowed so many of them to devote such energy to a task that was virtually impossible; and it was the strong Giriama opposition to the imposition of a new economic system, that of wage-labor, alongside threats to their most productive land, to their sales of ivory, and to the fees customarily due to senior councillors which encouraged the Giriama to go on resisting so strong a power as the British in what had to be, in the end, a losing battle. The Giriama became further divided as they were forced to take a stand either for or against the British government. When, in 1913, they did become sufficiently unified to oppose British actions, internal contradictions were still potent enough to prevent success.

Beyond the strong determination of British officials to succeed and the Giriama determination to protect their political economy were the differences in the previous British and Giriama experiences. The Giriama were enough like the Kikuyu, Luo, Nandi, and Kamba for the officers to feel that tested ideas and practices would work. But the Giriama differed in crucial ways— ways that had more to do with their economy than with their political struc-ture. Some British officers stressed what they perceived as obstinacy, indiffer-ence, or "unbendable pride," or they called the Giriama "pertinacious," "dem-ocratic," "undisciplined," "apathetic," or "anarchists."[52] Whatever the label, they were describing an independent spirit in cultural terms and failing to recognize its economic basis.

Traill wrote that the strength of Giriama opposition to wage-labor was rare among the agricultural peoples of Africa.[53] Hobley seemed incredulous of the Giriama psychology as he saw it: "Their psychology is perhaps the most complex of all the tribes; they knew the power of Government, but always seemed to think that by the adoption of a persistent attitude of *non possumus* they could wear us down so that we should become tired, thus relaxing our efforts"; but he concluded, "Their reasoning was more or less sound."[54]

The Giriama learned that the government held ultimate authority over them, but they also learned that a show of deference toward the British administration was sometimes sufficient to keep the rulers satisfied while preventing them from wielding their power effectively. They retained much control over their internal affairs. They also learned that they could survive economically through the continuation of their agricultural production.

British officers learned less that they could apply; the value systems re-mained different. In 1926, an officer was making the same oversimplified diagnosis and prescribing the same ineffective remedies that had been offered in 1912: "The Wayika suffer from five grave disabilities: drunkenness, apathy, lack of discipline, incompetent and apathetic headmen, and loose administra-tion. Special attempts have been made to tighten administration. Labour, with good employers, is at the moment one of the best medicines available for the WaNyika ills."[55] In 1936 the district officer at Kilifi wrote, "The back-wardness of Nyika can largely be attributed to drink, venereal disease, or malaria."[56]

The long-range assessment of British officers was that it had been "the weakness of the Giriama tribal structure which proved to be its strongest weapon."[57] These officers, who had dealt with weak structures elsewhere, failed to remember earlier situations. In those instances they had bolstered the British position of superiority with much authority, and with military force, over a long period of interaction. Among the Giriama the British lacked missionary agents to interpret the two cultures to one another, and they had minimal numbers of administrative officers and police. The Giriama, on the other hand, simply had no organization for indirect rule. Under pressure of the British demands, they soon became aware that they no longer possessed sufficient traditional machinery and power to govern themselves as a single people. In 1921, after the British abandoned their hinterland station, even Rabai station was closed down. The British administration would henceforth for all practical purposes ignore the Giriama, particularly regarding land and wage labor. They left a once-viable economy shattered and they offered little administrative assistance for recovery. The Giriama had originally maintained their successful political economy without British support; now they had to try to recover economic stability without British support. Despite all the efforts and money expended, British administration of the Giriama was a failure. The Giriama were never to serve the Protectorate as laborers. Moreover, the British had tied the Giriama economy to their own without offering a way to facilitate its integration. By so doing, they had accomplished the opposite of their intention and thwarted any development of the coast and its hinterland.

9
Conclusions

Proponents of the dependency theory for third-world countries have argued that African participation as traders in worldwide capitalist systems has long benefited the metropole at the expense of local economies.[1] E. A. Alpers has demonstrated that such underdevelopment on the southcentral African coast had its roots in the system of international trade begun by Arabs in the thirteenth century, continued by Portuguese in the sixteenth and seventeenth centuries, dominated by Indians in the eighteenth century, and expanded to include Indian, Arab, and Western capitalism in the nineteenth century.[2] It is very likely that this same basic phenomenon also occurred among coastal peoples in Tanzania and Kenya. This study has examined the Giriama as a society that had been successful both as trading partners in an Afro-Arab system in the nineteenth century and as producers of grain for export.

The roots of underdevelopment for the Giriama lay in their trading role as dependents in a capitalist system, but underdevelopment became inescapable when in 1912 the British undermined Giriama productive capacity in order to acquire labor to support the colonial economy. British colonialism interfered to such a degree with the prosperous Giriama economy that the Giriama were never to recover their prosperity during the colonial period. The British based their early twentieth-century colonial economic development in Kenya on only two production systems. The colonial system, which centered in the central highlands and focused on settler agriculture, required initial artificial assistance and heavy labor resources. The Afro-Arabs, whose coastal plantations had collapsed at the end of the nineteenth century when the end of the slave trade removed their labor base, still claimed their widespread plantation land; they thus prevented newcomers easy access to land. These plantations were seen as units to be taken over by British capitalists. African production systems were generally ignored. The hinterland production of the Giriama, who had marketed their grain regionally and exported it to Arabia through the Afro-Arab network, was still thriving in 1912. Rather than drawing the Giriama into their colonial production system, British officers failed to offer assistance in continued marketing of Giriama goods, and they relegated the Giriama to the periphery of the major economic system by concentrating on the Mombasa-Nairobi railway, bypassing Giriama territory. As the Giriama accommodated themselves to a regional market by squatting on Afro-Arab lands, British restrictions on land usage and demands for young Giriama men as wage-laborers threatened to undercut Giriama production. Giriama refusal to cooperate brought repressive measures and increased restrictions. When the British pressure became relentless and conditions deteriorated, the Giriama rebelled.

In this study, I have tried simultaneously to provide a longitudinal economic history of the Giriama, to bring new dimensions to Kenya coastal history, to view the difficulties of early colonial rule from the perspective of the colonized, and to examine African resistance, in the hope that we may better understand why Africans chose that response against such great odds.

GIRIAMA HISTORY

This longitudinal history of the Giriama has unraveled a sequence of changes in their noncentralized political system and uncovered the significance of their economic development. Long-term analysis of the Giriama economy demonstrates the degree of disruption the early colonial experience brought to the Giriama economy. In the decades prior to 1912 the Giriama underwent many changes in response to new economic options; these changes, which prepared them to take individual economic risks supported by families and local communities, proved disadvantageous when they were confronted with British demands for labor. Their political organization, which was effective under circumstances of expansion, migration, and prosperity, could not facilitate a unified response to British demands for drastic economic change. The economic changes the British tried to impose after 1912 reduced Giriama options so severely that the Giriama were finally virtually forced to fight in a last, desperate effort. The Giriama historical experience had left them decidedly unprepared for and unreceptive to British colonial needs.

COASTAL HISTORY

The Kenya coast is an interwoven cultural zone of Afro-Arab enclaves and hinterland peoples, joint participants in the coastal economy. Changes in one group directly influenced the other. The British demand for Giriama laborers was not their first direct intervention into the coastal economy: British abolition of the slave trade ruined the Afro-Arab plantations by removing their labor base, and British removal of the faction of Takaungu Mazrui Arabs who had been the primary Giriama trading partners had severe repercussions on the Giriama economy. The British demand for Giriama laborers was viewed by the Giriama in the context of these events in the coastal economy, not in the context of the colonial economy based in the highlands; it is no wonder that the Giriama were perplexed that the British would put an end to a successful labor system and then put pressure on them to become replacements for these ex-slaves.

The Giriama struggle to maintain a viable coastal economy at the same time that settlers were establishing themselves up-country provides a useful contrast between early colonial development and neglect. On the coast, British investors were absentee landlords. Pressure in London was more significant than pressure from local European residents, who had no way to coerce laborers without administrative assistance. The coast was treated almost as a distinct colonization effort, unrelated to the up-country settlement.

PROBLEMS OF COLONIAL RULE

To establish colonial rule, the colonizers had to bring the Africans under control, find useful African agents to assist their efforts, and bring Africans into compliance with colonial economic goals. With the Giriama, the British had difficulty in accomplishing any of these ends.

Conquest and Control

Since the history of the conquest of Kenya is still in a formative stage,[3] and since the history of the establishment of colonial rule has focused on the central highlands and western region at the expense of the remainder of the colony, the conditions and responses of the Giriama may serve to place both conquest and colonization in a new perspective. Although the participating officers could not see it at the time, by 1912 they were involved in a third phase of British conquest in Kenya.

In the first phase, from 1895 to 1905, the British were dependent on Africans as producers of food, as guides and porters, for security, and as fighting allies—all necessary to make possible a secure route from the coast to Uganda. Africans who interrupted communications, disturbed caravans, or raided British allies had to be dealt with by force, but the British were fighting from a position of insecurity and had to rely on African troops organized in traditional regiments to fight at their side, with payment made in the form of cattle confiscated in battle.

In the second phase, after about 1905, when British armed forces were better established and Africans fought with British expeditions as paid mercenaries, British troops were in full control. They not only won their battles easily, but they used measures that were severe beyond all need, and they sold confiscated cattle to settlers.[4]

In the third phase of conquest, to maximize economic resources in Kenya, the British wanted much more than political and administrative control. They needed a specific kind of participation from Africans. Only if sufficiently large numbers of Africans would serve as wage-laborers could the labor needs of the Protectorate be met. The only alternatives were to import workers or to redesign the economic plan. Under such desperate conditions of labor shortage, the British turned to the Giriama.

As economic and political pressures to draw the Giriama into the labor market proved increasingly unsuccessful, realization of their lack of political control caused the British great alarm. Ironically, the British position was not much different from that of the first stage of the Protectorate in 1895, when they were dependent on African cooperation and used economic debilitation to achieve political control over those Africans who acted as obstacles to the overall plan. The British had always faced difficulties in trying to control the noncentralized societies of Kenya. They were at a loss as to how to deal with what appeared to be a lack of leaders among those societies which refused to cooperate. Unable to identify agents with whom to negotiate, the British opted to punish the society by debilitating the economy to such an extent that the people became unable to muster resources to oppose them. In Kenya, they had continued to fight the Bukusu, the Kabra, the Nandi, and the Gusii until the society's economy had suffered so great a loss of cattle, crops, and personnel that it was clear that the British were the political masters. In the case of the Nandi it has been demonstrated that the British succeeded in undermining an expanding economy. This amounted to using economic disability as a means to obtain political ends.[5]

Economic Colonization

The primary goal of the British in the East African Protectorate, contradictory as it may seem in terms of their actions, was economic colonization. European conquest and colonization of Africa meant more than establishment of political control within boundaries designated by Europeans making agreements among themselves. In most cases, the colonizer needed more than an internationally recognized claim to the land and the people's acceptance of their presence in the colonized territory; too often, he needed the labor of the colonized. With a capitalist model determining the form of the colonial economic system, the colonized were left, ultimately, with two options: either they could serve as wage-laborers, or they could produce cash crops. In Kenya, the demand for wage-laborers predominated, because European settlers and administrators needed workers. Settlers insisted on restrictions upon African cash-crop production because such crops offered competition to their own endeavors; further, such production provided the Africans with an alternative to wage-labor, making recruitment difficult. The people most likely to become wage-laborers were those in poor economic situations who could not raise cash crops.

By 1912, the colonial economy had been launched but faced a severe labor shortage. Although official British policy from London stated in no uncertain terms that the colonial administration was not to participate in labor recruitment, officers in the Protectorate, from the governor on down, acted as if they had no choice but to put forward their best efforts to end the labor crisis.

When the Labour Commission designated the Giriama as the most significant untapped labor resource, the potential Giriama labor pool was, at best, 15,000 men. At its peak the African labor force in the Protectorate was approximately 100,000 men. The Public Works Department employed from 3,000 to 5,000 men, and the railway, including private contractors, employed another 7,000 men. The remaining Africans worked in the private sector. Prior to 1912, labor had been provided by the three most numerous ethnic groups in the Protectorate, whose economic situation had made them receptive to service as wage-laborers. The Kikuyu of the central highlands had lost much of their land to settlers, resided near Nairobi, the capital, and were under pressure from their elders to relieve the overcrowded conditions of the reserves by seeking wage-labor. The Luyia and Luo of western Kenya did not lose land to Europeans, but they had no cash crops and their land was overcrowded, so wage-labor was attractive. The next largest group, the Kamba, who resided between the coast and the central highlands, had already responded to economically stressful conditions by establishing small communities along trade routes to Mombasa and through Taveta and by herding more cattle in marginal areas, and they were notorious for their unwillingness to work for wages. The Labour Commission pinpointed the Kamba and the Giriama as the groups crucial for obtaining the needed labor, with the most active administrative attention given to the Giriama.[6]

Why the Giriama, considering their small numbers? More than anything else it was the fact that the Giriama lived in the coastal hinterland that made them the most likely labor force. The greatest labor demands came from European planters along the coast and from various governmental agencies at Mombasa. Through London, officials in Nairobi and on the coast were being pressured by irate speculators who had invested in coastal plantation developments only to see little or no profit. Since up-country Africans who filled the existing labor positions suffered, in the warm coastal climate, from malaria and other diseases, administrators hoped that the Giriama, who were accustomed to life in the coastal climate, would free the Kikuyu, Luo, and Luyia to work up-country, where they were better acclimatized. Drawing the Giriama into the wage-labor market would also solve the problem of their encroachment onto coastal lands, on which, it was feared, they might make permanent claims. The hopes placed upon the Giriama potential were far higher than the reality would support.

African Agents

To find Giriama agents to assist the British administrative efforts proved to be almost impossible. The Giriama ruled themselves through local councils: individuals lacked authority and no henchmen were immediately available to follow a newly created leader. British officers chose to aim for political control when they could more effectively have met their economic goals by assessing the economic situation of the Giriama as well as the economic plans for the coast. Failing to remember that in previous cases they had gained political control only through economic debilitation, in the case of the

Giriama they tried to use an extremely weak, artificially created political mechanism, that of the headmen, to force specific economic behavior. By trying simultaneously to establish political authority and obtain workers, the British eliminated the possibility of achieving either goal.

As they attempted to work within the Giriama situation, British officers were confused by their prior perceptions of the effectiveness of appointed "chiefs." Among the Kikuyu, these men had been able to fulfill demands for laborers, but there they had been backed by colonial police forces and they had political and economic favors with which to reward young men who agreed to be their agents for labor recruiting. Kikuyu chiefs, in particular, developed local organizations strong enough to coerce young men into working. In contrast, Giriama headmen were given no police force, had little interest in encouraging young men to go to work, and lacked the support of the elders. Whereas the Kikuyu had lost their land to powerful settlers, were restricted from growing cash crops, and lived in extremely overcrowded reserves, the Giriama were still participating in economic expansion and had very little incentive for wage-labor. They had witnessed the British dismantling of the slave-labor force—an act which implied to the Giriama that labor was no longer needed.

Giriama headmen were actually the first wage-laborers, although initially they were given few duties and their salary was very low. As British demands increased and the headmen's jobs became increasingly difficult, the headmen's position proved to be a poor model for encouraging additional wage-labor. In no case was a Giriama serving as a headman because he lacked a place in Giriama society or was destitute. As soon as the costs came to outweigh the benefits, the headmen became reluctant in their support of the British effort.

In the course of Giriama resistance, realization of the lack of political control became so embarrassing to the British that economic goals gave way to political needs. The Giriama had to be controlled. This attitude helps to explain why the punishment was made so severe even though it became clear that the economy would become seriously undermined if the terms were met. It also helps to explain why the British continued to uphold their appointed headmen even when those headmen proved to be ineffective. In the last resort, the British needed the headmen more than the headmen needed the British. Ironically, it was much easier for a British officer to fire a headman than it was for a headman to resign. The divisions uncovered within Giriama society demonstrate the problems faced by headmen who were unwilling to use coercion against their own people unless they were rewarded. Without the advantages of access to land or the attraction of mission education, and without the opportunity to advance their own clan at the expense of another or with the support of police, Giriama headmen had few incentives to be effective agents for British colonialism.

AFRICAN RESISTANCE

With the exception of a few headmen and some individuals in various locations, Giriama had resisted the British administration ever since its inception
in 1912. The Giriama are unique in the consistency with which they defied
British colonial efforts. They, more than any other of Kenya's peoples, were
immediately confronted with the economic implications of colonialism. The
demand for laborers asked more than the Giriama were willing to give:
meeting that request risked forfeiture of their own economic production.
Headmen underwent much pressure from their own people not to work for
the British. There were almost no British agents who could facilitate Giriama
integration into a well-established colonial system. Officers on the coast had
come and gone without making much impact or providing a sense of consistency in the government's presence. The mission experience had been minimal and was distorted by its connection with ex-slaves. Colonial education
never became attractive to the Giriama. The British came to their task of
bringing the Giriama into the administrative network only after seventeen
successful years of work up-country; they failed to consider the extent to
which the Giriama had been free of colonial influence, and they tried to do
too much too quickly.

Initial Giriama resistance did not take the form of open attack upon the
British. The more the British pushed, however, the more determined and
defiant the Giriama became. Finally, unrelenting British efforts escalated the
situation into war. Why were the British so unrelenting? The need for laborers overshadowed all other considerations. Their dream of an economic
revival of the coast that would bring profits to investors and a stable economic base for the Protectorate caused administrators to deny evidence concerning the unavailability of labor, the failure of cash crops, and effective use
of coastal land. The First World War distorted the Giriama situation; Giriama proximity to the war front prevented their struggle from being regarded
separately from the larger effort; and the possibility that the Giriama might
divert troops and supplies threatened British security. Charles Hobley, as
senior officer responsible for the development of the coast, was under personal and political pressure to deal firmly with the Giriama. British need for
political organization through which they could rule indirectly, their assumptions about the totality of warfare and the conclusiveness of its outcome, and
their tendency to be unrealistic about the economic upheaval they were causing all hampered their efforts seriously.

One of the most difficult questions for colonial powers centered around
the organization of African opposition, particularly in those societies that
lacked chiefs or kings to serve as leaders or act as spokesmen for the society
as a whole. Europeans presumed that African societies, mirroring European
societies, would opt to relate to the outsiders on a political level, but political
alliances and oppositions imply a kind of permanence of political organization that is alien to the conditions of most noncentralized peoples of Kenya.

The advantage the noncentralized society has lies in its ability to respond to circumstances, to be in the right place at the right time and to make the most effective decisions. This demands an awareness of the environment and schooling in the techniques of how best to take advantage of that environment. This kind of synchronicity cannot be pursued if a society has an overloaded bureaucratic structure whose primary goal is the survival of the polity.

The British officers proceeded on the basis that disturbance of the political structure and removal of leaders who urged rebellion would destroy the basis for resistance. Neither Giriama who held positions of traditional prominence nor people with charismatic personalities such as Mekatalili had, however, caused the Giriama defiant response; they had only articulated the grievances of the population at large and facilitated a unified response. The Giriama tried a number of tactics prior to open rebellion. First, women incited the elders to support Giriama grievances and protect young men from being sent away as laborers. This alliance, aimed at headmen and supported by general dissension and proscriptive oaths, created a campaign of non-cooperation to which the British responded with severe punishment. Once the elders had been discredited and young men still faced labor demands, the latter responded in keeping with their traditional role, launching defensive warfare. They fought without defined strategies or long-term goals, and leadership was spontaneous and short-lived. As juniors in a society divided by age, the dissidents lacked a framework to lead their own fight or to negotiate their own peace, and in Kenya, warfare was itself a limited venture. In most noncentralized societies, warfare was a tactic to obtain specific, short-term goals—usually to settle a matter of conflict or to obtain an economic edge; African societies in Kenya did not use warfare to force one group to submit totally to another. Moreover, up to the end of the nineteenth century there were almost no instances where an entire society fought—until the British demanded that societies deliver coordinated responses and adhere to them. In most cases, the ethnic units that we refer to as the Kikuyu, the Kamba, the Giriama, the Nandi, or the Gusii were in fact composites or multi-units. The basis of the societies had often changed from exclusive kinship units to units which had a territorial component. Often there was also a division according to age. Many of the units with which the British came into conflict were economic, territorial, and in the process of change. Under the circumstances, British demands for permanence, unity, and political response were impossible to meet.

It is possible, of course, that British officers wished to escalate the conflict with the Giriama into open warfare because they considered war to be the most certain way to bring the Giriama to accept their terms. The experiences of the colonizer and of the colonized inform their perception of the situation and their options for response. While most factions within Giriama had determined the British presence and continuous demands to be detrimental to their economy, they had never been required to respond to imposed economic demands. The British, on the other hand, had found warfare to be the most effective means of dealing with "recalcitrant" Africans. The Giriama used armed resistance as a last resort, involving widespread participation through the society as a whole; British used warfare as a means to bind ethnic groups into single units and to coerce them into submission. The British experience with the Giriama, however, by 1914 indicated the inconclusiveness of warfare as an effective tactic for colonial control.

In the final analysis, economic considerations proved to be the most important in determining the Giriama response to colonialism. The Giriama fought not so much against British political control, which was particularly difficult to understand in the early stages of colonialism, but for the opportunity to maintain their economic production. Had they been allowed permanent rights to land and palm trees along the coastal belt, and had the British helped to maintain export centers at Malindi and Takaungu rather than contributing to their decline in favor of Mombasa, Giriama could have participated in expanded cash-cropping of maize and could have entered the export market in copra. Instead, the British systematically undercut the Giriama economy. They made trade in ivory illegal and policed it strenuously; they restricted the sale of palm wine; they limited Giriama squatting on coastal lands; they ordered the evacuation of the most productive Giriama lands; they inaugurated a thorough collection of tax; and they demanded laborers. The Giriama response was to fight back against the destroyers of their economy.

In the long run, the conditions created by the First World War in East Africa intensified British insecurity and led to their decision to call in the military against the Giriama, which did end the open conflict but also destroyed any basis for firm administration. Still, the war with Germany provided a focus for African and European energies in the East African Protectorate and helped the British to complete their conquest of Kenya and to stabilize their administration. War conditions helped to ensure that the British had not only won internationally recognized claims to the land and the people's acceptance of their presence in the colonized territory, but had also obtained access to the labor potential of the colonized. The war offered a basis for Protectorate-wide labor recruiting and at the same time offered the additional argument of national security: Africans were needed to protect their homelands from a strong European enemy.

CONCLUSION

Giriama offers the only prewar instance in Kenya of the colonizer's demand for wage-labor working in direct competition with a society's expanding economy. Without the Giriama and their determination, we might have overlooked the intricacies of the economic systems of noncentralized societies in the early colonial period and have continued to assume that they were simple and inefficient. The Giriama case establishes criteria different from those we had been using to understand many noncentralized African societies and to interpret their goals.

It is in assessing the overall impact of the Giriama response to colonial demands that the issues of short-term and long-range goals can be clarified. The British won the war against the Giriama, and the Giriama were forced into a stringent peace settlement. When famine brought the condition of the Giriama to the attention of authorities in London and the severity of the penalties came to be questioned, the British government removed land restrictions and lightened labor demands. In this policy reversal the Giriama achieved the main goals for which they had originally fought. They even watched British administrators move away from the interior stations, back to the coast.

But the British had not abandoned the Giriama simply in compliance with Giriama wishes; they left because the benefits to be derived from administering the coastal hinterland had dwindled. Since the coastal plantations had failed, the Giriama were no longer badly needed as laborers. It might even be argued that Giriama had never intended the British agencies to remove themselves so totally. Although the Giriama had fought against a form of capitalist penetration that would relegate them to wage-labor, they had not necessarily been desirous of being excluded from participation in the capitalist economy on any basis. They had not wanted economic isolation; they had wanted to participate in the economy as producers. With virtual withdrawal of the colonial administration, their marketing structures were even further reduced, and they lacked administrative channels through which they could redesign their economy according to the colonial framework. They found themselves unable to compete with the sophisticated marketing systems of the settlers up-country or with some of their fellow Africans such as the Kikuyu and Kamba who, though on the periphery of the colonial market, did benefit from it. The Giriama remained alone in the hinterland to fend for themselves while the fertile coastal strip of land went begging. Giriama links to worldwide capitalist systems had been unequal and disadvantageous, particularly in their lack of control over their participation, both as traders in the Indian Ocean network in the nineteenth century and as wage-laborers for the British in the twentieth. Moreover, viritual colonial abandonment—by denying them access to unused coastal lands and markets—of a society that had potential for production was tantamount to ensuring the worst form of economic dependency. Undercutting the Giriama base with unfulfilled promises of economic prosperity was debilitating beyond all measure.

As the colonial economy passed them by, the Giriama were left to become small-scale producers. Their local economy became subordinated to the colonial economy but was not linked to it in any productive way. The Giriama were relegated to the backwater, both economically and politically, from

1920 onward. As we get a better sense of the economic conditions of African societies such as the Giriama, and of how they have experienced linkage to colonial economies during the initial period of colonization, we shall be in a better position to understand the responses Africans made to colonization and to identify more accurately the components of their underdevelopment.

Note on Methodology

Methodology for this project was determined by the scarcity of written documentation. The Kenya National Archives contained five files on the Giriama rising, but general administrative files were exceptionally meager. Almost no historical or anthropological studies existed for any of the Mijikenda peoples. This was primarily true because the Giriama are noncentralized and were excluded from the mainstream of colonial development—two conditions which discouraged scholarly investigation. They also lacked translators such as missionaries or Islamic leaders. Nor, as it follows, were there many educated articulators among their people. Thus, I had to rely heavily on oral evidence, not only for the rising, but also to reconstruct the precolonial kaya system and its subsequent modifications.

The dispersed population developed localized councils which still operate with flexibility alongside a recently revived Kaya Council. Since I was pursuing questions of organization, religious influence, economic determinants, and local circumstances, I sought elders in communities throughout the scattered Giriama homesteads before going to the kaya. In the local councils it was relatively easy to identify those who were most knowledgeable about Giriama tradition, precolonial change, and the war with the British. Older women offered interpretations of Mekatalili's role as an articulator of women's concerns and as a potentially religious figure.

Although the ideal interview is conducted with only one informant, and I tried as often as possible to achieve this goal, sometimes it was virtually impossible—when interviews were held out of doors, for example, or in small houses during the rainy season—among people whose decisions are made by councils. Other elders insisted on listening and challenging, a practice which helped me to clarify some of the ambiguities that arose as I talked with people in various locations. I worked with two interpreters (both Giriama students at the University of Nairobi) who conducted the interviews in kiGiriama, but my own knowledge of kiSwahili, a language extremely close to kiGiriama, allowed me extensive participation. When it became clear that the Giriama had not been organized to fight by either military, political, or religious leaders, I turned to economic and social conditions to explain the consistent mass response to the British colonial demands and to understand the degree to which the Giriama were responding defensively. Detailed information and a list of informants are given in the bibliography.

Notes

PREFACE

1. Carl G. Rosberg, Jr., and John Nottingham, *The Myth of "Mau Mau": Nationalism in Kenya* (New York, 1970), p. 11 n. 20.

2. Cynthia Brantley Smith, "The Giriama Rising, 1914: Focus for Political Development in the Kenya Hinterland, 1850-1963" (Ph.D. dissertation, University of California, Los Angeles, 1973).

3. The only material I could find was as follows: W. E. Taylor, *Giriama Vocabulary and Collections* (London, 1891); Alice Werner, "The Bantu Coast Tribe of the East Africa Protectorate," *Journal of the Royal Anthropological Institute of Great Britain and Ireland* 45 (1915): 326-54; idem, "The Native Tribes of British East Africa," *Journal of the Royal African Society* 19 (1919/20): 285-94; idem, "WaNyika," *Encyclopedia of Religion and Ethics* 9 (1917): 424-27; Arthur Champion, *The Agiryama of Kenya*, ed. John Middleton (London, 1967); A. H. J. Prins, *The Coastal Tribes of the North-Eastern Bantu* (London, 1952)—this work discusses the Mijikenda generally as the Nyika, making it hard to identify the political, economic, and social systems of the Giriama; and David Parkin, "Medicines and Men of Influence," *Man* 3 (1968): 425-39; idem, "Politics of Ritual Syncretism: Islam among the Non-Muslim Giriama of Kenya," *Africa* 40:3 (1970): 218-33. Parkin's full study of Kaloleni was completed as I was finishing my thesis: David Parkin, *Palms, Wine, and Witnesses: Public Spirit and Private Gain in an African Farming Community* (San Francisco, 1972). This excellent work concentrates on Kaloleni Giriama, an unusual group of Giriama who have had access to coconut trees for cash crops.

4. Reginald Coupland, *East Africa and Its Invaders: From the Earliest Times to the Death of Seyyid Said in 1856* (Oxford, 1938); idem, *The Exploitation of East Africa, 1856-1890* (London, 1939).

5. Christine Stephanie Nicholls, *The Swahili Coast: Politics, Diplomacy and Trade on the East African Littoral, 1798-1856* (London, 1971); A. I. Salim, *The Swahili-Speaking Peoples of Kenya's Coast, 1895-1965* (Nairobi, 1973); Fred James Berg, "Mombasa under the Busaidi Sultanate: The City and Its Hinterland in the Nineteenth Century" (Ph.D. dissertation, University of Wisconsin, 1971).

6. My interviews, under the title "Giriama Historical Texts," are on file at the Archives, Dept. of History, University of Nairobi, Kenya.

CHAPTER 1. INTRODUCTION

1. Roland Oliver and J. D. Fage, *A Short History of Africa* (London, 1960), p. 203.

2. T. O. Ranger, "African Reactions to the Imposition of Colonial Rule in East and Central Africa," in *Colonialism in Africa, 1870-1914*, ed. L. H. Gann and Peter Duignan (Cambridge, England, 1969), pp. 293-324.

3. Republic of Kenya, Ministry of Finance and Economic Planning, "Kenya Population Census, 1969" (Nairobi, 1970).

CHAPTER 2. NINETEENTH-CENTURY ADAPTATION, 1800-1890

1. For an extensive discussion of the Giriama political system in the kaya period, see Cynthia Brantley, "Gerontocratic Government: Age-Sets in Pre-Colonial Giriama," *Africa* 48:3 (1978): 248-64.

2. "Giriama Historical Texts" (hereafter GHT): Luganje wa Masha (Vitengeni), 23 December 1970; Pembe wa Bembere (Kayafungo), 31 December 1970; Bakardi Nzovu (Mwabayanyundo), 30 December 1970; Mwinga wa Gunga (Kinarani), 6 May 1971. The information in this chapter comes primarily from GHT and personal observation, but also draws on Arthur Champion, *The Agiryama of Kenya*, pp. 5-9; A. H. J. Prins, *The Coastal Tribes of the North-Eastern Bantu*; and William Walter Augustine FitzGerald, *Travels in the Coastlands of British East Africa and the Islands of Zanzibar and Pemba: Their Agricultural Resources and General Characteristics* (London, 1898; reprinted Folkestone and London, 1970).

3. See Brantley, "Gerontocratic Government," for the components of these three ritual processes.

4. For a full discussion of the precolonial Mijikenda, see T. T. Spear, "The Kaya Complex: A History of the Mijikenda Peoples of the Kenya Coast to 1900" (Ph.D. dissertation, University of Wisconsin, 1974).

5. Ibid., pp. 123-24.

6. John Lamphear, "The Kamba and the Northern Mrima Coast," in *Precolonial African Trade: Essays on Trade in Central and Eastern Africa before 1900*, ed. Richard Gray and David Birmingham (London, 1970), pp. 75-101.

7. Kennell A. Jackson, "An Ethnohistorical Study of the Oral Traditions of the Akamba of Kenya" (Ph.D. dissertation, University of California, Los Angeles, 1972), pp. 57-99; Lamphear, "Kamba," pp. 80-83; Spear, "Kaya Complex," p. 53.

8. Brantley, "Gerontocratic Government"; Spear, "Kaya Complex"; GHT.

9. Charles New, *Life, Wanderings and Labours in Eastern Africa* (London, 1873), pp. 162-63, 195, 199.

10. J. Ludwig Krapf, "Forty Mile Journey to Takaungu, 28 June-4 July 1845" (CMS: CA 5/016/168).

11. Kenneth MacDougall, "Notes on the Decline and Extermination of the Gallas," 31 March 1914. (KNA: DC/MAL/2/3).

12. GHT: Mwinga wa Gunga (Kinarani), 14 May 1971; Pembe wa Bembere (Kayafungo), 30 December 1970.

13. Frederick Cooper, *Plantation Slavery on the East Coast of Africa* (New Haven, Connecticut, 1977), pp. 97-106; Marguerite Helen Ylvisaker, "The Political and Economic Relationship of the Lamu Archipelago to the Adjacent Kenya Coast in the Nineteenth Century" (Ph.D. dissertation, Boston University, 1975).

14. J. M. Gray, *The British in Mombasa, 1824-1826* (London, 1957), pp. 22-25; Cooper, *Plantation Slavery*, pp. 156-57.

15. Gray, *The British in Mombasa*, pp. 22-33; G. S. P. Freeman-Grenville, "The Coast, 1798-1840," in *History of East Africa*, vol. 1, ed. Roland Oliver and Gervase Mathew (Oxford, 1963), pp. 158-61; Cooper, *Plantation Slavery*, pp. 28-32; Abdul Sheriff, "The Rise of a Commercial Empire: An Aspect of the Economic History of Zanzibar, 1770-1873" (Ph.D. dissertation, University of London, 1971).

16. Christine Stephanie Nicholls, *The Swahili Coast*, p. 360.

17. Fred James Berg, "Mombasa under the Busaidi Sultanate," pp. 35-56.

18. Freeman-Grenville, "The Coast," pp. 158-60; Cooper, *Plantation Slavery*, p. 97; Spear, "Kaya Complex," p. 177.

19. Thomas Boteler, *Narrative of a Voyage of Discovery to Africa and Arabia Performed by His Majesty's Ships Levin and Barracouta from 1821 to 1826* (London, 1935), vol. 1, pp. 375-77; Lt. James B. Emery, "Journal of the British Establishment of Mombas and Remarks on Mombas," from his journey on H.M.S. Barracouta, 1824-1826 (PRO: Admiralty Files, 52/3940).

20. J. Krapf, "Journal," 29 December 1848 (CMS: CA 5/016/74).

21. New, *Life, Wanderings and Labours*, pp. 52-54.

22. For a history of Takaungu, see Peter Koffsky, "A History of Takaungu, East Africa, 1830-1896" (Ph.D. dissertation, University of Wisconsin, 1977).

23. GHT: Mwinga wa Gunga (Kinarani), 14 May 1971; Pembre wa Bembere (Kayafungo), 30 December 1970.

24. GHT: Bambare wa Charo (Garashi), 18 December 1970; Kazungu wa Kigande (Mavueni), 30 March 1971.

25. GHT: Mungela wa Kalama (Bamba), 22 December 1970; Luganje wa Masha (Vitengeni), 23 December 1970.

26. GHT: Champion, *Agiryama of Kenya*, p. 36.

27. Charles Guillain, *Documents sur l'histoire, la géographie et le commerce de l'Afrique Orientale* (Paris, 1856), vol. 2, pp. 2, 265-66.

28. Spear, "Kaya Complex," pp. 150-53.

29. Ibid., p. 155.

30. Claims for compensation made by Rashid bin Salim Al-Mazrui in 1908 indicate that, by that time, only a few of his slaves were cultivators: "Slave Compensations" (KNA: CP 1/62/46). I am grateful to Frederick Cooper for this information.

31. GHT; Kenneth MacDougall, "Notes on the History of the Wanyika," Kilifi District Book, compiled 31 March 1914 (KNA: CP 75/46).

32. Krapf, "Journals" (CMS: CA 5/016/74).

33. Cooper, *Plantation Slavery*, p. 83.

34. Koffsky, "Takaungu," pp. 48-49.

35. A. Hardinge to Salisbury, 29 August 1895 (Further Correspondence, East Africa, PRO: FO 403/210); GHT: Mwavuo wa Menza (Marafa), 16 December 1970.

36. R. F. Morton, "Slaves, Fugitives, and Freedmen on the Kenya Coast, 1873-1907" (Ph.D. dissertation, Syracuse University, 1976), p. 265.

37. GHT: Kayafungo Elders (Kayafungo), 31 December 1970.

38. Brantley, "Gerontocratic Government."

39. Koffsky, "Takaungu," pp. 52-62, 67.

40. T. H. R. Cashmore, "Sheikh Mbaruk bin Rashid bin Salim el Mazrui," in *Leadership in Eastern Africa: Six Political Leaders*, ed. Norman Bennett (Boston, 1968), pp. 128-139.

41. Koffsky, "Takaungu," p. 61.

42. Ibid.

43. J. Forbes Munro, *Africa and the International Economy, 1800-1960* (London, 1976), pp. 10-14.

44. Cooper, *Plantation Slavery*, p. 40.

45. Gray, *The British in Mombasa*, p. 25.

46. Ibid., pp. 25-29.

47. Munro, *Africa and the International Economy*, p. 66.

48. Nicholls, *The Swahili Coast*, p. 221.

49. Ibid.

50. Reginald Coupland, *East Africa and Its Invaders*, pp. 87-95; J. M. Gray, "Zanzibar and the Coastal Belt, 1840-1848," in *History of East Africa*, ed. Roland Oliver and Gervase Mathew (Oxford, 1963), vol. 1, pp. 238-39.

51. Frederick Holmwood, "Report," in Prideaux to Derby, 24 November 1874 (PRO: FO 2915, 8); J. Frederick Elton, *Travels and Researches among the Lakes and Mountains of Eastern and Central Africa* (London, 1879), pp. 94, 98, 104.

52. British and Foreign State Papers, 1875-76 (PRO: FO 84, Slave Trade 1816-1892), pp. lxvii, 455-56.

53. Morton, "Slaves," pp. 183-98.

54. GHT: Kayafungo Elders (Kayafungo), 30 December 1970.

55. Morton, "Slaves," pp. 193-94.

56. Roland Oliver, *The Missionary Factor in East Africa* (London, 1952), pp. 4-7.

57. Morton, "Slaves," p. 201.

58. GHT: Mwavuo wa Menza (Marafa), 16 December 1970; Morton, "Slaves"; Koffsky, "Takaungu"; MacDougall, "Notes on the History of the Wanyika."

59. Morton, "Slaves," p. 221.

60. W. E. Taylor, "Papers and Diaries," 8 October 1887 to 18 December 1888 (CMS: Z13).

61. GHT: Kayafungo Elders (Kayafungo), 31 December 1970; MacDougall, "Notes on the History of the Wanyika"; Morton, "Slaves," pp. 193-97.

62. GHT: Mwinga wa Gunga (Kinarani), 14 May 1971; Luganje wa Masha (Vitengeni), 23 December 1970.

63. GHT: Mwavuo wa Menza (Marafa), 16 December 1970.

CHAPTER 3. SABAKI RIVER PROSPERITY, 1890-1900

1. Frederick Cooper, *Plantation Slavery on the East Coast of Africa*, chap. 3.

2. Ibid., pp. 81, 88.

3. Esmond Bradley Martin, *The History of Malindi: A Geographical Analysis of an East African Coastal Town from the Portuguese Period to the Present* (Nairobi, 1973), p. 66.

4. Cooper, *Plantation Slavery*, pp. 85, 88, 89.

5. Martin, *History of Malindi*, p. 66.

6. See Helge Kjekshus, *Ecology Control and Economic Development in East African History: The Case of Tanganyika, 1850-1950* (London, 1977).

7. Arthur Champion, "History of the Wagiryama," Rabai, n.d. (KNA: PRB/KFI/13).

8. See Parliamentary Debates, 4th Series, Vol. 30, col. 699, 14 February 1895. (PRO: FO 403, Confidential Prints, 1885-1900).

9. John Flint, "The Wider Background to Partition and Colonial Occupation," in *History of East Africa*, ed. Roland Oliver and Gervase Mathew (Oxford, 1963), vol. 1, pp. 352-90, esp. map on p. 375.

10. Marie de Kiewiet Hemphill, "The British Sphere, 1884-1894," in *History of East Africa*, vol. 1, pp. 391-432.

11. Mackenzie to C. B. Euan Smith, Correspondence, "Slave Trade," 15 November 1888 (PRO: FO 541/28).

12. Hardinge to Kemball, Anti-Slavery Society Papers, 26 November 1896 (CRP: MSS British Empire, 22/65).

13. Frederick Lugard, *The Rise of Our East African Empire* (Edinburgh, 1893), pp. 201-5; J. R. L. MacDonald and R. E. Major, *Soldiering and Surveying in British East Africa, 1891-94* (London, 1897), pp. 141-47.

14. Cooper, *Plantation Slavery*, pp. 132-34.

15. William Walter Augustine FitzGerald, *Travels in the Coastlands of British East Africa and the Islands of Zanzibar and Pemba*, p. 97.

16. Ibid., p. 55.

17. Champion, "History of the Wagiryama."

18. Lugard, *Rise of Empire*, p. 137.

19. FitzGerald, *Travels*, pp. 177-83.

20. Ibid., pp. 182-83.

21. Krapf, "Excursions to the Country of the WaNika Tribe at Rabai and Visit of the WaKamba People at Endila" (CMS: CA 5/016/165).

22. Cynthia Brantley, "Gerontocratic Government."

23. Arthur Champion, *The Agiryama of Kenya*, pp. 3-6; GHT: Kayafungo Elders (Kayafungo), 30 December 1970.

24. Brantley, "Gerontocratic Government."

25. Ibid.

26. T. T. Spear, "The Kaya Complex," p. 101.

27. Brantley, "Gerontocratic Government," is the source for the following discussion of the councillor ritual.

28. Ibid.

29. Hemphill, "British Sphere," p. 430.

30. Flint, "Wider Background," p. 362; "Correspondence with Imperial British East Africa Company re: Revocation of Its Charter," 1895 (PP: C. 7946).

31. Discussion of the Anglo-Mazrui war is based on the following sources: "Report of Sir Arthur Hardinge on the Conditions and Progress of the East African Protectorate from Its Establishment to 20 January 1897" (PP: LX 1898 C. 8683); Kenneth MacDougall, "The Mazrui Rebellion" (KNA: CP 75/46); Malindi District Reports, 1894-1898 (KNA: CP 75/46); "The Mbaruk Rebellion as Seen from Rabai" (KNA: CP 65/4).

32. Hardinge to Kimberley, 25 June 1895, and Hardinge to Salisbury, 6 July 1895 and 17 February 1896, in "Correspondence Respecting the Recent Rebellion" (PP: C. 8274, 7, 11, 63).

33. MacDougall to Pigott, 23 January and 2 and 19 February 1896 (KNA: CP 75/46); Hardinge to Salisbury, 17 and 25 February 1896, in "Correspondence Respecting the Recent Rebellion" (PP: C. 8274, 66-68, 72); MacDougall to Pigott, 15 February 1896 (KNA: CP 75/46).

34. Smith to Pigott, 25 August 1895, and Jones to Pigott, 25 August 1895 (KNA: CP 65/4); Hardinge to Salisbury, 17 February 1896, in "Correspondence Respecting the Recent Rebellion" (PP: C. 8274, 60-61).

35. Hardinge to Salisbury, 17 February 1896, in "Correspondence Respecting the Recent Rebellion."

36. GHT: Mwavuo wa Menza (Marafa), 12 December 1970.

37. W. E. Taylor, *Giriama Vocabulary and Collections*, p. 43.

38. Hardinge, in "Rebellion in East Africa" (PP: C. 8274, 66).

39. MacDougall, "Mazrui Rebellion."

40. Hardinge, in "Rebellion in East Africa."

41. GHT: Mwavuo wa Menza (Marafa), 12 December 1970; James Ponda (Marafa), 12 December 1970.

42. Hardinge, in "Rebellion in East Africa."

43. MacDougall, "Mazrui Rebellion."

44. Ibid.

45. Hardinge, in "Rebellion in East Africa."

46. GHT: Kayafungo Elders (Kayafungo), 30 December 1970.

47. GHT: Mwavuo wa Menza (Marafa), 12 December 1970.

48. Hardinge, in "Rebellion in East Africa."

49. Hardinge to Salisbury, 17 and 19 February, 26 March, 17 and 22 April 1896, in "Correspondence Respecting the Recent Rebellion" (PP: C. 8274, 57-70, 81-82, 94); Kenneth Mac-Dougall, "The Mazrui War," 28 and 30 March and 18 April 1896 (KNA: CP 75/46).

50. GHT: Kayafungo Elders (Kayafungo), 22 December 1970; Mwavuo wa Menza (Marafa), 12 December 1970; MacDougall, "Mazrui Rebellion"; Arthur Champion, "October Report on the Present Condition of the Administration of the Wagiriama and Kindred Wanyika Tribes," 28 October 1913 (KNA: CP 5/336-I).

51. Peter Koffsky, "A History of Takaungu, East Africa," pp. 190-92, esp. table 7, "Indian Compensation Claims."

52. Weaver to Crauford, 23 July 1896 (KNA: CP 75/46).

53. MacDougall to Pigott, 30 March and 18 April 1896 (KNA: CP 75/46); Hardinge, "Report" (PP: LX 1898 C. 8683, 61); Hardinge to H. K. Binns, "Correspondence Respecting the Status of Slavery in East Africa," 9 February 1899 (PP: C. 9502, 14).

54. W. A. F. Platts, Rabai, 1910 (KNA: CP 65/4); Hollis to Crauford, 9 October 1898 (KNA: CP 67/15).

55. MacDougall to Crauford, 3 February 1897 (KNA: CP 75/46); 1896/97 requests for slave returns (KNA: CP 67/14).

56. Hardinge, "Report" (PP: LX 1898 C. 8683, 6, 14, 21); Famine Committee report to Crauford, 4 July 1899 (KNA: CP 90/154).

57. Hardinge, "Report on the Condition and Progress of the Protectorate, to 20th July 1897" (PP: Africa, no. 7, 1897, 26).

58. Martin, *History of Malindi*, p. 74.

59. Salisbury to Hardinge, 16 December 1897, in response to Hardinge to Salisbury, 5 July 1897, in Correspondence, "Abolition of Slavery" (PP: C. 8858, 8, 14, 26).

60. Hardinge to Crauford, "Petition of the People of Takaungu," 1898 (KNA: CP 90/154); "Description of Coastal Province," 1899/1900 (KNA: CP 90/154).

61. "Takaungu Sub-District Population," 1908/09 (KNA: DC/MSA/1/1).

62. Republic of Kenya: Ministry of Finance and Economic Planning, "Kenya Population Census, 1969" (Nairobi, 1970), vol. 1.

63. "African Population of Kenya Colony and Protectorate" (Nairobi, 1950).

64. "Annual Report, Coast Province," 1924 (KNA: CP 2/1043).

65. P.C., "Coast Political Report," 1912 (KNA: DC/MAL/2/1).

66. J. Rebmann, "Journal," 1847-1848 (CMS: CA 5/024/52). J. L. Krapf estimates the total Wanyika population to have been about 50,000 in 1846, but in 1863 Charles New suggested that that figure was rather high: J. L. Krapf, *Travels, Researches and Missionary Labours during an Eighteen Years Residence in Eastern Africa* (London, 1860), p. 159; Charles New, *Life, Wanderings and Labours in Eastern Africa*, pp. 128-29.

67. Visit to Kaya Giriama, 30 December 1970.

68. Republic of Kenya, "Kenya Population Census, 1969," vol. 1.

69. GHT: Kayafungo Elders (Kayafungo), 30 December 1970; Spear, "Kaya Complex," p. 184.

70. GHT: Kayafungo Elders (Kayafungo), 31 December 1970.

CHAPTER 4. BRITAIN AND THE COASTAL ECONOMY, 1900-1912

1. The best account of the establishment of the British colonial economy is in Richard D. Wolff, *The Economics of Capitalism: Britain and Kenya, 1870-1930* (New Haven, Connecticut, 1974), chaps. 3-5. See also M. P. K. Sorrenson, *Origins of European Settlement in Kenya* (Nairobi, 1968); G. H. Mungeam, *British Rule in Kenya, 1895-1912* (Oxford, 1966); Anthony Clayton and Donald C. Savage, *Government and Labour in Kenya, 1895-1963* (London, 1974), chap. 2; and Robert Tignor, *The Colonial Transformation of Kenya: The Kamba, Kikuyu, and Maasai from 1900 to 1939* (Princeton, 1976).

2. See Wolff, *Economics of Capitalism*, chap. 7.

3. Ibid., p. 62.

4. Marjorie Ruth Dilley, *British Policy in Kenya Colony* (2nd ed., London, 1966).

5. Clayton and Savage, *Government and Labour*, chap. 2.

6. "East Africa Protectorate, Native Labour Commission, 1912-1913, Report and Evidence" (Nairobi, 1913).

7. Tignor, *Colonial Transformation of Kenya*, chap. 3.

8. D. A. Low, "British East Africa: The Establishment of British Rule, 1895-1912," in *History of East Africa*, ed. V. Harlow, E. M. Chilver, and A. Smith (Oxford, 1965), vol. 2, p. 47.

9. "Rules under Village Headmen's Ordinance, 1902." Note by Secretary for Native Affairs to Chief Secretary Nairobi, 22 August 1907 (KNA: CP 62/13).

10. Mungeam, *British Rule in Kenya*, p. 211.

11. Ibid., p. 213.

12. Ibid., p. 215.

13. Wolff, *Economics of Capitalism*, p. 74.

14. Ibid., p. 86.

15. "Native Labour Commission, Report."

16. *The Leader of British East Africa*, 13 April 1912.

17. Elspeth Huxley, *White Man's Country* (London, 1952), vol. 1, p. 81.

18. Wolff, *Economics of Capitalism*, p. 136.

19. GHT: Thuva wa Konde and Jefwa wa Muyaya (Hadu), 18 December 1970; Erastus Hare (Sekoke), 22 December 1960; Muganda wa Biria (Ganze), 23 December 1970.

20. Crauford, "Report on the Present Condition of the Administration of the Wagiriama and Kindred Wanyika Tribes," 28 October 1913 (KNA: PRB/KFI/13); J. M. Pearson to P.C., 22

March 1914 (KNA: CP 11/101); S.L. Hinde, "Inspection Report, Malindi District," 4 July 1913 (KNA: CP 64/261).

21. O.F. Watkins, "Takaungu Sub-District Annual Report," 1908/1909 (KNA: DC/MSA/1/1).

22. Arthur Champion, *The Agiryama of Kenya*, p. 50.

23. R.F. Morton, "Slaves, Fugitives, and Freedmen on the Kenya Coast, 1873-1907," pp. 327-28.

24. H.R. Tate, "Malindi District Quarterly Report ending 31 December 1911," 17 January 1912 (KNA: CP 1/37).

25. F.S. Traill, "Annual Report, Nyika District, 1914/15," 18 June 1915 (KNA: CP 16/49).

26. Sheikh Ali bin Salim, assistant liwali, Mombasa, witness no. 69, "Native Labour Commission, Evidence," p. 98.

27. A.D.C. Mangea to P.C., 22 March 1914 (KNA: CP 11/105).

28. A.G. report, 1913-1914, Memorandum on the Coconut Commission (KNA: CP 11/105).

29. "Coast Province Annual Report," 14 January 1902 (KNA: DC/MAL/3/52).

30. I am grateful to Frederick Cooper for this information, which is taken from chapter 5 of his manuscript on "Agriculture on Zanzibar and the Kenya Coast, 1890-1925."

31. F.I. Bretts, "Giriama Labour: Memo," 14 September 1912 (KNA: CP 4/308).

32. A.I. Salim, *The Swahili-Speaking Peoples of Kenya's Coast, 1895-1965*, pp. 104-9.

33. Mungeam, *British Rule in Kenya*, p. 243.

34. Salim, *Swahili-Speaking Peoples*, pp. 114-17.

35. Sorrenson, *Origins of European Settlement*, p. 220.

36. Cooper, "Agriculture," ms. chap. 5, p. 29.

37. Enclosure in Sadler to Elgin, 22 October 1907 (PRO: CO 33/32); Elgin to Sadler, 3 March 1908 (PRO: CO 533/41).

38. Malindi Commission of Inquiry, "Report and Evidence," 22 December 1916 (PRO: CO 533/180). See also map drawn by A.D.C. Malindi, 29 September 1916 (KNA: CP 5/132).

39. The best study is David Miller, "The Failure of European Plantations on the Coast of Kenya to 1914: A Case of Competing Economic Systems," Department of African Studies, Syracuse University, n.d. (mimeo). Note particularly his list of plantations on the coast between 1910 and 1913. I am grateful to John Lonsdale and Frederick Cooper for sharing this source.

40. H.E. Jones, "Native Cotton and Native Cultivation," January 1911 (KNA: CP 21/160); H.R. Tate, "Malindi District Quarterly Report," 17 January 1912 (KNA: CP 1/37); Skene, "Quarterly Report," 9 February 1912 (KNA: CP 1/4); R. Skene to H.R. Montgomery, 7 February 1914 (KNA: CP 63/270); MacDougall to D.C. Malindi, 7 June 1913 (KNA: PRB/KFI/11).

41. Blue Books, British East Africa Protectorate, totals for rubber exports, 1909-1915 (KNA). I am grateful to Frederick Cooper for this reference.

42. Miller "The Failure of European Plantations."

43. "Native Labour Commission, Evidence," pp. 88, 98.

44. D.D. Waller, director of Government Transport, Mombasa, witness no. 66, "Native Labour Commission, Evidence," p. 92.

45. Sheikh Ali bin Salim, assistant liwali of Mombasa, witness no. 69, "Native Labour Commission, Evidence."

46. "Native Labour Commission, Report."

47. Belfield to C.O., 2 March 1914 (PRO: CO 533/133).

48. "Native Labour Commission, Report," p. 325.

49. J.J. Cox, Manager BEAC, witness no. 79, "Native Labour Commission, Evidence."

50. Salim, *Swahili-Speaking Peoples*, p. 133.

51. Blue Books, BEA Protectorate, totals for rubber exports, 1909-1915 (KNA).

52. East Africa Coast Planters Association, "Report of the Proceedings," London, 25 June 1913 (KNA: CP 9/205).

53. GHT: Joshua Gohu wa Uyombo (Mavueni), 2 April 1971.

54. GHT: Mwinga wa Gunga (Kinarani), 4 June 1971; G.H.L. Murray, D.O. Malindi, to J.W.

Tritton, Senior Commissioner Mombasa, 8 August 1901 and 16 December 1901 (KNA: CP 2/1043).

55. GHT: Mwinga wa Gunga (Kinarani), 4 June 1971; and "Mijikenda Historical Texts," collected by T.T. Spear (University of Nairobi, Research Projects Archives), nos. 2, 2/2, 23.

56. Arthur Champion, "Report on the Wanyika covering a period from October 1912 to May 1913 by ADC Giryama," 30 May 1913 (KNA: CP 8/157).

57. For a full discussion of the precolonial Giriama political system, see Cynthia Brantley, "Gerontocratic Government.

58. D.C. Malindi to P.C. Mombasa, 30 December 1908 (KNA: CP 62/13); A.J. MacLean, D.C. Malindi, "Native Criminal Law Procedures and Customs as Found among the WaNyika Tribes," 7 May 1909 (KNA: DC/KFI/3/1).

CHAPTER 5. GIRIAMA OPPOSITION, 1913

1. Anthony Clayton and Donald C. Savage, *Government and Labour in Kenya, 1895-1963*, p. 56.

2. "Native Labour Commission, Report and Evidence"; Clayton and Savage, *Government and Labour*, p. 55.

3. "Native Labour Commission, Report."

4. Clayton and Savage, *Government and Labour*, p. 55.

5. J.E. Jones, letter, witness no. 64, 4 January 1913, "Native Labour Commission, Evidence,"

6. East Africa Protectorate, "Debates," as cited in Clayton and Savage, *Government and Labour*, p. 80 n. 129.

7. S.L. Hinde, D.C. Mombasa, 30 June 1909, to H.R. Tate, D.C. Malindi, 20 July 1909 (KNA: CP 65/4).

8. See D.A. Low, "British East Africa: The Establishment of British Rule, 1895-1912," in *History of East Africa*, ed. V. Harlow and E.M. Chilver (Oxford, 1965), vol. 2, pp. 1-56.

9. "Native Labour Commission, Evidence," pp. 85-87.

10. G.H. Mungeam, *British Rule in Kenya*, p. 216.

11. "Instructions to New A.D.C. Giryama," 24 December 1912 (KNA: CP 6/425).

12. H.W. Montgomery, "Attitudes of the Wanyika," 4 June 1914 (KNA: CP 5/336-I); A.M. Champion, "Report on the Present Political Situation in Giriama and the Attitude of the Natives towards the General Order to Vacate the North Bank of the Sabaki," 29 April 1914 (KNA: CP 5/336-I).

13. "Instructions to New A.D.C. Giriama," 24 December 1912.

14. H.R. Tate to C.W. Hobley, 27 December 1912 (KNA: CP 6/425).

15. GHT: Mwavuo wa Menza (Marafa), 12 December 1970; Pembe wa Bembere (Kayafungo), 31 December 1970.

16. C.W. Hobley, "Giriama District Report on Political Situation and Evidence," Mombasa, 19 November 1913 (KNA: CP 5/336-I).

17. Cynthia Brantley, "Gerontocratic Government."

18. Arthur M. Champion, "October Report on the Present Condition of the WaGiriama," October 1913 (KNA: CP 5/336-I).

19. Ibid.

20. Ibid.

21. A.M. Champion, "Report on the Wanyika Covering a Period from October 1912 to May 1913 by A.D.C. Giriama," 30 May 1913 (KNA: CP 8/157); "Notes from Baraza at Biryaa, 11 November through 13 November, 1913," 14 November 1913 (KNA: CP 5/336-I).

22. Champion, "October Report."

23. F.S. Traill, "Annual Report, Nyika District, April 1, 1914-March 31, 1915," 16 June 1915 (KNA: CP 16/49).

24. Ibid.; W.F.P. Kelley, compiler, Kilifi District Gazetteer, "Chronological Conspectus," 1960 (a copy of this was kindly lent to me by Dr. J. Milton-Thompson of Kaloleni).

25. Champion, "October Report,"

26. W.S. Marchant, "Kilifi Diary," 1925 (KNA: DC/KFI/4/1).

27. Champion, "October Report."

28. Ibid.

29. Tate to Hobley, 6 June 1913 (KNA: CP 8/157).

30. A.T. Matson, personal correspondence and conversation.

31. Hobley, "1913 Tour," 29 July 1913 (KNA: DC/MAL/2/1).

32. Ibid.

33. "Native Labour Commission, Evidence," pp. 86-87.

34. Hobley, "1913 Tour."

35. Champion to Skene, 17 August 1913, Skene to Hobley, 19 August 1913 (KNA: CP 5/336-I); GHT: Kadzumbi wa Ngari (Chakama), 15 December 1970.

36. Champion to Hobley, 8 October 1913 (KNA: CP 5/336-I); GHT: Karisa wa Gona (Chakama,) 15 December 1970.

37. Hobley to Chief Secretary Nairobi, 26 August 1913 (KNA: CP 5/336-I).

38. Skene to Hobley, 3 November 1913 (KNA: CP 5/336-I); GHT: Kadzumbi wa Ngari (Chakama), 15 December 1970.

39. Telegram, Hobley to Chief Secretary Nairobi, 28 August 1913, Skene to Hobley, 31 October 1913 and 31 November 1913 (KNA: CP 5/336-I); GHT: Mwavuo wa Menza (Marafa), 16 December 1970.

40. Champion, "October Report."

41. D.C. Malindi to D.C. Mombasa, 31 October 1913 (KNA: CP 5/336-I); GHT: Joshua Gohu wa Uyombo (Mavueni), 15 February 1971.

42. These grievances are evident from several sources: Wanje wa Mwadorikola, "Statement," 15 November 1913, Nziji wa Yaa, "Statement," 14 November 1913, Mekatalili, "Statement," 14 November 1913 (KNA: CP 9/403); "Women's Statement," 14 October 1913 (KNA: CP 5/336-I); "Notes from Baraza at Biryaa," 14 November 1913 (KNA: CP 5/336-I); "Elders' Statement at Biryaa Baraza," 11 November 1913 (KNA: CP 5/336-I); Ziro wa Luganje, "Statement," 4 October 1913, Kombi wa Yeri, "Statement," 7 October 1913 (KNA: CP 5/336-I); "Notes from Baraza outside *Kaya Giriama*," 14 November 1913 (KNA: CP 5/336-I); GHT: Karezi wa Mwasada (Bamba), 3 March 1971.

43. Kadidi wa Bembere, "Statement made at the *Baraza* at Biryaa," 12 November 1913 (KNA: CP 5/336-I).

44. GHT: Kayafungo Elders (Kayafungo), 31 December 1970; Katoi wa Kiti (Kajiweni), 2 April 1971; Mwinga wa Gunga (Kinarani), 14 June 1971; Mwangoto wa Kalama (Mwembekati) 16 June 1971.

45. Ziro wa Luganje, "Second Statement," 15 November 1913, Kombi wa Yeri, "Statement," 7 October 1913 (KNA: CP 5/336-I); GHT: Katoi wa Kiti (Kajiweni), 2 April 1971; Mwinga wa Gunga (Kinarani), 6 April 1971 and 14 June 1971; Hawe Charo (Takaungu), 2 April 1971; Kaleso wa Ruwa wa Jumwa (Malemweni), 8 December 1970; Hawe Karisa Nyevu Makarye (Jilore), 15 December 1970; Champion, "October Report."

46. GHT: Mulanda wa Wanje (Msabaha), 5 May 1971; Kibogo wa Masha (Kajiweni), 2 April 1971; "Notes from Baraza at Biryaa," 14 November 1913; Cynthia Brantley, "An Historical Perspective of the Giriama and Witchcraft Control," *Africa* 49:3 (1979): 112-133.

47. C.. Hobley, *Kenya: From Chartered Company to Crown Colony* (2nd ed., London, 1970), p. 197; Champion, "October Report"; Charles Dundas, *African Crossroads* (London, 1955), p. 77. Most Giriama referred to "witch medicine" rather than calling her a witch; see statements by Ziro wa Luganje, 4 October 1913, and Kombi wa Yeri, 7 October 1913, in KNA: CP 5/336-I; GHT: Nzaro wa Chai (Garashi), 18 December 1970, Bambare wa Charo (Garashi), 18 December 1970; Mekatalili, "Statement," 14 November 1913. Mekatalili was apparently ineligible to issue any of the oaths herself: Kadidi wa Bembere, "Statement Made at the *Baraza* at Biryaa," 12 November 1913 (KNA: CP 5/336-I).

48. Cf. Champion, "October Report."

49. Wanje wa Mwadorikola, "Statement," 15 November 1913; "Statement Made by the Woman Menyazi wa Menza, alias Katalili Before Me [Champion] at Her Own Request at Garashi, 17 October 1913" (KNA: CP 5/336-I); Mekatalili, "Statement," 14 November 1913.

50. Champion had collected only 900 rupees, with 30,000 to be collected in the following three months: Champion, "October Report." Quote is from Mkowa wa Gobwe, "Statement Made in the Presence of Champion at Garashi," 23 September 1913 (KNA: CP 5/336-I).

51. Mkowa wa Gobwe to Champion, 29 September 1913 (KNA: CP 5/336-I).

52. Later Kombi was to serve as a witness to Mekatalili's "sedition"; Kombi wa Yeri, "Statement," 7 October 1913; Champion, "October Report"; Mkowa wa Gobwe, "Second Statement," 15 November 1913 (KNA: CP 5/336-I); Ziro wa Luganje, "Statement," 4 October 1913; "Deposition of Deportation of Mekatalili and Wanje," 23 November 1913 (KNA: CP 9/403).

53. Mekatalili, "Statement," 17 October 1913.

54. Champion, "October Report."

55. Ibid.

CHAPTER 6. BRITISH PUNISHMENT, 1913-1914

1. East Africa Coast Planters Association, "Report of the Proceedings," 25 June 1913 (KNA: CP 9/205).

2. Letter from the East Africa Coast Planters Association to the Secretary of State for the Colonies, 11 August 1913 (KNA: CP 9/292).

3. Ibid.

4. Ibid.

5. "Native Labour Commission, Report," p. 322.

6. Ibid., p. 324.

7. Ibid., p. 321.

8. Ibid.

9. Ibid., pp. 334, 328.

10. Arthur Champion, "October Report."

11. Ibid.; Hobley, "Giriama District Report on Political Situation and Evidence," Mombasa, 19 November 1913 (KNA: CP 5/336-I).

12. W.M. Logan, A.D.C. Takaungu, to P.C. Mombasa, 31 October 1913 and 4 November 1913 (KNA: CP 5/336-I).

13. Report of the Rev. Harris as told to Skene, 29 October 1913, Skene to Hobley, 3 November 1913 (KNA: CP 5/226-I).

14. Report of the Rev. Harris, 29 October 1913.

15. Hobley, "Report on Political Situation"; "Statement of Some Giriama Elders before Hobley at Waa (Mombasa)," 4 November 1913 (KNA: CP 5/336-I).

16. Hobley, "Report on Political Situation."

17. "Statement at Waa," 4 November 1913.

18. Hobley, "Report on Political Situation."

19. "Notes from Baraza at Biryaa," 14 November 1913 (KNA: CP 5/336-I).

20. Hobley, "Report on Political Situation."

21. Ibid.; "Notes from Baraza at Biryaa."

22. "Notes from Baraza at Biryaa"; "Women's Statement," 4 October 1913 (KNA: CP 5/336-I).

23. GHT: Mwinga wa Gunga (Kinarani), 14 June 1971; H.R. Montgomery, "Oath in Favour of Government," 19 March 1914, S.F. Traill, "Annual Report, Nyika District, 1 April 1914-31 March 1915," 16 June 1915.

24. "Notes from Baraza at Biryaa"; Nziji wa Yaa, "Statement," 14 November 1913.

25. Hobley, "Notes from Baraza at Biryaa"; Hobley to J.M. Pearson, A.D.C. Rabai, 25 November 1913 (KNA: CP 5/336-I).

26. Pearson to Hobley, 1 December 1913 (KNA: CP 5/336-I).

27. G.E. Spencer, D.C. Kisumu, to Hobley, 18 December 1913 (KNA: CP 9/403).

28. C.W. Hobley, Kenya, pp. 163, 165.

29. Hobley, "Report on Political Situation."

30. Kitu wa Sirya, "Statement," 7 October 1913 (KNA: CP 5/336-I).

31. Hobley to A.D.C. Rabai, 25 December 1913 (KNA: CP 5/336-I).

32. Ibid.

33. Hobley, "Report on Political Situation."

34. Hobley, "Notes from Baraza at Biryaa."

35. "Minute by the Governor Forwarded to P.C. 2 Jan. 1914," 25 November 1913 (KNA: CP 5/336-I).

36. C.W. Hobley, "Giriama: Plan of Campaign," 21 November 1913 (KNA: CP 5/336-I).

37. Skene to Hobley, "Giriama Reserve—Area to be Evacuated by Giriama," 4 December 1913 (KNA: CP 5/336-I).

38. Skene to Hobley, 4 December 1913.

39. C.W. Hobley, "Seyyidie Province Annual Report, 1 August 1913," 1912-1913 (KNA: CP 8/157).

40. D.C. Malindi to P.C. Mombasa, 6 June 1913 (KNA: CP 8/157).

41. P.C. Mombasa to Chief Secretary Nairobi, 5 May 1913 (KNA: CP 9/925).

42. The letter of complaint was sent to Montgomery through liwali Said bin Abdulla Bakswein. The translation is enclosed in Montgomery to Hobley, 16 May 1914 (KNA: CP 5/336-II).

43. Hobley, "1913 Tour," 29 July 1913.

44. Hobley to Montgomery, 27 May 1914 (KNA: CP 5/336-II).

45. "Memo from Arthur Champion," 11 February 1914 (KNA: CP 5/336-II).

46. Pearson to Hobley, 9 December 1913 (KNA: CP 5/336-II).

47. Ibid.

48. Hobley to Pearson, 17 December 1913 (KNA: CP 5/336-II).

49. Montgomery, "Native Affairs, Giriama," 27 February 1914, Montgomery, "Report on Tour in Giriama," 19 March (KNA: CP 5/336-I); Hobley to Chief Secretary Nairobi, 1 April 1914 (KNA: CP 5/336-II).

50. Montgomery, "Report on Tour," 19 March 1914; Hobley to Chief Secretary Nairobi, 1 March 1914 (KNA: CP 5/336-II).

51. J.M. Pearson, "Account of the Taking of an Oath of the Hyaena by the Giriama Elders of Godoma and Gallana . . .," 12 March 1914 (KNA: CP 5/336-II).

52. C.W. Hobley, "The Giriama Oath," Mombasa, 22 November 1913 (C.W. Hobley Collection, Royal Anthropological Institute of Great Britain and Ireland, London, MS 27).

53. Montgomery, "Report on Tour," 19 March 1914.

54. Champion, "Attitude of Wanyika," reported by Montgomery to Mombasa, 2 July 1914 (KNA: DC/KFI/13).

55. Champion to Montgomery, 2 July 1914, Montgomery to Hemsted, 4 July 1914, Champion, Safari Report, n.d. (KNA: CP 5/336-II).

56. Hazleriggs to Hemsted, 4 July 1914, Hemsted to Chief Secretary Nairobi, 22 July 1914, and Hemsted to Champion 28 July 1914 (KNA: CP 5/336-II).

57. Champion, "Attitude of Wanyika."

58. Ibid.

59. Ibid.

60. Ibid.

61. I am grateful to John Lonsdale, who allowed me to see a paper in preparation (J.M. Lonsdale, "The Politics of Conquest: The British in Western Kenya, 1894-1908," *Historical Journal* 20:4 [1977]: 841-70), and to A.T. Matson for personal conversation confirming this material.

62. Lonsdale, "Politics of Conquest"; A.D.C. Rabai to P.C. Mombasa, "Deportation of the Prisoners Katalili and Wanje," 7 August 1914 (KNA: CP 9/403); "Destruction of *Kaya Giriama*," 4 August 1914 (KNA: DC/KFI/13).

CHAPTER 7. REBELLION, 1914

1. Champion, "Confidential Report," 29 July 1914 (KNA: DC/KFI/13); "Destruction of Kaya Giriama," 4 August 1914; GHT: Mwinga wa Gunga (Kinarani), 14 June 1971.

2. "Destruction of *Kaya Giriama*," 4 August 1914.

3. GHT: Joseph Denge (Kibwabwani), 17 June 1971; Mwinga wa Gunga (Kinarani), 15 June 1971; Ziro wa Mae (Madzimbani), 28 December 1970.

4. Champion, "Summary of Incidents on Outbreak of Giriama Rising," n.d. (KNA: CP 5/336-III).

5. GHT: Mwinga wa Gunga (Kinarani), 14 June 1970.

6. Statement made by Giriama interpreter Jonathan Wanje wa Mugaya, 23 July 1915 (KNA: CP 16/38).

7. S. F. Traill, "Annual Report, Nyika District," 1 April 1914 to 31 March 1915 (KNA: CP 16/49).

8. Sheikh Fathili bin Omar, former Mudir of Arabuko, reported this matter: Montgomery to Hemsted, 28 August 1914 (KNA: CP 5/336-IV).

9. Champion, "Summary of Incidents."

10. Hemsted to Governor, 2 February 1915 (KNA: CP 5/336-V).

11. Champion to D.C. Rabai, 17 August 1914 (KNA: CP 5/336-III).

12. Champion, "Summary of Incidents."

13. Ibid.

14. 17 August 1914 (KNA: CP 5/336-III).

15. L. Henry, manager of Sekoke Plantations, to Vidal, A.D.C. Takaungu, 22 August 1914, notes from Hemsted's notebook, 24 August 1914 (KNA: CP 5/336-III).

16. Champion, "Summary of Incidents"; idem, "Report on Armed Disturbance at Vitengeni," 21 August 1914 (KNA: CP 5/336-III).

17. Florence Deed, entries in "Log Book of the Church Missionary Society, Kaloleni, Aug. 1914-Oct. 1939," between 5 August and 10 September 1914. I am most grateful to Dr. and Mrs. D. Milton-Thompson of Kaloleni, who kindly lent me this manuscript for a few days.

18. GHT: Mwinga wa Gunga (Kinarani), 15 June 1971.

19. Ibid.; Kayafungo Elders (Kayafungo), 29 December 1970.

20. GHT: Cyril Kenya (Maluwani), 14 June 1971; Willie Katifu Fondo (Vishakani), 17 June 1971; Paul Nyamwi (Vishakani), 17 June 1971; Joseph Denge (Kibwabwani), 17 June 1971.

21. GHT: Mwinga wa Gunga (Kinarani), 15 June 1971.

22. GHT: Muganda wa Biria (Ganze), 23 December 1970; Karezi wa Mwasada (Bamba), 22 December 1970.

23. Telegrams, 20 August 1914 and 21 August 1914 (KNA: CP 5/336-III).

24. Hemsted to Governor, code telegram, 23 August 1914 (KNA: CP 5/336-III).

25. Champion, "Report on Armed Disturbance."

26. Dundas to A.D.C. Takaungu, telegram (KNA: CP 5/336-IV). The inked copy appears to indicate that it was received on 18 August 1914, but such an early date is impossible; it is more likely that it arrived on 23 August 1914.

27. Dundas to Hemsted, 24 August 1914 (KNA: CP 5/336-III).

28. Champion, "Attack on Government Station," 23 August 1914, Dundas to Hemsted, 24 August 1914 (KNA: CP 5/336-III); Dundas to Hemsted, 5 September 1914 (KNA: CP 5/336-IV).

29. Montgomery to Hemsted, 25 August 1914 (KNA: CP 5/336-III); Acting Chief Secretary Nairobi to A.D.C. Mombasa, telegram, 7 September 1914 (KNA: CP 5/336-IV).

30. Charles Dundas, "Report on the Giriama Rising," 25 October 1914 (KNA: CP 5/336-IV); Major Hawthorne to Commander, Troops in BEA and Uganda, 31 August 1914 (KNA: CP 5/336-IV).

31. Dundas to Hemsted, 26 August 1941 (KNA: CP 5/336-IV).

32. Hawthorne to Commander, Troops in BEA and Uganda, 31 August 1914 (KNA: CP 5/336-IV).

33. Ibid.

34. Dundas to Hemsted, 4 September 1914 (KNA: CP 5/336-IV).

35. GHT: Pembe wa Bembere (Kayafungo), 31 December 1970; Mwinga wa Gunga (Kinarani), 5 June 1971.

36. Dundas to Hemsted, 11 September 1914 (KNA: CP 12/222).

37. Montgomery to Hemsted, 13 September 1914 (KNA: CP 5/336-IV).

38. G.H.L. Murray to Tritton, 11 August 1901 (KNA: CP 2/1043).

39. Champion, "Memorandum on the Labour Supply and the Wa Giriama," Political Record Book, Malindi, n.d. (included in correspondence for 2 December 1914) (KNA: KFI/72/6/13); GHT: Wilson Kajaro (Jilore), 15 December 1970.

40. Dundas (Mangea) to Hemsted, 29 August 1914, Dundas to Acting P.C. Mombasa, 4 September 1914, Montgomery (Malindi) to Hemsted, 5 September 1914 (KNA: CP 5/336).

41. Dundas, "Report on the Giriama Rising," 25 October 1914; R. Skene, D.C. Malindi, "Report on Removal of Wanyika," 22 April 1915 (KNA: MAL/20/128).

42. Dundas (Mangea) to Hemsted, 4 September 1914 (KNA: CP 5/336-IV).

43. H.J. Lascelles, "Annual Report for Rabai," 29 May 1915 (KNA: CP 14/49).

44. GHT: Mwinga wa Gunga (Kinarani), 15 June 1971.

45. Ibid.; Lascelles (Rabai) to Hemsted, 23 September 1914 (KNA: CP 12/222).

46. MacDougall (Malindi) to Hemsted, 29 August 1914 (KNA: CP 5/336-IV).

47. Montgomery (Malindi) to Dundas, 28 September 1914, Dundas to Hemsted, 27 September 1914 (KNA: CP 12/222).

48. Hemsted to Chief Secretary Nairobi, 30 September 1914 (KNA: CP 5/336-IV).

49. Ibid.

50. Lascelles (Rabai) to Hemsted, 3 October 1914 (KNA: CP 12/222); GHT: Mwinga wa Gunga (Kinarani), 14 June 1971; Anderson Kenga (Vitengeni), 23 December 1970.

51. Lascelles to Hemsted, 3 October 1914; GHT: Mwinga wa Gunga (Kinarani), 14 June 1971.

52. R.M. Rose, Captain 3rd KAR, to Officer in Charge of Troops Mombasa, from Jilore, 16 October 1914 (KNA: CP 5/336-IV).

53. Dundas, "Memorandum," n.d. (KNA: CP 5/336-IV).

54. S.F. Traill, "Annual Report, Nyika District, 1 April 1914-31 March 1915," 16 June 1915.

55. Champion to Traill, D.C. Nyika, 19 November 1914 (KNA: CP 5/336-IV); Traill to Hobley, 24 November 1914 (KNA: CP 5/336-IV).

56. Traill (Jilore) to Hemsted, 19 November 1914 (KNA: CP 5/336-IV).

57. Champion, "Memorandum," 8 October 1914 (KNA: CP 5/336-IV).

58. Traill, "Annual Report, Nyika District," 16 June 1915; Pearson, "Giriama Report," 2 January 1916 (KNA: CP 21/163).

59. Hemsted, "Memorandum Regarding Punitive Measures in Giriama," 21 December 1914 (KNA: CP 5/336-V).

CHAPTER 8. AFTERMATH, 1915-1920

1. Traill to Hobley, 1 January 1915 (KNA: CP 12/222).

2. S.F. Traill, "Annual Report, Nyika District," 16 June 1915.

3. Traill (Jilore) to Hobley, 10 May 1915, Hobley to Traill, 21 May 1915 (KNA: CP 16/38).

4. Traill, "Annual Report, Nyika District," 16 June 1915.

5. Hobley, "Tour of Giriama—Inspection Report," 19 July 1915, and "Notes on P.C.'s Meeting at Jilore Camp," 27 June 1915 (KNA: CP 17/62).

6. Traill to Hobley, 10 February 1915 and 20 February 1915, Beech, D.C. Malindi, to Traill, 22 February 1915, W.J. Monson (for the Chief Secretary Nairobi) to Hobley, 6 March 1915 (KNA: CP 5/336-V).

7. Traill to Hobley, 8 August 1915 and 27 August 1915 (KNA: CP 17/62).

8. Traill to Hobley, 18 September 1915, Traill, "Giriama Affairs," 25 October 1915 (KNA: CP 16/38).

9. Traill, "Giriama Affairs," 25 October 1915.

10. Ibid.

11. Ibid.

12. "Deportation of Makiziro Giriama, including Statement Made by Tsumu wa Iha, Government Headman," 16 March 1915, Traill to Hobley, 2 October 1915, Pearson (Jilore) to Hobley, 12 November 1915, Lt. J.W. Barth to Chief Secretary Nairobi, 13 September 1915 (KNA: CP 19/97).

13. Traill to Hobley, 30 August 1915 (KNA: CP 16/68).

14. Traill, "Handing-Over Report," 12 November 1915 (KNA: CP 20/136).

15. Traill, "Giriama Affairs," 25 October 1915.

16. Traill, "Handing-Over Report," 12 November 1915.

17. J. M. Pearson (Jilore), "Collection of Giriama Fine," 25 November 1915 (KNA: CP 21/132).

18. "Crown Land Ordinance," Section 54, 4 March 1916 (EAP: OG).

19. Traill, "Annual Report, Nyika District," 16 June 1915; Pearson, "Giriama Report," 2 January 1916 (KNA: CP 21/163).

20. Hobley, "Tour in Giriama," 14 September 1916 (KNA: DC/MAL/2/1).

21. Ibid.

22. Traill, "Annual Report, Nyika District," 16 June 1915.

23. Hobley, "Tour in Giriama," 14 September 1916.

24. Hobley to D.C. Nyika, 17 January 1916 (KNA: HOR/MSA/20/136).

25. Pearson, "Collection of Giriama Fine," 25 November 1915.

26. W. F. P. Kelley, compiler, Kilifi District Gazetteer, "Chronological Conspectus," 1960. A copy of this was kindly lent to the author by Dr. J. Milton-Thompson of Kaloleni.

27. "Malindi Commission of Inquiry, Report and Evidence"; and letter from A. G. Bowring, 17 April 1917 (PRO: CO 533/180).

28. Ibid.

29. A.G.'s file 25/17, des. 23 April 1917 para. 5, as cited in T. H. R. Cashmore, "Studies in District Administration in the East Africa Protectorate, 1895-1918" (Ph.D. dissertation, Cambridge University, 1965), p. 240.

30. "Malindi Commission of Inquiry, Report and Evidence," and letter from A. G. Bowring, 17 April 1917.

31. GHT: Mwavuo wa Menza (Marafa), 16 December 1970.

32. "Malindi Commission of Inquiry, Report and Evidence."

33. Hobley, "1913 Tour," 29 July 1913; Champion, "October Report"; Skene, "Giriama Reserve: Western Boundary North of the Sabaki: Area to be Evacuated by Giriama," 4 December 1913 (KNA: CP 2/154); Governor to Secretary of State for the Colonies, 4 May 1914 (KNA: CP 5/336-I).

34. Governor to Secretary of State for the Colonies, 4 May 1914.

35. C. C. Bowring, A.G., to Walter Long, Secretary of State for the Colonies, 3 January 1917 (KNA: DC/KFI/1/1).

36. Champion, "History"; MacDougall, "Galla" (KNA: CP 5/336-I).

37. James Weaver, A.D.C. Malindi, to C. H. Crauford, Acting Commissioner Mombasa, "Malindi Inward, 1895-1898," 23 July 1916 (KNA: CP 75/46).

38. Ibid.

39. Hobley, "Notes on Nyika Land and Development," 15 November 1917 (KNA: DC/MAL/72/6).

40. "Malindi Commission of Inquiry, Report and Evidence."

41. See the summary in Bowring to Long, 3 January 1917 (KNA: DC/KFI/13).

42. Hobley to Chief Secretary, Nairobi, 15 November 1917 (KNA: DC/MAL/2/1); Cashmore, "Studies in District Administration," pp. 244-45.

43. Bowring to Long, 3 January 1917.

44. "Malindi District Annual Report," 1917-1918 (KNA: DC/KFI/1/1).

45. Vol. XXI, O + R, Notice 169, 20 May 1919.

46. R. F. Palethorpe, "Handing-Over Report," January 1917 (KNA: CP 21/168).

47. Cynthia Brantley, "Gerontocratic Government."

48. R. W. Lambert, "Nyika District Annual Report, Rabai," 27 June 1919 (KNA: CP 16/49).

49. GHT: Kayafungo Elders (Kayafungo), 30 December 1970.

50. Hobley to Principal Medical Officer Nairobi, 28 June 1919 (KNA: CP 21/161).

51. Champion, "October Report."

52. Champion, "Labour Supply and the WaGiryama," n.d. (from its contents it must have been written after June 1914, and probably after the August 1914 rising) (KNA: DC/KFI/13);

Hobley, "Tour in North Giriama," 24 September 1916 (KNA: DC/MAL/2/1); R.W. Lambert, "Annual Report, 1924," n.d. (KNA: DC/MAL/1/2); "Annual Report, 1925" (KNA: CP 2/1043); Pearson, "Handing-Over Report," 10 August 1914 (KNA: CP 4/375); GHT: Kayafungo Elders (Kayafungo), 31 December 1970.

    53. Traill, "Handing-Over Report," 12 November 1915.

    54. C.W. Hobley, *Kenya*, p. 165.

    55. L.A. Weaving, "Annual Report, 1926" (KNA: DC/KFI/1/1).

    56. E.St.J. Tisdall, "Annual Report, 1926" (KNA: DC/KFI/1/1).

    57. Cashmore, "Studies in District Administration," p. 247.

CHAPTER 9. CONCLUSIONS

    1. A number of studies on dependency theory are applicable here: André Gunder Frank, "The Development of Underdevelopment," *Latin America: Underdevelopment or Revolution* (New York, 1969), chap. 1; André Gunder Frank and Dale Johnson, eds., *Dependency and Underdevelopment* (New York, 1972); Roger Owen and Bob Sutcliffe, eds., *Studies in the Theory of Imperialism* (London, 1972); Henry Bernstein, ed., *Underdevelopment and Development* (Harmondsworth, 1973); Samir Amin, "Underdevelopment and Dependence in Black Africa—Origins and Contemporary Forms," *Journal of Modern African Studies* 10:4 (1972): 503-24; Giovanni Arrighi and John S. Saul, *The Political Economy of Africa* (New York, 1973). For work on the analysis of class formation, see Claude Meillassoux, "From Reproduction to Production: A Marxist Approach to Economic Anthropology," *Economy and Society* 1 (1972): 93-105; Catherine Coquery-Vidrovitch, "Research on an African Mode of Production," in *Perspectives on the African Past*, ed. Martin Klein and G. Wesley Johnson (Boston, 1972), pp. 33-52; Emmanuel Terray, *Marxism and Primitive Societies*, trans. Mary Klopper (New York, 1972); idem, "Long Distance Exchange and the Formation of the State: The Case of the Abron Kingdom of Gyaman," *Economy and Society* 3 (1974): 315-45; Maurice Godelier, "Modes of Production, Kinship and Demographic Structure," in *Marxist Analysis and Social Anthropology*, ed. Maurice Bloch (London, 1975), pp. 3-29.

    2. E.A. Alpers, *Ivory and Slaves: Changing Patterns of International Trade in East Central Africa to the Later Nineteenth Century* (Berkeley and Los Angeles, 1975), esp. p. 267.

    3. For western Kenya see J.M. Lonsdale, "The Politics of Conquest." For the Nandi in particular, see A.T. Matson, *Nandi Resistance to British Rule, 1890-1906* (Nairobi, 1972); idem, *The Nandi Campaign against the British, 1895-1906*, vol. 1 (Transafrica Historical Papers no. 1, Nairobi, 1974) (vol. 2 is forthcoming); Alice Gold, "The 'Intransigent,' 'Truculent' Nandi and the *Chumbek* Who Stayed: Background to the Nandi Resistance to British Rule, 1895-1906" (African Studies Association Conference, Houston, Texas, November 1977) (mimeo.). For the Gusii see Robert Mead Maxon, "British Rule in Gusiiland, 1907-1963" (Ph.D. thesis, Syracuse University, 1971). For British-Maasai relations see Richard Waller, "The Maasai and the British, 1895-1905: The Origins of an Alliance," *Journal of African History* 17:4 (1976): 529-53. For Kikuyu response see Godfrey Muriuki, *A History of the Kikuyu, 1500-1900* (London, 1974), chap. 6.

    4. Lonsdale, "Politics of Conquest," pp. 858-59, 869-70.

    5. Gold, "The 'Intransigent,' 'Truculent' Nandi"; Matson, *Nandi Campaign*.

    6. "Native Labour Commission, Report and Evidence."

Bibliography

I. PRIMARY SOURCES AND UNPUBLISHED WORKS

A. Oral Sources: Giriama Historical Texts (GHT). Interviews collected by Cynthia Brantley Smith, October 1970 to June 1971, and by Victor Gona Kazungu, July/August 1971. Transcripts of these oral interviews are deposited in the History Department Archives, University of Nairobi, Kenya, and are also in the possession of the author. The informants who provided the basis for these interviews, with their nearest village location, are listed below.

A second stage of oral investigation, with the purpose of clarifying answers to specific questions, was conducted in five phases through informal interviews throughout Giriamaland.

An asterisk indicates an interview conducted by Victor Gona Kazungu; (f) indicates that the informant is female. All informants are Giriama, unless otherwise noted; all Giriama clans are represented.

Anderson Kenga, Vitengeni
Bakardi Nzovu, Mwabayanyundo
Bambare wa Charo, Garashi
Baya wa Toya, Bungale
*Biria wa Masha, Kaloleni
Boniface Kahindi wa Konde, Kanyumbani
Chakuku wa Nguyete (Chonyi), Mwembekati
Charo wa Maita, Bungale
Chembe wa Kajoro, Jilore
Cyril Kenga, Maluwani
Danieli Mwavuo Thoya, Mikomani
Daniel Ngumbao, Jilore
Erastus Hare, Sekoke
Gona wa Nguma, Jilore
Gona wa Rimba, Bungale
Hawe Charo (Kahonzi wa Kiti) (f), Takaungu
Hawe Chengo (f), Jilore
Hawedema Nzingo Mashe (Kambe) (f), Mikoba Chenda
Hawe Karisa Nyevu Makarye (f), Jilore
*Haweside Kabuche (f), Mwabayanyundo
Hawe Sidi Katsoe (f), Jilore
Ishamael Kenga, Bungale
Ishamael Toya, Jilore
Jambo wa Toloko, Marafa
James Mudhengi, Jilore

James Ponda, Marafa
Jefwa wa Muyaya, Hadu
Joseph Denge, Kibwabwani
Joseph Kalume, Kanamai
Joshua Gohu wa Uyombo, Mavueni
*Kabunda wa Kuchu (f), Mwabayanyundo
Kadu wa Baya (f), Mkomboani
Kadzumbi wa Ngari, Chakama
Kalama wa Nzaro, Mavueni
Kaleso wa Ruwa wa Jumwa (f), Malemweni
Kalume wa Koi, Ganze
Karezi wa Mwasada, Bamba
Karisa Kifudu, Bamba
Karisa wa Gona, Chakama
Karisa wa Mweni, Garashi
Katoi wa Kiti, Kajiweni
Kayafungo Elders, Kayafungo
Kazungu wa Kigande, Mavueni
Kenga wa Hare, Vitengeni
Kenga wa Mwanenge, Mwabayanyundo
Kibogo wa Masha, Kajiweni
Kithi wa Mrimi Charo, Kayafungo
Knazi wa Finga (f), Chakama
Kuronga (f), Mkomboani
Luganje wa Masha, Vitengeni
Luvuno wa Kalama (f) (Chonyi), Maluwani
Maita wa Mweni, Kayafungo
Masha Murumwengu, Kizurini
Masha wa Kaluma, Ganze
Mboga wa Galoa, Kayafungo
Michael Kachaa (Chonyi), Mwembekati
Mole wa Munyaya, Kayafungo
Muganda wa Biria, Ganze
Mukiza wa Birya, Hadu
Mulanda wa Wanje, Msabaha
Mungela wa Kalama, Bamba
Musage wa Magongo, Kayafungo
Mutsunga, Bungale
Mwalimu Hamisi, Vitengeni
Mwamoto wa Nzaro, Kajiweni
Mwangoto wa Kalama (Chonyi), Mwembekati
Mwavuo wa Menza, Marafa
Mwilo wa Simba, Hadu
Mwinga wa Gunga, Kinarani
Ngala wa Pembe, Kayafungo
Nguma wa Kalama, Mutsara wa Mavindi
Nyundo wa Mwamure, Sekoke
Nzaro wa Chai, Garashi
Nzingo Pengu, Mwabayanyundo
Paul Mitsanze, Mwabayanyundo
Paul Nyamwi, Vishakani
Pembe we Bembere, Kayafungo
Rebecca Kadzo (f), Vishakani
Samuel Baya Mose, Kibwabwani

Samuel Jefwa Gumbe, Mikomani
Samuel Ngale, Ganze
Sayo Ngala Mose, Kayafungo
Shadrack Kambi, Jilore
Sidi Ruwa (f), Muleji
Thomas Kalume (Kauma), Nairobi
Thuva wa Kajambo, Kayafungo
Thuva wa Konde, Hadu
Toya wa Iha, Bamba
Tsangwa Ngala, Kinarani
Victor Gona Kazungu, Vipingoni
Willie Katifu Fondo, Vishakani
Wilson Gona Nguma, Malindi
Wilson Kajoro, Jilore
Yaa (Godha) wa Mangi, Kayafungo
Ziro wa Mae, Madzimbani

B. Archival Material
  1. Kenya
     a. Kenya National Archives, Nairobi (KNA)
        Although some provincial records and district records are still available at local
        centers, the major collection is at the National Archives in Nairobi. Giriama and coastal
        material is scattered through files from Mombasa (MSA), Kilifi (KFI), and Malindi
        (MAL) districts and from the Coast Province (CP). Also valuable are Political Record
        Books (PRB), Annual Reports (AR), and Miscellaneous (M). The central material is
        found in "Giriama Rising" (five volumes), CP 5/336.
     b. Fort Jesus Library, Mombasa
     c. University of Nairobi, Research Projects Archives, Nairobi
        Kazungu, Victor Gona. "Agiryama, the Rise of a Tribe and Its Traditions."
        Spear, T.T. "Mijikenda Historical Texts."
  2. London
     a. Public Record Office, London (PRO)
        Relevant material for the coast is filed under the Foreign Office (FO) records until 1905,
        when the jurisdiction changed to the Colonial Office (CO).

        Some of the most pertinent files consulted include:
        FO 2 (Africa, 1825-1905)
        FO 2/138 Title deeds of the I.B.E.A. Co. (1886-
            1890)
        FO 54 (Muscat, 1834-1905)
        FO 84 (Slave Trade, 1816-1892) (40 vols.)
        FO 107 (Zanzibar, 1893-1898)
        FO 403 Confidential Prints 1885-1900 (60 vols.)
        FO 541 Confidential Prints 1859-1892 (25 vols.)
        CO 519 Original correspondence on the hand-
            over of the Protectorates from the Foreign
            Office to the Colonial Office 1904-1905
            (1 vol.)
        CO 533 Original correspondence, East Africa
            Protectorate/Kenya, from 1903 (515 vols.)
        CO 533/180 "Malindi Commission of Inquiry.
            Report and Evidence." 22 December 1916.
        CO 534 K.A.R. Files (57 vols.)
        CO 544 Sessional Papers, East Africa Protec-
            torate, Kenya, from 1905 (58 vols.)

CO 628 Register of Correspondence, East Africa Protectorate/Kenya, 1904-1926 (17 vols.)

CO 879 Colonial Office Confidential Prints, Africa

b. Church Missionary Society, London (CMS)

The records from the coastal CMS stations after 1844 in Rabai, Freretown, Jilore, Kaloleni, and other Giriama areas are in the central archives in London. The letters of Krapf, Rebman, W. A. Taylor, H. D. Hooper, and H. K. Binns are the most valuable. The CA 5 series covers events until 1881 and the G3A5 series covers material since 1881.

c. Colonial Records Project, Rhodes House, Oxford (CRP)

Collections of private papers of colonial officers and agents have been housed here. Although this collection includes papers of many who worked in the coastal areas, no full papers exist for either Charles Hobley or Arthur Champion. See British and Foreign Anti-Slavery Society Papers; East Africa and the IBEA; Lugard Papers; A. C. Hollis, Autobiography; T. H. R. Cashmore, "Your Obedient Servants, 1895-1918" (MS)

d. University Library, School of Oriental and African Studies, London

William Mackinnon Papers

W. E. Taylor Manuscripts

C. Official Publications

1. United Kingdom Government Publications (published in London)

a. Parliamentary Papers (PP)

Annual Reports of the East African Protectorate

1890 C. 725	"Correspondence respecting the Punitive Expedition against Witu"
1895 C. 7646	"Correspondence with Imperial British East Africa Company re: Revocation of Its Charter"
1896 C. 8274	"Correspondence respecting the Recent Rebellion—1896 Disturbance near Takaungu, a Place on the Coast between Mombasa and Malindi and within the IBEA District"
1896 C. 8683	"Report of Sir Arthur Hardinge on the Conditions and Progress of the East Africa Protectorate from Its Establishment to 20th January 1897 with Map"
1899 C. 1925	"Report by Sir A. Hardinge on British East Africa Protectorate for 1897-98"
1899 C. 9502	"Correspondence Respecting the Status of Slavery in East Africa"
1903 C. 1631	"Report on Slavery and Free Labour"
1906 Cd. 2740	"Reports relating to the Administration of the East Africa Protectorate (Ainsworth Report)"
1908 Cd. 4117	"Correspondence relating to the Tenure of Land in the East Africa Protectorate"
1913 Cd. 6939	"Judgment of the High Court in the Case brought by the Masai tribe against the Attorney-General of the East Africa Protectorate and Others, Dated 26th May, 1913"
1934 Cmd. 4556	"Report of the Kenya Land Commission, September 1933"
1962 Cmnd. 1899	"Kenya: Report of the Regional Boundaries Commission"

b. Others

"Handbook for British East Africa, 1893"

"Report on Famine and Floods in Kenya, 1902"

2. Kenya Government Publications (published in East Africa)

1903-1920	East Africa Protectorate/Kenya *Official Gazette*
1905	"Report of the Land Committee"
1905-1946	Blue Books for the East African Protectorate and Kenya Colony

1910	"Memoranda for Provincial and District Commissioners"
1912	"Minutes of the Proceedings of the Legislative Council, 1907-1912"
1913	"East Africa Protectorate. Native Labour Commission, Report and Evidence, 1912-1913"
1916	"Crown Land Ordinance"
1919	"Final Report of the Economic Commission of the East Africa Protectorate, 1919, Part I"
1919	"Land Settlement Commission"
1962	"Kenya Population Census, 1960" (Nairobi: Republic of Kenya, Ministry of Finance and Economic Planning)
1970	"Kenya Population Census, 1969" (Nairobi: Republic of Kenya, Ministry of Economic Planning and Development)

D. Unpublished Materials

Austin, H. H. "East African Railway Survey. Mombasa-Lake Victoria, Nyanza-Mombasa, 4 December 1919." Diary. McMillan Library, Nairobi.

Berg, Fred James. "Mombasa under the Busaidi Sultanate: The City and Its Hinterland in the Nineteenth Century." Ph.D. dissertation, University of Wisconsin, 1971.

Cashmore, T. H. R. "Studies in District Administration in the East Africa Protectorate, 1895-1918." Ph.D. dissertation, Cambridge University, 1965.

Chittick, Neville. "Observations on Early Bantu-Speaking People in the Horn of Africa." History Department, University of Nairobi, Staff Seminar Paper no. 12, 1977. (mimeo.)

Cummings, Robert. "Aspects of Human Porterage with Special Reference to Akamba of Kenya: Towards an Economic History, 1820-1920." Ph.D. dissertation, University of California, Los Angeles, 1975.

Deed, Florence. "Giryama Exercise." N.d. (mimeo.)

———. "Log Book of the Church Missionary Society, Kaloleni, Aug. 1914-Oct. 1939." In the possession of Dr. and Mrs. J. Milton-Thompson, Kaloleni.

De Kiewiet [Hemphill], M. J. "History of the Imperial British East Africa Company—1876-1895." Ph.D. dissertation, University of London, 1955.

Dunda, Said K. "Giriama Resistance to Government Labour Policy in the British East Africa Protectorate: 1912-1914." Syracuse University, 1970. (mimeo.)

Gold, Alice. "The 'Intransigent,' 'Truculent' Nandi and the *Chumbek* Who Stayed: Background to the Nandi Resistance to British Rule, 1895-1906." African Studies Association Conference, Houston, Texas, November 1977. (mimeo.)

Greenstein, Lewis J. "Africans in a European War: The First World War in East Africa with Special Reference to the Nandi of Kenya." Ph.D. dissertation, University of Indiana, 1975.

Hay, Margaret Jean. "Economic Change in Luoland: Kowe, 1890-1945." Ph.D. dissertation, University of Wisconsin, 1972.

Hinnebusch, Thomas. "Prefixes, Sound Change and Sub-Grouping in the Coastal Kenya Bantu Languages." Ph.D. dissertation, University of California, Los Angeles, 1973.

Hodges, G. W. T. "African Responses to European Rule in Kenya to 1914." Historical Association of Kenya Conference, 1970. (mimeo.)

Hollis, A. C. "Some of the Customs of the WaNyika People of the Mombasa District, 1898." In "Native Tribes and Their Customs," vol. 1, part 2, 2:d (located in the Kenya National Archives reading room).

Jackson, Kennell A. "An Ethnohistorical Study of the Oral Traditions of the Akamba of Kenya." Ph.D. dissertation, University of California, Los Angeles, 1972.

Jacobs, Alan. "The Traditional Political Organization of the Pastoral Masai." Ph.D. dissertation, Oxford University, 1965.

Johnson, Marguerite Bradley. "Dispute Settlement among the Giriama of Kenya." Ph.D. dissertation, University of Pennsylvania, 1976.

Kelley, W. F. P. "Kilifi District Gazette, 1960." In the possession of the Methodist Mission, Ribe.

Koffsky, Peter. "A History of Takaungu, East Africa, 1830-1896." Ph.D. dissertation, University of Wisconsin, 1977.

Larson, Lorne. "A History of the Mahenge (Ulanga) District, c. 1860-1957." Ph.D. dissertation, University of Dar-es-Salaam, 1976.

Livro das Monco es #94-B, folio 618 anon., n.d. Enclosed in Viceroy to Crown, Goa, folio 615r, Historical Archives of India, Panjim, Goa. Translation in the possession of E. A. Alpers, University of California, Los Angeles.

McKay, William Francis. "A Preclonial History of the Southern Kenya Coast." Ph.D. dissertation, Boston University, 1975.

Maxon, Robert Mead. "British Rule in Gusiiland, 1907-1962." Ph.D. dissertation, Syracuse University, 1971.

Merritt, Hollis. "A History of the Taita of Kenya to 1900." Ph.D. dissertation, Indiana University, 1975.

Miller, David. "The Failure of European Plantations on the Coast of Kenya to 1914: A Case of Competing Economic Systems." Department of African Studies, Syracuse University, n.d. (mimeo.)

Morton, R.F. "The Present State of Mijikenda History: A Critical Review." Department of History, University of Nairobi, Kenya, 1970. (mimeo.)

―――. "Slaves, Fugitives, and Freedmen on the Kenya Coast, 1873-1907." Ph.D. dissertation, Syracuse University, 1976.

Odaga, Asenath Bole. "Giriama Oral Tradition." Institute of African Studies, 1977. (mimeo.)

Pyarali, Ali Memon. "Mercantile Intermediaries in a Colonial Spatial System: Wholesaling in Kenya, 1830-1940." Ph.D. dissertation, University of Western Ontario, Canada, 1974.

Rassner, Ronald. "Symbols and Symbol-Systems in Wagiryama Ngano." Discussion paper no. 74, University of Nairobi, 1977. (mimeo.)

Remole, R.A. "White Settlers and the Foundation of Agricultural Settlement in Kenya." Ph.D. dissertation, Harvard University, 1959.

Schecter, R. "Kanonyesha and Kazembe: The Influence of Ecology on State Formation." Institute for African Studies, Lusaka, Zambia, 30 September 1971. (mimeo.)

Shaykh al-Amin b. "Ali al-Mazrui (1890-), Tao'rikh al Mazrui (a History of the Mazru'is of Mombasa)." N.d. In the possession of B.G. Martin, University of Indiana.

Sheriff, Abdul. "The Rise of a Commercial Empire: An Aspect of the Economic History of Zanzibar, 1770-1873." Ph.D. dissertation, University of London, 1971.

Smith, Cynthia Brantley. "The Adaptation Struggle: The Giriama in the Twentieth Century." Department of History, University of Nairobi, Kenya, August 1971. (mimeo.)

―――. "The Giriama Rising, 1914: Focus for Political Development in the Kenya Hinterland, 1850-1963." Ph.D. dissertation, University of California, Los Angeles, 1973.

Spear, T.T. "The Kaya Complex: A History of the Mijikenda Peoples of the Kenya Coast to 1900." Ph.D. dissertation, University of Wisconsin, 1974.

―――. "The Mijikenda in the Nineteenth Century." Department of History, University of Nairobi, Kenya, October 1971. (mimeo.)

Sperling, D.C. "Some Aspects of Islamization in East Africa with Particular Reference to the Digo of Southern Kenya." Department of History, University of Nairobi, Kenya, 1970. (mimeo.)

Strobel, Margaret. "Muslim Women in Mombasa, Kenya, 1890-1973." Ph.D. dissertation, University of California, Los Angeles, 1975.

Temu, A.J. "The Giriama War, 1914-1915." Department of History, University of Dar-es-Salaam, Tanzania, 1970. (mimeo.)

Ylvisaker, Marguerite Helen. "The Political and Economic Relationship of the Lamu Archipelago to the Adjacent Kenya Coast in the Nineteenth Century." Ph.D. dissertation, Boston University, 1975.

II. PUBLISHED WORKS

Acland, J.D. *East African Crops*. London, 1971.

Ajayi, J.F. Ade. "The Continuity of African Institutions under Colonialism." In *Emerging Themes in African History*, edited by T.O. Ranger. Nairobi, 1968. Pp. 189-200.

Akinola, G. Akin. "The Mazrui of Mombasa." *Tarikh: Six Aspects of African History* 2:3 (1968): 26-48.

Allan, W.A. *The African Husbandman*. Edinburgh, 1965.

Alpers, E.A. *Ivory and Slaves: Changing Patterns of International Trade in East Central Africa to the Later Nineteenth Century*. Berkeley and Los Angeles, 1975.

_____. "Re-Thinking African Economic History." *Kenya Historical Review* 1 (1973): 163-188.

Amin, Samir. "Underdevelopment and Dependence in Black Africa—Origins and Contemporary Forms." *Journal of Modern African Studies* 10:4 (1972): 503-524.

Arrighi, Giovanni, and John S. Saul. *The Political Economy of Africa*. New York, 1973.

Austen, Ralph. "Economic History." *African Studies Review* 14:3 (December 1971): 425-438.

_____. "Patterns of Development in Nineteenth Century East Africa." *African Historical Studies* 4:3 (1971): 645-657.

Austin, Herbert H. *With Macdonald in Uganda, a Narrative Account of the Uganda Mutiny and Macdonald Expedition in the Uganda Protectorate and the Territories to the North*. London, 1903.

Axelson, E. *South-East Africa, 1488-1530*. London, 1940.

Bahrey. "History of the Galla" (c. 1593). In *Some Records of Ethiopia, 1593-1646*, edited by C.F. Beckingham and G.W.B. Huntingford. London, 1954. Pp. 53-79.

Baker, E.C. "Notes on the History of the Wasegeju." *Tanganyika Notes and Records* 27 (1949): 16-41.

Barnes, J.A. "Some Ethical Problems in Modern Field Work." *British Journal of Sociology* 14:2 (1963): 118-134.

Barrett, W.E.H. "Notes on the Customs of the WaGiriama." *Journal of the Royal Anthropological Institute of Great Britain and Ireland* 41 (1911): 20-40.

Bartlett, H. Moyse. *The King's African Rifles: A Study in the Military History of East and Central Africa, 1890-1945*. Aldershot, 1956.

Beachey, R.W. "The East African Ivory Trade in the Nineteenth Century." *Journal of African History* 8:2 (1967): 269-290.

Bennett, George. *Kenya: A Political History*. London, 1963.

Bennett, Norman. *The Church Missionary Society of Mombasa, 1873-1894*. Boston University Papers in African History, vol. 1. Boston, 1964.

Berg, Fred James. "The Coast before the Arrival of the Portuguese." In *Zamani*, edited by B.A. Ogot and J.A. Kieran. Nairobi, 1968. Pp. 100-118.

_____. "The Swahili Community of Mombasa, 1500-1900." *Journal of African History* 9 (1968): 35-56.

Bernstein, Henry, ed. *Underdevelopment and Development*. London, 1973.

Boteler, Thomas. *Narrative of a Voyage of Discovery to Africa and Arabia Performed by His Majesty's Ships Levin and Barracouta from 1821 to 1826*. 2 vol. London, 1835.

Brantley, Cynthia. "Gerontocratic Government: Age Sets in Pre-Colonial Giriama." *Africa* 48:3 (1978): 248-264.

_____. "An Historical Perspective of the Giriama and Witchcraft Control." *Africa* 49:3 (1979): 112-133.

Braudel, Fernand. *The Mediterranean and the Mediterranean World in the Age of Philip II*. New York, 1972.

Brett, E.A. *Colonialism and Underdevelopment in East Africa: The Politics of Economic Change, 1919-1939*. London, 1973.

Brewin, R. *Memoirs of Mrs. Rebecca Wakefield*. London, 1888.

Brooke, Clarke. "The Heritage of Famine in Central Africa." *Tanganyika Notes and Records* 67 (June 1967): 15-22.

Brown, Paula. "Patterns of Authority in West Africa." *Africa* 21 (1951): 261-278.

Burton, Richard F. *Zanzibar: City, Island and Coast.* 2 vols. London, 1872.

Capon, M.G. *Towards Unity in Kenya: The Story of Cooperation between Missions and Churches in Kenya, 1913-1947.* Nairobi, 1962.

Cashmore, T.H.R. "A Note on the Chronology of the WaNyika of the Kenya Coast." *Tanganyika Notes and Records* 57 (September 1961): 167-178.

———. "Sheikh Mbaruk bin Rashid bin Salim el Mazrui." In *Leadership in Eastern Africa: Six Political Leaders,* edited by Norman Bennett. Boston, 1968. Pp. 128-139.

Caulfield, Mina Davis. "Imperialism, the Family, and Cultures of Resistance." *Socialist Revolution* 20 (1974): 67-85.

Cerulli, Enrico. *Somalia, scritti vari editi ed inediti.* 3 vols. Rome, 1957-1964.

Champion, Arthur. *The Agiryama of Kenya,* edited by John Middleton. London, 1967.

———. "Some Notes on the Wasanye." *Journal of the East Africa and Uganda Natural History Society* 17 (1922): 21-24.

Chirot, Daniel. "The Growth of the Market and Service Labor Systems in Agriculture." *Journal of Social History* (1975): 67-80.

Chittick, Neville. "An Archeological Reconnaissance of the Southern Somali Coast." *Azania* 4 (1969): 115-130.

———. "The Coast before the Arrival of the Portuguese." In *Zamani: A Survey of East African History,* edited by B.A. Ogot and J.A. Kieran. Nairobi, 1968. Pp. 100-118.

Christie, James. *Cholera Epidemics in East Africa.* London, 1876.

Church Missionary Intelligencer 6:45 (1881) (London).

Clayton, Anthony, and Donald C. Savage. *Government and Labour in Kenya, 1895-1963.* London, 1974.

Cobbing, Julian. "The Absent Priesthood: Another Look at the Rhodesian Rising of 1896-1897." *Journal of African History* 18:1 (1977): 61-84.

Cone, L., and G. Lipscomb. *The History of Kenya Agriculture.* Nairobi, 1972.

Cooper, Frederick. *Plantation Slavery on the East Coast of Africa.* New Haven, Connecticut, 1977.

———. "The Treatment of Slaves on the Kenya Coast in the Nineteenth Century." *Kenya Historical Review* 1 (1973): 87-108.

Coquery-Vidrovitch, Catherine. "Research on an African Mode of Production." In *Perspectives on the African Past,* edited by Martin Klein and G. Wesley Johnson. Boston, 1972. Pp. 33-51.

Coupland, Reginald. *East Africa and Its Invaders: From the Earliest Times to the Death of Seyyid Sa'id in 1856.* Oxford: 1938, 1965.

———. *The Exploitation of East Africa, 1856-1890.* London, 1939.

Cranworth, Lord. *A Colony in the Making, or, Sport and Profit in British East Africa.* London, 1912.

Cummings, Robert. "A Note on the History of Caravan Porters in East Africa." *Kenya Historical Review* 1:2 (1973): 21-37.

Curtin, Philip D. "Field Techniques for Collecting and Processing Oral Data." *Journal of African History* 9:3 (1968): 367-385.

Darroch, R.G. "Some Notes on the Early History of the Tribes Living on the Lower Tana, Collected by Mikael Samson and Others." *Journal of the East Africa and Uganda Natural History Society* 17 (1943/44): 244-254, 370-394.

Davidson, Basil. *The African Awakening.* London, 1955.

Dawson, E.C. *James Hannington, a History of His Life and Work.* London, 1887.

Deed, Florence. *Giryama-English Dictionary.* Nairobi, 1964.

Dilley, Marjorie Ruth. *British Policy in Kenya Colony.* New York, 1937; 2nd ed., London, 1966.

Doke, Clement M. *Bantu: Modern Grammatical, Phonetical, and Lexicographical Studies since 1860.* London, 1945.

Douglas, Mary. "Techniques of Sorcery Control in Central Africa." In *Witchcraft and Sorcery in East Africa*, cited by John Middleton and E. H. Winter. London, 1963. Pp. 123-141.

Duarte, Barbosa. *Viage por Malabar y Costas de Africa d. A. 1512. A Description of the Coasts of East Africa and Malabar in the Beginning of the Sixteenth Century*. Translated by H.E.J. Stanley. London, 1866.

Dundas, Charles. *African Crossroads*. London, 1955.

———. "Native Laws of Some Bantu Tribes of East Africa." *Journal of the Royal Anthropological Institute* 51 (1921): 217-278.

Dyson-Hudson, Neville. "Factors Inhibiting Change in an African Pastoral Society: The Karimojong of Northeast Uganda." In *Black Africa: Its People and Their Cultures Today*, edited by John Middleton. London, 1970. Pp. 49-77.

———. "The Karimojong Age System." *Ethnology* 2 (1963): 353-401.

"East African Protectorate: Treaty." Signed at Zanzibar, 14 December, 1895, by Sir Arthur Hardinge and Sultan Hamed. In Zoe Marsh, ed., *East Africa through Contemporary Records*. Cambridge, 1961. Pp. 57-58.

Ehret, Christopher. "Linguistics as a Tool for Historians." In *Hadith 1*, edited by B.A. Ogot. Nairobi, 1968. Pp. 49-77.

Eisenstadt, S.N. *From Generation to Generation*. New York, 1956.

Eliot, Charles. *The East African Protectorate*. London, 1905.

Elkan, Walter. *Migrants and Proletarians: Urban Labour in the Economic Development of Uganda*. London, 1960.

Ellis, Diana. "The Nandi Protest of 1923 in the Context of African Resistance to Colonial Rule in Kenya." *Journal of African History* 17:4 (1976): 555-575.

Elton, J. Frederick. *Travels and Researches among the Lakes and Mountains of Eastern and Central Africa*. Edited and completed by H.B. Cotterill. London, 1968.

Emery, J.B. "A Short Account of Mombasa." *Journal of the Royal Geographic Society* 3 (1833): 280-283.

Fadiman, Jeffrey. *Mountain Warriors: The Pre-Colonial Meru of Mt. Kenya*. Papers in International Studies 27. Athens, Ohio, 1976.

Fearn, Hugh. *An African Economy: A Study of the Economic Development of the Nyanza Province of Kenya, 1903-1953*. London, 1961.

Feierman, Steven. *The Shambaa Kingdom: A History*. Madison, Wisconsin, 1974.

FitzGerald, William Walter Augustine. *Travels in the Coastlands of British East Africa and the Islands of Zanzibar and Pemba: Their Agricultural Resources and General Characteristics*. London, 1898; reprinted Folkestone and London, 1970.

Flint, John. "The Wider Background to Partition and Colonial Occupation." In *History of East Africa*, edited by Roland Oliver and Gervase Mathew. Oxford, 1963. Vol. 1, pp. 352-390.

Foran, W. Robert. *A Cuckoo in Kenya: The Reminiscences of a Pioneer Police Officer in British East Africa*. London, 1936.

———. *The Kenya Police, 1887-1960*. London, 1962.

Forbes-Munro, J. "Migrations of the Bantu-Speaking Peoples of the Eastern Kenya Highlands: A Reappraisal." *Journal of African History* 8:1 (1967): 25-28.

Forde, Daryll. "The Governmental Roles of Associations among the Yako." *Africa* 31:4 (1961): 309-323.

Forster, Kent. "The Quest for East African Neutrality in 1914." *African Studies Review* 22:1 (April 1979): 73-82.

Frank, André Gunder. "The Development of Underdevelopment," *Latin America: Underdevelopment or Revolution*. New York, 1969. Chap. 1.

Frank, André Gunder, and Dale Johnson, eds. *Dependence and Underdevelopment*. New York, 1972.

Freeman-Grenville, G.S.P. "The Coast, 1798-1840." In *History of East Africa*, edited by Roland Oliver and Gervase Mathew. Oxford, 1963. Vol. 1, pp. 129-168.

————. *The East African Coast: Select Documents from the First to the Earlier Nineteenth Century.* Oxford, 1962.

Fried, Morton. *The Notion of Tribe.* Menlo Park, California, 1975.

Frontera, Ann. *Persistence and Change: A History of Taveta.* Waltham, Massachusetts, 1978.

Galbraith, John S. *Mackinnon and East Africa, 1878-1895: A Study in the "New Imperialism."* Cambridge, England, 1972.

Garlake, P. S. *The Early Islamic Architecture of the East African Coast.* Oxford, 1966.

Gedge, E. "A Recent Exploration, under Captain F. G. Dundas, up the River Tana to Mt. Kenia." *Proceedings of the Royal Geographic Society* (London), 1892.

Geertz, Clifford. "Religion as a Cultural System." In *Reader in Comparative Religion, an Anthropological Approach*, edited by W. Lesa and E. Vogt. New York, 1965. Pp. 204-216.

Gerlach, Luther P. "Nutrition in Its Sociocultural Matrix: Food-Getting and Using along the East African Coast." In *Ecology and Economic Development in Tropical Africa*, edited by David Brokensha. Research Series no. 9. Berkeley, California, 1965. Pp. 245-268.

Godelier, Maurice. "Modes of Production, Kinship and Demographic Structure." In *Marxist Analysis and Social Anthropology*, edited by Maurice Bloch. London, 1975. Pp. 3-29.

Goldthorpe, J. E. *Outlines of East African History.* Kampala, Uganda, 1958.

Gray, J. M. *The British in Mombasa, 1824-1826.* London, 1957.

————. "Rezende's Description of East Africa in 1634." *Tanganyika Notes and Records* 23 (June 1947): 2-28.

————. "Zanzibar and the Coastal Belt, 1840-1848." In *History of East Africa*, vol. I, pp. 212-251, edited by Roland Oliver and Gervase Mathew. Oxford, 1963.

Gregory, Robert, Robert M. Maxon, and Leon Spencer, eds. *A Guide to the Kenya National Archive.* Syracuse, New York, 1968.

Griffeths, J. B. "Glimpses of a Nyika Tribe: WaDuruma." *Journal of the Royal Anthropological Institute* (1935): 267-296.

Grottanelli, V. L. "A Lost African Metropolis." *Afrikanistische Studien* (Berlin) 26 (1955): 231-242.

Guillain, Charles. *Documents sur l'histoire, la géographie, et le commerce de l'Afrique Orientale.* 3 vols. Paris, 1856.

Gulliver, P. H. *Tradition and Transition in East Africa: Studies of the Tribal Element in the Modern Era.* Los Angeles, 1969.

————. "The Turkana Age Organization." *American Anthropologist* 60 (1958): 900-922.

Guthrie, Malcolm. "The Age-Set Organization of the Jie Tribe." *Journal of the Royal Anthropological Institute* 83 (1953): 147-168.

————. *The Classification of the Bantu Languages.* London, 1948.

Gutkind, Peter. *The Emergent African Proletariat Employment and Housing of Servants in Nairobi.* Montreal, 1974.

Gwassa, Gilbert C. K. "The German Intervention and African Resistance in Tanzania." In *A History of Tanzania*, edited by I. N. Kimambo and A. J. Temu. Nairobi, 1969. Pp. 85-122.

Gwassa, Gilbert C. K., and Iliffe, John. *Records of the Maji Maji Rising.* Historical Association of Tanzania Paper No. 4. Dar-es-Salaam, 1968.

Hailey, William Michael. *An African Survey.* London, 1938.

Hamilton, Robert W. "Land Tenure among the Bantu WaNyika of East Africa." *Journal of the Royal African Society* 20:77 (October 1920): 13-18.

Hardinge, Sir Arthur. *A Diplomatist in the East, 1844-99.* 8 vols. London, 1928.

Harries, Lyndon, ed. "The Founding of Rabai: A Swahili Chronicle by Midani bin Mwidad." *Swahili* n.s. 1:2 (September 1960): 140-149.

Hechter, Michael. *Internal Colonialism: The Celtic Fringe in British National Development, 1536-1966.* Berkeley and Los Angeles, 1975.

Hellen, John. *Rural Economic Development in Zambia, 1890-1964.* London, 1968.

Hemphill, Marie de Kiewiet. "The British Sphere, 1884-94." In *History of East Africa*, edited by Roland Oliver and Gervase Mathew. Oxford, 1963. Vol. 1, pp. 391-432.

Henige, David. "The Problem of Feedback in Oral Tradition: Four Examples from the Fante Coastlines." *Journal of African History* 14 (1973): 223-235.

Hertslet, E. *Map of Africa by Treaty*. 3 vols. Third edition, London, 1909.

Hill, M. F. *Permanent Way: The Story of the Kenya and Uganda Railroad*. 2 vols. Nairobi, n.d.

Hinnebusch, Thomas. "The Shungwaya Hypothesis: A Linguistic Reappraisal." In *East African Cultural History*, edited by J. Gallagher. Syracuse, New York, 1976. Pp. 1-42.

Hobley, C. W. *Kenya: From Chartered Company to Crown Colony*. Second edition, London, 1970.

―――. "Upon a Visit to Tsavo and the Taita Highlands." *Geographical Journal* 5:6 (June 1895): 21-36.

―――. "The Wa-Langulu or Ariangulu of the Taru Desert." *Man* 12:9 (1912): 18-21.

Hollingsworth, L. W. *Zanzibar under the Foreign Office 1890-1913*. London, 1953.

Hollis, A. C. "Notes on the Graves of WaNyika." *Man* 9 (1909): 145.

―――. "Notes on the History of Vumba, East Africa." *Journal of the Royal Anthropological Institute* 30 (1900): 276-277.

―――. "Nyika Enigmas." *Journal of the Royal African Society* 16 (1917): 135-142.

―――. "Nyika Proverbs." *Journal of the Royal African Society* 16 (1916): 62-70.

Holway, James. "The Religious Composition of the Population of the Coast Province of Kenya." *Journal of Religion in Africa* 3:3 (1970): 228-239.

Hordern, Lt. Col. Charles. "The Dual Policy in Kenya." Nakuru, Kenya Colony: *Kenya Weekly News*, 1944.

―――, comp. *History of the Great War: Military Operations in East Africa*. Vol. 1: *August 1914-September 1916*. London, 1941.

Humphrey, N. "The Gede Native Settlement Scheme." *East African Agricultural Journal* 4 (1939): 447-450.

Huntingford, G. W. B. "The Bantu Peoples of Eastern Kenya and North-Eastern Tanganyika." In *History and Archeology in Africa*, edited by R. E. Hamilton. London, 1955. Pp. 48-49.

―――. *The Galla of Ethiopia: The Kingdoms of Kafa and Junjero*. London, 1955.

Huxley, Elspeth. *Flame Trees of Thika*. London, 1949.

―――. *Race and Politics in Kenya*. London, 1956.

―――. *Red Strangers*. London, 1939.

―――. *White Man's Country*. London, 1952.

Iliffe, John. *Agricultural Change in Modern Tanganyika*. Nairobi, 1971.

―――. "The Organization of the Maji Maji Rebellion." *Journal of African History* 8:3 (1967): 495-512.

Ingham, Kenneth. *A History of East Africa*. New York, 1962.

Irvine, F. R. *A Textbook of West African Agriculture*. London, 1953.

Isaacman, Allen, and Barbara Isaacman. "Resistance and Collaboration in Southern and Central Africa, ca. 1850-1920." *The International Journal of African Historical Studies* 10:1 (1977): 31-62.

―――. "Social Banditry in Zimbabwe (Rhodesia) and Mozambique, 1894-1907: An Expression of Early Peasant Protest." *Journal of Southern African Studies* 4:1 (October 1977): 1-30.

―――. *The Tradition of Resistance in Mozambique: Anti-Colonial Activity in the Zambesi Valley, 1850-1921*. Berkeley and Los Angeles, 1976.

Jackson, Robert D. "Resistance to the German Invasion of the Tanganyika Coast, 1888-1891." In *Protest and Power in Black Africa*, edited by Robert I. Rotberg and Ali Mazrui. New York, 1970. Pp. 129-143.

Jacobs, Alan. "A Chronology of the Pastoral Maasai." In *Hadith I*, edited by B. A. Ogot. Nairobi, 1968. Pp. 10-31.

Janmohamed, K. K. "African Laborers in Mombasa, c. 1895-1940." In *Hadith 5: Economic and Social History of East Africa*, edited by B. A. Ogot. Nairobi, 1975. Pp. 154-176.

Johnstone, H. B. "Notes on the Customs of the Tribes Occupying Mombasa Sub-District, British East Africa." *Journal of the Anthropological Institute of Great Britain and Ireland* 32 (1902): 263-272.

"Kajiwe-Superwitch: His Magic Spell was Fear." *Drum* (January 1969): 1-2.

"Kenya Tribes: The Giriama." *Kenya Today* 3 (September 1957): 26-27.

Kieran, J.A. "Abushiri and the Germans." In *Hadith 2*, edited by B.A. Ogot. Nairobi, 1970. Pp. 198-212.

──────. "The Historian in East Africa." In *Zamani: A Survey of East African History*, edited by B.A. Ogot and J.A. Kieran. Nairobi, 1968. Pp. 1-21.

Kimambo, Isaria. *A Political History of the Pare of Tanzania c. 1500-1900.* Nairobi, 1969.

Kirkman, J.S. *The Arab City of Gedi.* London, 1964.

──────. *Fort Jesus, Mombasa.* Nairobi, 1970.

──────. "The Great Pillars of Malindi and Mambrui." *Oriental Art* 4:2 (1958). Pp. 4-9.

──────. *Men and Monuments on the East African Coast.* London, 1964.

Kjekshus, Helge. *Ecology Control and Economic Development in East African History: The Case of Tanganyika, 1850-1950.* London, 1977.

Krapf, J.L. *A Dictionary of the Swahili Language*, London, 1882; reprinted Ridgewood, New Jersey, 1964.

──────. *Reisen in Ost-Afrika.* 2 vols. Stuttgart, 1858.

──────. "Reports." In *Church Missionary Intelligencer*, vols. 2-4. London, 1851-1853.

──────. *Travels, Researches and Missionary Labours during an Eighteen Years Residence in Eastern Africa.* London, 1860; second edition, London and New York, 1968.

──────. *Vocabulary of Six East African Languages (Kisuaheli, Kinika, Kikamba, Kipokomo, Kihiau, Kigalla).* Tubingen, 1850; reprinted Farnborough, 1967.

Krapf, J.L., and J. Rebmann. *A Nyika-English Dictionary.* London, 1887.

Kuczynski, R.R. *Demographic Survey of the British Colonial Empire.* Vol. 2: *East Africa.* London, 1949.

Lambert, H.E. "The Background to Mau Mau: Widespread Use of Secret Oaths in Kenya." *Times British Colonies Review* 8 (Winter 1952): 21.

──────. *The Systems of Land Tenure in the Kikuyu Land Unit.* Capetown, 1950.

──────. *The Use of Indigenous Authorities in Tribal Administration: Studies of the Meru of Kenya Colony.* Communications School of African Studies publ. 16. Capetown, 1947.

Lamphear, John. "The Kamba and the Northern Mrima Coast." In *Pre-Colonial African Trade: Essays on Trade in Central and Eastern Africa before 1900*, edited by R. Gray and D. Birmingham. London, 1970. Pp. 75-101.

Legum, Colin. *Africa Contemporary Record.* London, 1973.

LeVine, Robert. "The Internalization of Political Values in Stateless Societies." *Human Organization* 19:2 (Summer 1960): 51-58.

LeVine, Robert, and Walter H. Sangree. "The Diffusion of Age-Group Organization in East Africa: A Controlled Comparison." *Africa* 32 (1962): 97-109.

Lewis, Herbert S. *A Galla Monarchy.* Madison, Wisconsin, 1965.

──────. "The Origins of the Galla and Somali." *Journal of African History* 7:1 (1966): 27-47.

Lewis, I.M. "The Galla in Northern Somaliland." *Rassegna de Studi Etiopia* (Rome) 15 (1959): 21-38.

──────. *Peoples of the Horn of Africa.* Part I: *Somali Afar and Saho.* London, 1955/1969.

──────. "Somali Conquest of the Horn of Africa." *Journal of African History* 1:2 (1960): 213-229.

Leys, Colin. *Underdevelopment in Kenya: The Political Economy of Neo-Colonialism.* Berkeley and Los Angeles, 1975.

Leys, Norman. *Kenya.* Fourth edition, London, 1973.

Lindblom, Gerhard. *The Akamba in British East Africa: An Ethnological Monograph.* Uppsala, 1920; reprinted New York, 1969.

Lloyd-Jones, W. *K.A.R., Being an Unofficial Account of the Origins and Activities of the King's African Rifles.* London, 1926.

Lobo, J. *A Voyage to Abyssinia.* New York, 1886.

Lock, G.W. *Sisal.* London, 1962.

Lonsdale, J.M. "The Politics of Conquest: The British in Western Kenya, 1894-1908." *Historical Journal* 20:4 (1977): 841-870.

————. "Some Origins of Nationalism in East Africa." *Journal of African History* 9:1 (1968): 119-146.

————. "When Did the Gusii (or Any Other Group) Become a 'Tribe'—A Review Essay." *Kenya Historical Review* 5:1 (1977): 123-133.

Louis, William Roger. *Imperialism: The Robinson and Gallagher Controversy*. New York, 1976.

Low, D. A. "British East Africa: The Establishment of British Rule, 1895-1912." In *History of East Africa*, edited by V. Harlow, E. M. Chilver, and A. Smith. Oxford, 1965. Vol. 2, pp. 1-56.

————. "The Northern Interior, 1840-1844." In *A History of East Africa*, edited by Roland Oliver and Gervase Mathew. Oxford, 1963. Vol. 1, pp. 297-351.

————. "Warbands and Ground-Level Imperialism in Uganda, 1870-1900." *Historical Studies* (Melbourne) 15 (October 1975): 584-597.

Lucas, C. P. *A Historiographical Geography of the British Colonies*. London, 1894.

Lugard, Frederick. *The Rise of Our East African Empire*. 2 vols. Edinburgh, 1893.

Lyne, R. N. *An Apostle of the Empire, Being the Life of Sir Lloyd Matthews*. London, 1936.

McDermott, P. L. *British East Africa or IBEA: A History of the Formation and Work of the Imperial British East Africa Company*. London, 1895.

MacDonald, J. R. L., and R. E. Major. *Soldiering and Surveying in British East Africa, 1891-94*. London, 1897.

McIntosh, B. G. "The Eastern Bantu Peoples." In *Zamani: A Survey of East African History*, edited by B. A. Ogot and J. A. Kieran. Nairobi, 1968. Pp. 198-215.

Mair, Lucy. *Primitive Government*. London, 1962.

Marks, Shula. "Khoisan Resistance to the Dutch in the Seventeenth and Eighteenth Centuries." *Journal of African History* 13:1 (1972): 55-80.

————. *Reluctant Rebellion: The 1906-1908 Disturbances in Natal*. Oxford, 1970.

Martin, Esmond Bradley. *The History of Malindi: A Geographical Analysis of an East African Coastal Town from the Portuguese Period to the Present*. Nairobi, 1973.

Matheson, J. K., and E. W. Bovill, eds. *East African Agriculture*. London, 1950.

Matson, A. T. *The Nandi Campaign against the British, 1895-1906*. Vol. 1. Transafrica Historical Papers no. 1. Nairobi, 1974.

————. *Nandi Resistance to British Rule, 1890-1906*. Nairobi, 1972.

————. "Nandi Traditions in Raiding." In *Hadith 2*, edited by B. A. Ogot. Nairobi, 1970. Pp. 61-78.

————. "The Pacification of Kenya." *Kenya Weekly News*, 14 September 1962.

————. "Reflections on the Growth of Political Consciousness in Nandi." In *Hadith 4: Politics and Nationalism in Colonial Kenya*, edited by B. A. Ogot. Nairobi, 1972. Pp. 18-45.

Maxon, Robert M. "Early Gusii Resistance to British Rule, 1905-1914." In *Protest Movements in Colonial East Africa*, edited by Robert Strayer, Edward Steinhart, and Robert Maxon. Syracuse, New York, 1973. Pp. 70-96.

————. "John Ainsworth and Agricultural Innovation in Kenya." *Kenya Historical Review Journal* 2:2 (1973): 151-162.

Mbotela, J. J. *The Freeing of the Slaves in East Africa*. London, 1956.

Meillassoux, Claude. "From Reproduction to Production: A Marxist Approach to Economic Anthropology." *Economy and Society* 1 (1972): 93-105.

Meinertzhagen, Richard. *Kenya Diary, 1902-1906*. Edinburgh, 1957.

Mettam, R. W. M. "A Short History of Rinderpest with Special Reference to Africa." *Uganda Journal* 5 (1937): 16-27.

Middleton, John. "Kenya: Changes in African Life 1912-1945." In *History of East Africa*, vol. 2, edited by Vincent Harlow, E. M. Chilver, and Alison Smith. Oxford, 1965. Pp. 115-129.

Middleton, John, and Greet Kershaw. *The Kikuyu and Kamba of Kenya*. London, 1965.

Miracle, Marvin P. *Agriculture in the Congo Basin: Tradition and Change in African Rural Economics*. Madison, Wisconsin, 1967.

Morton, R. F. "The Shungwaya Myth of Mijikenda Origins: A Problem of Late Nineteenth Century Kenya Coastal History." *International Journal of African Historical Studies* 5:3 (1973): 397-423.

Moyse-Bartlett, H. *The King's African Rifles: A Study of the Military History of East and Central Africa, 1890-1945.* London, 1950.

Mungeam, G. H. *British Rule in Kenya, 1895-1912.* Oxford, 1966.

Munro, J. Forbes. *Africa and the International Economy, 1800-1960.* London, 1976.

———. *Colonial Rule and the Kamba.* Oxford, 1975.

———. "Migrations of the Bantu Speaking Peoples of the Eastern Kenya Highlands: A Reappraisal." *Journal of African History* 8:1 (1967): 25-28.

Muriuki, Godfrey. *A History of the Kikuyu, 1500-1900.* London, 1974.

Nadel, S. F. "Witchcraft in Four African Societies: An Essay in Comparison." *American Anthropologist* 54 (1952): 13-29.

New, Charles. "Journey from the Pangani via Usambara to Mombasa." *Journal of the Royal Geographic Society* 45 (1875): 414-420.

———. "Journey from the Pangani via Wadigo to Mombasa." *Journal of the Royal Geographic Society* 19 (1874/75): 317-323.

———. *Life, Wanderings and Labours in Eastern Africa.* London, 1873.

Ngala, Ronald G. *Nchi na Desturi za Wagiriama* (Country and Customs of Giryama). Nairobi, 1949.

Nicholls, Christine Stephanie. *The Swahili Coast: Politics, Diplomacy and Trade on the East African Littoral, 1798-1856.* London, 1971.

Noble, D. S. "Demoniacal Possession among the Giriama." *Man* 2 (1961): 50-52.

Nurse, D., and G. Philippson. "The North-Eastern Bantu Languages of Tanzania and Kenya: A Classification." *Kiswahili* 45 (1975): 1-28.

O'Connor, Anthony Michael. *An Economic Geography of East Africa.* Second edition, London, 1971.

Ogot, B. A. *History of the Southern Luo.* Vol. 1: *Migration and Settlement 1500-1900.* Nairobi, 1967.

———. "Kenya under the British, 1895-1963." In *Zamani: A Survey of East African History*, edited by B. A. Ogot and G. A. Kieran. Nairobi, 1968. Pp. 255-289.

Oliver, Roland. *The Missionary Factor in East Africa.* London, 1952.

Oliver, Roland, and J. D. Fage. *A Short History of Africa.* London, 1960.

Oliver, Roland, and Gervase Mathew, eds. *History of East Africa*, vol. 1. Oxford, 1963.

Ominde, S. H. *Land and Population Movements in Kenya.* Evanston, Illinois, 1968.

Oruka, H. Odera. "Marxism and African History." *Kenya Historical Review Journal* 2:2 (1973): 139-150.

Osogo, John. *A History of the Baluyia.* Nairobi, 1966.

Owen, Roger, and Bob Sutcliffe, eds. *Studies in the Theory of Imperialism.* London, 1972.

Owen, W. F. W. *Narrative of Voyages to Explore the Shores of Africa, Arabia, and Madagascar.* 2 vols. London, 1833; reprinted Farnborough, 1968.

Parkin, David. "Medicines and Men of Influence." *Man* 3 (1968): 425-439.

———. "National Independence and Local Tradition in a Kenya Trading Centre." *Bulletin of the School of Oriental and African Studies* 37:1 (1974): 157-174.

———. *Palms, Wine, and Witnesses: Public Spirit and Private Gain in an African Farming Community.* San Francisco, 1972.

———. "Politics of Ritual Syncretism: Islam among the Non-Muslim Giriama of Kenya." *Africa* 40:3 (1970): 218-233.

Patterson, J. H. *In the Grip of the Nyika.* London, 1910.

Patterson, K. David. "The Giriama Rising of 1913-1914." *African Historical Studies* 3:3 (1970): 89-100.

———. *The Pokot of Western Kenya, 1910-1962: The Response of a Conservative People to Colonial Rule.* Program in East African Studies occasional paper no. 53. Syracuse, New York, 1969.

Peel, W. "Among the Wadigo and Wagiryama of British East Africa." *Church Missionary Review* 62 (1911): 163-169.

Pim, Sir Alan. *Colonial Agricultural Production.* London, 1946.

Prins, A. H. J. *The Coastal Tribes of the North-Eastern Bantu*. London, 1952.

———. *East African Age-Class Systems (Galla, Kipsigis, and Kikuyu)*. Groningen, 1953; reprinted New Haven, Connecticut, 1970.

———. *Sailing from Lamu*. Assen, 1965.

———. *The Swahili-Speaking Peoples of Zanzibar and the East Africa Coast*. London, 1961.

Proceedings of the CMS (1914-1915). London, 1916.

Ranger, T. O. "African Reactions to the Imposition of Colonial Rule in East and Central Africa." In *Colonialism in Africa, 1870-1914*, edited by L. H. Gann and Peter Duignan. Cambridge, 1969. Pp. 293-324.

———. "Connexions between 'Primary Resistance' Movements and Modern Mass Nationalism in East and Central Africa." *Journal of African History* 9:3 and 4 (1968): 437-453, 631-641.

———. "The People in African Resistance: A Review." *Journal of Southern African Studies* 4:1 (October 1977): 125-146.

———. *Revolt in Southern Rhodesia, 1896-7*. London, 1967.

Ranger, T. O., ed. *Emerging Themes in African History*. Nairobi, 1968.

Roberts, Andrew. "The Second Conference on Oral History." *Tanzania Zamani: A Bulletin of Research on Pre-Colonial History*, no. 2 (January 1968): 2-13.

Roberts, Andrew, ed. *Tanzania before 1900*. Nairobi, 1970.

Robinson, Ronald E., and John Gallagher. "The Partition of Africa." In *The New Cambridge Modern History*. Vol. 11: *Material Progress and Worldwide Problems, 1870-1898*, edited by F. H. Hinsley. Cambridge, 1962. Chap. 22.

Rodney, Walter. *How Europe Underdeveloped Africa*. Dar-es-Salaam, 1972.

Rosberg, Carl G., Jr., and John Nottingham. *The Myth of "Mau Mau": Nationalism in Kenya*. New York, 1970.

Rotberg, Robert I., and Ali A. Mazrui. *Protest and Power in Black Africa*. New York, 1970.

Ruel, M. G. "Kuria Generation Classes." *Africa* 32 (1962): 14-37.

Saberwal, Henry F., and Satish Saberwal, eds. *Stress and Response in Fieldwork*. New York, 1969.

Saberwal, Satish. "Historical Notes on the Embu of Central Kenya." *Journal of African History* 8:1 (1967): 29-38.

———. *The Traditional Political System of the Embu of Central Kenya*. Nairobi, 1970.

Sahlins, Marshall D. "The Segmentary Lineage: An Organization of Predatory Expansion." *American Anthropologist* 63 (1961): 322-343.

Salim, Ahmed Idha. "The Movement for 'Mwambao' or Coast Autonomy in Kenya, 1956-63." In *Hadith 2*, edited by B. A. Ogot. Nairobi, 1970. Pp. 212-228.

———. "Native or Non-Native?: The Problem of Identity and the Social Stratification of the Arab-Swahili of Kenya." In *Hadith 6: History and Social Change in East Africa*, edited by B. A. Ogot. Nairobi, 1976. Pp. 65-84.

———. *The Swahili-Speaking Peoples of Kenya's Coast, 1895-1965*. Nairobi, 1973.

Sandford, G. R. *An Administrative and Political History of the Masai Reserve*. London, 1919.

Schlippe, Pierre de. *Shifting Cultivation in Africa*. London, 1956.

Smith, A. Donaldson. *Through Unknown African Countries: The First Expedition from Somaliland to Lake Lamu*. New York, 1897; reprinted New York, 1969.

Sorrenson, M. P. K. *Origins of European Settlement in Kenya*. Nairobi, 1968.

Southall, A. W. "The Illusion of Tribe." In *The Passing of Tribal Man in Africa*, edited by Peter Gutkind. Leiden, 1970. Pp. 28-50.

Spear, T. T. *The Kaya Complex*. Nairobi, 1978.

———. "The Mijikenda." In *Kenya before 1900*, edited by B. A. Ogot. Nairobi, 1976.

———. "Traditional Myths and Historians' Myths: Variations on the Singwaya Theme of Mijikenda Origins." *History in Africa* 1 (1974): 67-84.

———. "Traditional Myths and Linguistic Analysis: Singwaya Revisited." *History in Africa* 4 (1977): 229-246.

Steinhart, Edward I. "Anti-Colonial Resistance and Nationalism: The Nyangire Rebellion." In *Protest Movements in Colonial East Africa*, edited by Robert Strayer, Edward Steinhart, and Robert Maxon. Syracuse, New York, 1973. Pp. 97-123.

Stahl, Kathleen Mary. *History of the Chagga People of Kilimanjaro*. London, 1964.

Stigand, C. H. *The Land of Zinj: Being an Account of British East Africa, Its Ancient History and Present Inhabitants*. London, 1913.

Stock, Eugene. *The History of the Church Missionary Society*. Vol. I. London, 1899.

Stovald, Kenneth E. *The CMS in Kenya*. Vol. 1: *The Coast 1844-1944*. Nairobi, 1949.

Strandes, Justus. *The Portuguese Period in East Africa*. Berlin, 1899; English edition edited by J. S. Kirkman, Nairobi, 1961.

Strayer, Robert. *The Making of Mission Communities in East Africa*. London, 1978.

Taylor, W. E. *Giriama Vocabulary and Collections*. London, 1891.

Temu, A. J. *British Protestant Missions*. London, 1972.

––––––. "The Giriama War, 1914-1915." In *War and Society in Africa*, edited by B. A. Ogot. London, 1972. Pp. 215-236.

Terray, Emmanuel. "Long Distance Exchange and the Formation of the State: The Case of the Abron Kingdom of Gyaman." *Economy and Society* 3 (1974): 315-345.

––––––. *Marxism and Primitive Societies*. Translated by Mary Klopper. New York, 1972.

Thomson, Joseph. *Through Masai Land*. London, 1885; reprinted London, 1968.

Tignor, Robert. *The Colonial Transformation of Kenya: The Kamba, Kikuyu, and Maasai from 1900 to 1939*. Princeton, 1976.

Uzoigwe, G. N. "The Mombasa-Victoria Railway, 1890-1902: Imperial Necessity, Humanitarian Venture, or Economic Imperialism?" *Kenya Historical Review* 4:1 (1976): 11-34.

Vansina, Jan. *Oral Tradition: A Study in Historical Methodology*. London, 1965.

Vansina, Jan, R. Mauny, and L. V. Thomas. *The Historian in Tropical Africa*. Oxford, 1964.

Van Zwanenberg, Robert, with Ann King. *An Economic History of Kenya and Uganda, 1800-1970*. London, 1975.

Vincent, Joan. *African Elite: The Big Men of a Small Town*. New York, 1971.

––––––. "Agrarian Society as Organized Flow: Process of Development Past and Present." *Peasant Studies* 1:2 (April 1977).

––––––. "The Changing Role of Small Towns in the Agrarian Structure of East Africa." *Journal of Commonwealth and Comparative Politics* 12:3 (November 1974): 261-275.

Wagner, G. *The Bantu of North Kavirondo*. Vol. I. Oxford, 1949.

Wakefield, E. S. *Thomas Wakefield: Missionary and Geographical Pioneer in East Equatorial Africa*. London, 1904.

Wakefield, Thomas. "New Route through Masai Country." *Proceedings of the Royal Geographical Society* 4 (1882): 742-746, 776.

––––––. "Routes of Native Caravans from the Coast to the Interior of Eastern Africa." *Journal of the Royal Geographical Society*, no. 40 (1870): 303-338.

––––––. "The Wakwafi Raid on the District near Mombasa." *Proceedings of the Royal Geographical Society* 5 (1883): 289-290.

Walker, D. A. "Giriama Arrow Poison: A Study in African Pharmacology and Ingenuity." *Central African Journal of Medicine* 3:6 (1957): 226-228.

Waller, Richard. "The Maasai and the British, 1895-1905: The Origins of an Alliance." *Journal of African History* 17:4 (1976): 529-553.

Wallerstein, Immanuel. "Africa in a Capitalist World," *Issue: A Quarterly Journal of Africanist Opinion* 3:3 (Fall 1973): 1-11.

––––––. *The Modern World System: Capitalist Agriculture and the Origins of the European World Economy in the Sixteenth Century*. New York and London, 1974.

––––––. "The Three Stages of African Involvement in the World Economy." In *The Political Economy of Contemporary Africa*, edited by P. C. W. Gutkind and Immanuel Wallerstein. Beverly Hills, 1976. Pp. 30-55.

Wards, H. F., and J. W. Milligan, comps. *Handbook of British East Africa 1912-13*. London, 1913.

Webster, John. *A Bibliography on Kenya*. Syracuse, New York, 1967.

Werner, Alice. "The Bantu Coast Tribe of the East Africa Protectorate." *Journal of the Royal Anthropological Institute of Great Britain and Ireland* 45 (1915): 326-354.

————. "The Galla of the East Africa Protectorate." *Journal of the African Society* 13:50 (January 1914): 121-142; and 13:51 (April 1914): 262-287.

————. "The Native Tribes of British East Africa." *Journal of the African Society* 19 (1919/20): 285-294.

————. "Some Notes on the WaPokomo of the Tana Valley." *Journal of the African Society* 12 (1912/13): 359-384.

————. "WaNyika." *Encyclopedia of Religion and Ethics* 9 (1917): 424-427.

Wipper, Audrey. "The Gusii Rebels." In *Protest and Power in Black Africa*, edited by Robert Rotberg and Ali Mazrui. London, 1970. Pp. 377-426.

Wolff, Richard D. *The Economics of Colonialism: Britain and Kenya, 1870-1930*. New Haven, Connecticut, 1974.

Wright, A.C.A. "Maize Names as Indicators of Economic Contacts." *Uganda Journal* 31:1 (March 1949): 61-81.

Wrigley, E.A. *Population and History*. New York, 1974.

Young, Roland, ed. *Through Masailand with Joseph Thomson*. Evanston, Illinois, 1962.

Index

Administrative system (British), 4-5, 57-60, 70-72, 73; Giriama opposition to, 76-90; loss of control over Giriama by, 91-109; after the Rebellion, 130-132; attempt to salvage, 138-140

Afro-Arabs, 1, 12, 51, 70, 102f, 120; Mazrui, 19, 44, 144; land and plantations of, 20, 133, 143-144; in Takaungu system, 22, 144; British and, 27, 44-45, 60-61, 64-66, 143f

Age-sets, 11, 42-43, 138. *See also* Ruling generations

Agriculture, 2, 5, 10-17 *passim*, 21, 34, 40, 141; as women's work, 5-6, 23*n*, 67, 93f, 102; slave labor for, 17, 22-23, 61-62, 67; British/European interest in developing, 37-38, 43-44, 55-56, 101-102. *See also* Crops

Akiza clan, 23, 42*n*

Alpers, E. A., 143

Anglo-Mazrui war, 43-51

Arabs. *See* Afro-Arabs; Omani Arabs

Aziz (rebel leader), 48-49

Bajuni Swahili, 22

Baratum Line (1908), 65, 133, 135

Baya wa Gunga of Manyimbo, 99

Baya wa Kadidi, 80

Belfield, Sir Henry, 75-76, 132, 134, 135-136

Biryac, 13, 19ff, 35, 40; headman at, 79, 83, 86, 88, 96, 98f; requests for laborers from, 113; during the Rebellion, 116, 119; after the Rebellion, 128

Birya wa Masha, 138*n*

Blood money (*kore*), 84

Bogosho wa Menza, 79, 83, 86, 88, 96, 98f

Bom Bom famine, 50

Borders/boundaries, 7, 65. *See also* Baratum Line; Sabaki River

Bowring, C. C., 134, 136

Bretts, A. J., 111

British colonialism, 1-7, 25-31, 33, 35, 38-39, 44; Giriama reactions to, 8-32, 74-90, 137-138; and coastal economy, 54-73; punishment tactics of, 91-109, 113, 120, 122-124, 125-130, 148; problems of, 145-148; and economic upheaval, *see* Economic system; labor to support, *see* Labor force. *See also* Anglo-Mazrui war; Imperial British East Africa Company

Buganda, 35, 36-37, 38, 44, 54-55, 57

Bugusu, 35

Bungale, 128

Busaidi dynasty, 17-18, 22, 26, 44

Capitalist development (European): versus African traditional rights, 101-102; land issues and, 132-133; dependency theory on, 143-144; Giriama exclusion from participation in, 152

Carrier Corps, 120, 140

Cash crops, 5, 58-59, 62-63, 65, 101-102, 146

Catholic White Fathers, 76

Cattlekeeping, 5, 6, 10-15 *passim*, 21, 35, 40

Ceara rubber trees, 69, 102

Cerebrospinal fever epidemic, 75

Chagga territory, 13, 21

Chakama incident, 83-84, 95, 113

Champion, Arthur, 34*n*, 62, 77-84 *passim*, 89-95 *passim*, 103-109 *passim*, 111-114, 115, 123-124, 126, 134, 136, 140

Chiefs. *See* Elders; Headmen

Chonyi, 9f, 20, 22, 52

Chula wa Dzala of Bungale, 126*n*

Church Missionary Society (CMS), 1, 22, 29, 36, 38f, 46

Clans. *See* Kinship patterns

Climate, 5

Clove plantations, 17, 27f

Coast Planters Association, 91

Coast Titles Ordinance (1908), 65